The
Copy
Book

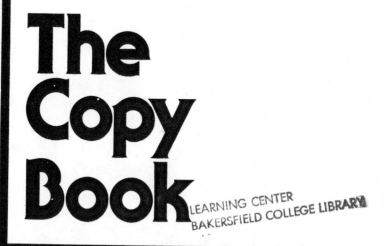

The Copy Book

Mastering Basic Grammar and Style

Thomas Friedmann
James MacKillop
Onondaga Community College

Holt, Rinehart and Winston
New York   Chicago   San Francisco
Atlanta   Dallas   Montreal   Toronto

To Ilana, Molly, and Colin, who have been teaching us

Library of Congress Cataloging in Publication Data

Friedmann, Thomas.
  The copy book.

  Includes index.
  1. English language—Rhetoric. 2. English language
—Grammar—1950–   I. MacKillop, James, joint author.
II. Title.
PE1408.F717   808'.042   79-27176

ISBN 0–03–051026–0

0 1 2 3   059   9 8 7 6 5 4 3 2

To Instructors Who Use The Copy Book

In writing *The Copy Book*, we have assumed that students trying to master basic English skills are primarily intelligent people. They already have a wide range of interests, often hold down jobs, and are experiencing few difficulties in their daily, informal communication with their peers. Yet, unquestionably, they make many errors in their writing. We believe that these errors reveal not the inability to learn but the accumulation of bad writing habits, learned in school or in social encounters. It is hardly likely that any of these students has passed through high school without having had *alright* circled in red on his or her paper—yet this error persists in appearing. In fact, we are sure that no "rule" for proper writing has ever been withheld from these students, none of their mistakes has ever been ignored, and no help was ever denied them. Yet here the students are, in introductory English, remedial, or developmental writing courses, seeking to master what is only "basic" about writing.

We suggest that these students make errors because they have developed bad writing habits. Students who have written *alright* two hundred times in the course of an academic career have undoubtedly had the error corrected for them by an instructor. Hence, while these students have "practiced" writing *alright* until it is automatic, they have not practiced the correct spelling of the two words. Small wonder then that while concentrating on an essay topic, the students' "automatic pilot" guides their hands into writing the incorrect form the way they have written it most often. How often do we find ourselves having performed some daily task—showering, dressing, driving to work—with no memory of the actual process? We perform the task effectively because we have done it the right way so often that we can rely on habit to carry ourselves through the activity. Our students, unfortunately, have not developed the right habits in their

v

writing. They will write a word down to see how it "looks" on paper, but they will have no clearly focused photograph of the correctly spelled word in their mind's eye. Their habitual behavior in writing classes is error-filled writing.

The Copy Book offers the opportunity for such students to develop good writing habits. "Copying" is very much an essential part of it. The first STEP, in fact, asks the students to do nothing more than copy a short essay and then proofread carefully, matching their own copy to the text. Invariably, students make errors in this STEP; they are used to proof*hearing*, not to proof*reading*. Once the students have been convinced of the importance of close, careful attention to the written word, they go on to other STEPs. These subsequent STEPs attempt to teach *one* grammatical skill at a time. Students copy short essays, changing one particular item per essay: the article, for example, or the tense, from past to present. Because the students are working on mastering one skill at a time, they can focus on it without being distracted by other tasks, such as might be present in a free essay. Because the task is within a complete and an organized essay, the students are provided with a context for the learning of that skill. You, the instructor, of course, are similarly provided with the opportunity to teach only one skill or to correct only one type of error because any other errors the students might make would be *copying errors*. You need only point to the correct version in the text. You should find the obviousness of the error a more effective teaching tool than writing, "Stop being careless!" in the margins of papers. In any case, even as the students are learning one skill, they are habituating themselves to the correct writing of such previously mislearned forms as "it's" for "its," as well as such often overlooked elements as comma placement and paragraph divisions. The essays themselves are on subjects that should interest students, making the work of copying and changing a more enjoyable experience than filling in blanks in uninteresting sentences, the typical activity in most grammar texts.

How to Use This Book. Begin by having students choose one of the first two exercises in STEP 1. *Do not skip this STEP.* If you prefer, you might actually begin with the "Sample Passage" in the introduction to the student, page 1. Encourage students not to rush, but to take their time in matching their written copy to the text. Try to go over the students' written copy in class so that you can return the papers immediately. As you do not have to write lengthy marginal comments, correction (or merely an indication in the margin that a copying errors exists) should be quick. If a student has made an error, have him or her correct it, list it, then go on to another exercise in STEP 1. If the student has made no error, you may choose to have the student go on to STEP 2, or to try another STEP 1, just to be sure of mastery. In later STEPs, we have asked students to underline any changes they have made, making your correction all the quicker.

While there may be a slight jam at your desk at the very beginning, soon the rush will cease as students work at different rates and on different STEPs. You will find that you have sufficient time to run in-class tutorials, explaining things to students individually as problems occur. You might also discover that students waiting to have their papers checked by you will begin to proofread each other's essays. We have found such interaction among students helpful, but have tried to make sure that they proofread "downwards," that is, a student should have mastered a STEP that he or she is going to proofread in another student's essay.

Finding Mistakes. Such is the power of habit that in copying, students will make an error, have it pointed out as being different from the original in the text, and still not see the mistake. For this reason, we have at times simply told students that there was an error in a particular paragraph, sentence, or line, and required the students to locate the error by themselves. You might want to bypass this and point out the error immediately. If the mistake is in copying, you need only point out the original. If the error pertains to the STEP, you might ask the student what the correct answer might have been, or, once again, show what was expected, with as much explanation as you feel may be necessary. Our "Introduction" to each STEP and the "Helpful Hints and Special Situations" within each STEP should be of assistance, but you may want to provide more explanation. All the exercises in a STEP are of comparable difficulty, but they do vary somewhat in size. You might let students choose the exercise that interests them for any work they need to do in a STEP beyond the first two exercises. When students working on a later STEP make a mistake on something that had been covered in an earlier STEP, they should do an additional exercise in that earlier STEP.

Determining Mastery. Students must be able to do at least one exercise in a STEP *without a single mistake*. An error you allow to pass is one that students will not learn to master. If students continue to make errors that pertain to a STEP, they should continue with other exercises until they have completed all five or seven; if that is not sufficient, they should start again with the first exercise chosen. Thorough mastery of the first thirteen STEPS should establish minimum competency in the course. How grades or standing is determined beyond that is a matter for your professional standards or those of your institution. In our experience, a large number of students can master all twenty-six STEPS, even when they also write summaries of different miniessays and also write freer assignments.

Branching Off. No one would claim that students writing the exercises in *The Copy Book* are doing creative writing. Students are, instead, trying to master the basics. Students can begin to move toward freer expression by writing summaries of the different miniessays of exercises, which gives students experience in paragraph construction as well as sharpens their reading skills. The writing assignments at the end of each STEP are designed to give students a wide selection of topics yet still oblige them to face some of the basic conventions taught in the STEP. Instructors who like to have students keep journals could still assign them, checking at intervals to see how many habits from different steps have been incorporated in the looser form of the journal.

Last Words. The *Instructor's Manual* for *The Copy Book* gives more advice about what you can expect to see as students work out the different STEPs, tips on how to arrange your grade book so as to accommodate the large amount of writing *The Copy Book* will elicit from students, and suggestions about related matters. The essays in *The Copy Book* itself, while designed with specific grammatical or stylistic lessons in mind, are also carefully organized. They are "miniessays," their brevity not eliminating the necessary parts of an essay: introduction, thesis sentence, paragraphs in defense (each with a main idea), and conclusion. In general, each of the essays also contains clear transitions between paragraphs. In essence, then, we have made an attempt to make the essays models for organization as well, and as such, useful for teaching outlining and summarization. Sentences have been numbered to facilitate reference to particular paragraphs, sentences, or words. Some basic English questions, such as vocabulary building, we have left to individual initiative. In most instances, the vocabulary found in the essays is not too challenging and should not limit the students' understanding. Meanwhile, you should find that your basic English students have never written more—or better.

The *Instructor's Manual* may be obtained through a local Holt representative or by writing to the English Editor, College Department, Holt, Rinehart and Winston, 383 Madison Avenue, New York, NY 10017.

We wish to thank Cerisa Shopkow for introducing us to the concepts of habituation and controlled composition, and for voicing her support for the book. Our thanks also to Kathy Forrest for making valuable suggestions about the arrangement of materials in the first half of *The Copy Book*. The library staff at Onondaga Community College has been extremely helpful as well; Lil Kinney and Frank Doble were particularly on the lookout for fascinating bits of information that proved useful. Bonita Kalwara has made our proposal presentable and has also been a willing audience, along with other members of our department, for our recitals about odd events and people.

We wish to thank the following reviewers who have offered us extensive and incisive comments that have greatly improved the book: Richard S. Beal; Robert Christopher, Ramapo College; William Coggin, Oklahoma State University, Stillwater; Phyllis Mehranian, Los Angeles City College; James W. Peck, Jefferson State Junior College; Audrey Roth, Miami-Dade Community College; David Skwire, Cuyahoga Community College; Fred Wood, Cleveland State Community College.

Finally, we are grateful to the people at Holt, Rinehart and Winston—Kenney Withers, Susan Katz, and Lester A. Sheinis—who have supported our project enthusiastically.

T.F.
J.MacK.

Contents

The
Copy
Book

To Students Who Use
The Copy Book

If you are like most people, you find writing difficult—especially writing for classes in school. There is so much to remember, how to spell a certain word, where to put a comma, where a paragraph should end—to say nothing about what idea you want to get across. Everyone who writes feels this, even someone who wins the Pulitzer Prize. This book is designed to help you reduce some of that uneasy feeling.

All the miniessays in *The Copy Book* are correct as they are printed on the page. To begin with, you must just copy a page out of the book. Sound easy? Try this one:

SAMPLE PASSAGE

Bug Facts

[1]There are five million different species of insects in the world. [2]They live in different environments. [3]Here are five facts about them. [4]There are more beetles on earth than any other living creature. [5]Mosquitoes are attracted to blue twice as often as to any other color. [6]There is a fly that can go faster than a jet airplane; the deer botfly has been clocked at a speed of 818 miles per hour. [7]Honeybees kill more people each year worldwide than do poisonous snakes. [8]It takes 27,000 spiders, each spinning a single web, to produce a pound of web.

Were you able to do it? When we asked beginning students to do this, nineteen out of twenty made at least one mistake. Their problem was that they were in too much of a hurry, did not proofread, and tried to get the assignment out of the way as soon as possible. Rushing like that causes more mistakes in beginning college writing than anything else.

Now, once you have the copying done, we ask you to make slight changes in the rest of the essays in the book. The changes start small and grow more complicated. With each essay you have only one kind of thing to worry about, changing single subjects to plural ones, changing the tense of a verb, and so on. If you make the changes correctly and copy everything else in the essay correctly, you will always be producing A essays.

You will notice there is no chapter in *The Copy Book* called "Grammar" or "Thirteen Uses of the Comma You Must Memorize." We are not asking you to memorize any grammar rules. We think that you will learn—master— all you need to know about grammar and style in a freshman English course by simply writing correctly, and writing a great deal. To help you develop good writing habits, we ask you do a great deal of copying even as you are making small changes in the essays. Everything you will be copying will be correct. We want you to develop good habits. To make sure you will do so, we have tried to write correct essays. We have not planted any mistakes we want you to uncover. We are hoping that by working with these models, you will get used to them and make them part of your skills. If spelling "receive" correctly becomes part of your habit, you know you will be able to concentrate on other aspects of the essay and let your "automatic pilot" worry about spelling.

There is more to writing, of course, than what is available to you in this book. Some people spend their lives trying to become better writers. But if you do every STEP in this book, you will have mastered the basics of English writing.

How to Use *The Copy Book*

In Class:

1. Read the Introduction to the STEP. (It provides explanations and examples of the work you will have to do in the STEP.)
2. Choose Exercise A or B in the STEP, and write it.
3. Proofread carefully your completed copy, underlining any changes you have made.
4. Have your instructor check your copy for any errors. Do not go on until your essay has been checked.
5. A. If you have made any errors:
   a. correct them on your copy,
   b. list any misspelled words,
   c. complete your progress chart on back cover,
   d. read the "Hints and Situations" section,
   e. choose another exercise in the STEP or ask your instructor to assign one,
   f. write your exercise.

   B. If you have made no errors (not a single one):
   a. complete your progress chart,
   b. list any words you find unfamiliar,
   c. either go on to the next STEP or do another exercise in the same STEP.

   Follow this procedure throughout *The Copy Book:*
   a. choose Exercise A or B,
   b. have it checked by instructor,
   c. complete progress chart,
   d. make corrections (if necessary),
   e. do another exercise (if necessary).

At Home:

The previous STEPs can and should be done in class, where your instructor can review your copy immediately. However, you can certainly write an exercise at home and hand it in when you come to your next class. Remember to do only *one* exercise at a time. Each should be checked before you go on to the next one.

Your instructor might allow another student in your class to check your essay if that student has already mastered the STEP you are working on. Your STEP 4 essay might be checked, for example, by your classmate who is on STEP 6.

The assignments that are found at the end of each STEP should also be written at home. Although they are controlled composition assignments that focus on the STEP you have completed, they are "free" to the extent that you will be composing them, not copying them. As such, you will require the additional time and concentration working at home provides.

If your instructor locates a STEP 4 error in a STEP 8 assignment, you should return to STEP 4, choosing an exercise and mastering the STEP. Then you should continue at the STEP 8 or 9 level.

Part 1

Grammar in Context

Step 1

Proofreading

Proofreading is not a simple matter. First of all, it is *reading*, not *hearing*. When you look over something you have just written, you may "hear" a word that is missing or not hear a letter that is there. It takes patience and training to find those little mistakes that you would be able to correct if only you could notice them. Hasty proofreading contributes more errors to student writing than any other single act in putting a composition together.

Professional proofreaders, such as those who work for newspapers or publishers, often read passages both backwards and forwards. They read forwards for the sense of each sentence, and they read backwards to catch little printing errors that the sense of the passage might encourage them to "hear" as if they were correct.

Most proofreading mistakes come with familiar words rather than unfamiliar ones. Few students misspell "psychoanalysis" or "Czechoslovakia" on their papers because they are cautious in dealing with such words. Students are more likely to have problems with words like "receive," "separate," or "existence." Again, the eye is a better guide than the ear. For example, a child may pull a little red wagon, but an adult drives a little red Volkswagen. Washington may be the capital of the United States, but the white-domed building there is the Capitol.

The passage above has tried to draw your attention mostly to variations in spelling, but there are other details to "check out" during proofreading. Capitalization is one; punctuation is another. Quotation marks and apostrophes cannot be heard in speech but must be noticed in reading. Notice, for example, that the commas and period in the previous paragraph were placed *inside* the quotation marks. Similarly, a girl may be described as being *blue-eyed* (with a hyphen), but she may work as a *bookkeeper* (one word). However, if you reached the end of the line while in the middle of the word *bookkeeper*, you might have separated the word where the dictionary indicates its syllables to be (book·keep·er), putting one syllable on one line, adding a hyphen, and then completing the word in the next line.

When writing original compositions, you should use from one-fifth to one-third of your time in proofreading and going over what you have written. It is a rare writer, student or professional, who can reach perfection on the first attempt.

A good idea is to write clearly and neatly, skipping a line between each line of writing and leaving wide margins. You will notice errors more easily.

STEP 1   Copy the short essay below, paying particular attention to punctuation and capitalization. After you have finished, proofread your copy carefully.

Games with Capitals

---

¹A rose by another name will certainly retain its sweet smell, but would Formica Corporation manage to hold on to its share of the market if all plastic laminates became known as formica? ²Formica Corporation thinks not and is fighting the attempts of rival companies to sell plastic laminates under the name "formica." ³The competing companies, backed by the Federal Trade Commission, argue that the trademark has become so popular that it now stands for the product. ⁴Because it has become a generic or descriptive term, they feel it should no longer be the exclusive property of Formica Corporation.

⁵In the past, the courts have allowed other companies to use terms that were once trademarks. ⁶The vacuum bottles that are popularly known as "thermos bottles" were once marketed by Thermos Company. ⁷The name of the heat- and cold-retaining containers was the same as the capitalized name of the company. ⁸When another manufacturer, Aladdin Company, wanted to market vacuum bottles, it had to sue for the right to call its product "Thermos." ⁹The right was granted, but Aladdin was ordered to use the term only with lowercase letters, that is, "thermos," not "Thermos." ¹⁰Aladdin appealed and won the right to capitalize the word provided it used the word according to grammatical rules, specifically, as the first word in a sentence where capitalization is obligatory. ¹¹Similarly, "escalator" was once the property of Otis Escalator, "aspirin" belonged to Bayer Aspirin, and "shredded wheat," "linoleum," "cellophane," and "cola" were once written as Shredded Wheat, Linoleum, Cellophane, and Cola, and they were restricted for the use of the particular company that first invented, marketed, or named the product. ¹²The brand names, however, proved too popular. ¹³Once they came to mean any brand of the product, their capitalization was no longer mandatory, and they became common property.

¹⁴To keep their trademarks from falling into common use, companies such as Coca-Cola, Xerox, and Kleenex are careful to insist that their names are trademarks. ¹⁵For this reason, a customer asking for "coke" must be told by the waiter that "Pepsi" is available if Coca-Cola is not sold, and Xerox Corporation advises its employees and customers to "copy" or "zero" materials, not "xerox" them.

NO. OF ERRORS

If you have made any errors, correct them, listing any misspelled words below. Then choose another selection from STEP 1.

_____   _____   _____

STEP 1   Copy the short passage that follows. Many words in the English language are not spelled as they are pronounced. Other words have look-alikes and sound-alikes with which they are frequently confused. Be sure to proofread what you have copied after you have written it.

How Did They Begin?

[1]We cannot always judge what people will make of themselves by looking at the jobs they hold now. [2]An eventual Nobel Prize winner, an international celebrity, or a world leader may be trying to sell us a vacuum cleaner at the front door or may be weighing chocolates at a candy counter.

[3]American philosopher and writer Henry David Thoreau gained perspective on our economic system by working as a pencil maker. [4]Albert Einstein polished his mathematics by working as a patent office clerk. [5]Poet Robert Burns learned to appreciate simple beauties by working as a tenant farmer, the Scottish equivalent of what we would call a sharecropper. [6]Novelist William Faulkner reached his first heights by painting antebellum houses in Mississippi. [7]But who could expect that political philosopher Thomas Paine could chart the course of his career when starting out as a corsetmaker?

[8]Some famous people once had jobs some of us might not want to accept. [9]Desi Arnaz, for example, once cleaned birdcages. [10]Both Elvis Presley and Sean Connery drove trucks before truck driving came to be thought of as glamorous. [11]Bob Hope began his career among the coarse world of professional boxers, and Dean Martin was a steelworker. [12]Marilyn Monroe was a factory worker, and Clark Gable was a lumberjack. [13]Some show business people began by performing services for other people. [14]Carol Burnett was an usherette, James Cagney was a waiter, and Perry Como was a barber. [15]President Harry S. Truman worked in a haberdashery, which is what men's shops were called when he was young. [16]Another president made a living by wearing men's clothes: Gerald R. Ford was a professional male model who appeared in many national advertisements.

[17]Although dictator Adolf Hitler is often described as a "paper hanger," he was also a poster artist. [18]Who knows how many people would still be alive today if he had been a success at his first profession and had not gone on to a job for which he was unfit?

NO. OF ERRORS

If you have made any errors, correct them, listing any misspelled words below. Then choose another selection in STEP 1.

_____   _____   _____

Step 1

Proofreading

Helpful Hints
and Special Situations

We tend to forget things and often need to jog our memories.

Use *i* before *e* except after *c* (but there are always exceptions).
There is *a rat* in "separate."
A "principal" is your *pal*.
A chicken *lays* eggs, do you?

Such devices can be helpful. There are additional hints below. You might devise some for particular words that give you trouble. Use these clues when you need them, but remember that checking the dictionary works best. And after you have checked on the use or spelling of a word, *write that word down*. Get to be so familiar with it that you will be able to write it correctly *automatically*. The proof of mastery is not only in getting the word right on a spelling test, but also in using it correctly in your essays or letters. Again, these "rules" do not describe all situation. There are exceptions to all of them. *Learn those words that are exceptions as you come across them.*

When you add an ending to a word, consider the last letter of the word and the first letter of the addition. If the word ends in a silent *e* and the addition begins with a vowel (*a, e, i, o, u*), *drop* the silent *e*.

love + able = lovable   race + ed = raced   clone + ing = cloning

Words that end in *y* need special care. No one rule covers all the possibilities. When you add a suffix (an ending) to such a word, check it against the text or the dictionary. Look. Do not listen.

As many errors in spelling and usage have to do with sound, one way to cut down on the errors is to avoid using contractions. In general, formal writing does not use contractions. Speech, even formal speech, does use them. Emphasize the distinctions between writing and speaking by not using contractions.

Use: *they are, does not, do not, is not, it is, will not*.

There is a troublesome word. Here is a simple method for checking whether you are using it correctly. Cross off the *t*. That leaves you with *here*. Read the sentence. If *here* makes sense, *there* has been used correctly. *Here* is part of *there* and *where*.

STEP 1   Copy the essay below, paying close attention to capitalization in particular. When you are done, proofread your copy carefully.

Gestures

---

[1]Anthropologists have theorized that the handshake developed out of an attempt by two suspicious strangers to reassure each other that they carried no concealed weapons. [2]The proferred handshake does, in fact, suggest friendship around the world. [3]Other gestures, however, change their meaning from country to country and have also varied over the centuries.

[4]To an American, touching the lobe of the ear, for example, means only that the earlobe itches. [5]When a Southern Italian or Yugoslavian man touches his ear, he is sending an insulting message, suggesting that another man is not sufficiently masculine. [6]To Greek children, the sight of a parent scratching the ear is a warning of coming punishment. [7]In Portugal the same gesture is a sign of extreme approval. [8]In Turkey it wards off evil spirits, in Scotland it questions the accuracy of a statement, and in the Canary Islands it refers to someone who is living off another person.

[9]Kissing the tips of the fingers, while universally accepted today as a gesture of approval, had varying meanings in the past. [10]At one time it was used to worship deities from afar. [11]For the Roman Tacitus and later for Shakespeare it was a sign of insincere flattery. [12]Only recently has it become a lighthearted sign of pleasure. [13]In fact, a group of researchers led by Desmond Morris found only one element common to most of the gestures. [14]Of the twenty movements the researchers had designated as "key gestures," seventeen contained an obscenity, an insult, or a combination of the two.

[15]Why gestures come to mean what they do often remains mysterious, but the researchers did clear up one misconception. [16]"Thumbs up," the supposed Roman sign for the gift of life in the arena, actually meant the opposite. [17]They blame the confusion on shoddy translators.

NO. OF ERRORS

If you have made any errors, correct them, listing any misspelled words below. Then choose another selection from STEP 1.

---   ---   ---

STEP 1   Copy the essay below. Do not change anything. You are being asked to develop your attention to details. Pay particular attention to the punctuation. If you reach the end of a line in the middle of a word, do not separate it at random. Check the dictionary to see how the word is separated into syllables, and divide the word at one of those points before completing it in the next line. Proofread your copy carefully.

Forgotten Laws

---

[1]A lot of state and federal laws remain on the books even though their usefulness is long past and their original purposes are long forgotten. [2]New York State has a particularly curious group of such laws.

[3]Part of the state's Agricultural and Markets Law is a regulation regarding horses' tails. [4]"Any person," states the law, "who cuts the bone, tissues, muscles, or tendons of the tail of any horse, mare, or gelding" is committing a misdemeanor. [5]The penalty? [6]Ninety days in jail and a $500 fine.

[7]The state's Environmental Conservation Law opposes building walls around your pond if these walls would prevent frogs from "having free access to and egress from water." [8]Clearly, this is part of some frogs' Bill of Rights.

[9]Other New York State penal laws prohibit people from participating in a public exhibition that involves throwing baseballs, softballs, or melons at people's heads, from competing in a bicycle race or dance marathon for more than eight straight hours without rest, and from selling fewer than six live baby turkeys. That is exactly what the law says. [10]Sell six or more but not fewer than six baby turkeys.

NO. OF ERRORS

If you have made any errors, correct them, listing any misspelled words below. Then choose another selection from STEP 1.

---   ---   ---

Step 1   Copy the short passage below. Many words in the passage are not spelled as they are pronounced. Other words have look-alikes and sound-alikes with which they are frequently confused. Be sure to proofread what you have copied after you have written it.

Sneezing

¹Although sneezing nowadays is considered merely a symptom of the common cold, earlier peoples had a variety of attitudes on the subject. ²The ancient Hebrews believed that when a person sneezed, he or she was nearest death. ³This fear was based on the erroneous notion that the essence of life would be blown from a person in sneezing. ⁴The fact that a dead person never breathed led to the deduction that one's soul must be one's breath. ⁵The association of sneezing with dreaded disease, especially the plague, goes back at least as far as the Athenians. ⁶Later, when a plague destroyed most of the population of medieval Rome, Pope Gregory the Great introduced the custom of saying, "God bless you," to anyone who sneezed. ⁷The custom survives and is also behind our use of the German word *Gesundheit,* which means "health."

⁸During the seventeenth and eighteenth centuries people had a more positive attitude toward sneezing. ⁹Not only did they think it cleared the mind, but they also thought sneezing brought a pleasure just this side of ecstasy. ¹⁰Men of leisure liked to carry quantities of pulverized tobacco called snuff to help induce sneezing. ¹¹They carried the snuff in bejeweled miniature boxes, some of which were highly precious indeed. ¹²Because only the idle and rich could afford snuff or have the time to sneeze at will, the self-induced sneeze became synonymous with aristocratic living. ¹³The sneezer had status, but the person who could not sneeze at will did not. ¹⁴Thus to sneeze at a person became a code for saying he or she was boring or insignificant. ¹⁵This custom helped to give rise to the expression, "He's not to be sneezed at."

¹⁶Some aspects of sneezing are still mysterious to us. ¹⁷For example, it is apparently impossible to sneeze and keep one's eyes open at the same time. ¹⁸Another oddity about a sneeze is that it can travel as fast as 100 miles per hour.

NO. OF ERRORS

If you have made copying errors, choose another selection in STEP 1. If your error was in misspelling a word, check the word's spelling and write the correct spelling here.

_____   _____   _____

STEP 1   Copy the selection printed below. After copying, proofread carefully. If you must separate a word, look it up in the dictionary, and see how it separates into syllables. Remember that there is no need to correct this essay. You need only copy it and proofread your copy.

When Lightning Strikes

[1]There is one important fact to keep in mind about lightning. [2]A bolt of lightning takes the shortest route to the ground, usually striking the tallest object in the area. [3]Thus, if you would like to be safe during a thunderstorm, avoid being the tallest or being near the tallest object in the vicinity.

[4]The safest place to be, of course, is inside some shelter. [5]An open convertible is not safe, but a car with its windows closed would be a secure place. [6]A structure with a lightning rod would provide the best refuge. [7]If no building is available, try to "lie low." [8]Seek out a ditch or a ravine, and avoid contact with metal or water while waiting for the storm's end.

[9]The least safe place to be is under a tree. [10]Many golfers and other sports figures get hurt when lightning strikes the tree they are under. [11]Two well-known golfers, Lee Trevino and Jerry Heard, were injured during a recent tournament while they tried to wait out a storm under a tree. [12]Open water holds the same danger as the area beneath the branches of a tree. [13]Swimmers in open water are usually the tallest objects around, attracting lightning to themselves. [14]In addition, water conducts electricity, enabling lightning to shock and sometimes even kill swimmers.

[15]All in all, lightning is a tremendous, as yet uncontrollable force. [16]It kills 125 Americans each year and causes millions of dollars of property damage. [17]Even a massive structure like the Statue of Liberty must wear a lightning rod for protection.

NO. OF ERRORS

If you have made any errors, correct them, listing any misspelled words below. Then choose another selection from STEP 1.

_____ _____ _____

Step 1   Copy the short essay that follows. After copying, proofread what
you have written.

Who Is in the Secretarial Pool?

---

[1]By law, advertisements for secretaries cannot be listed exclusively in the "Females Wanted" column. [2]In spite of this, few male applicants have rushed to enter the field. [3]According to Labor Department statistics, 99.1 percent of the nation's secretaries are female.

[4]But women were not always the ones to fill secretarial positions. [5]A lot of early business tycoons, particularly railroad executives, preferred to hire male secretaries. [6]Often known as "administrative assistants," these men had to take dictation, transcribe, and cope with the hardships of travel. [7]They often had to spend long periods of time on the road, living and working in special railroad cars. [8]One of those early railroad secretaries eventually became president of the Santa Fe railroad. [9]Chicago's late mayor, Richard Daley, was another who served as a secretary early in his career. [10]He worked for four different Cook County treasurers.

[11]Perhaps if fewer bosses would require that their secretaries prepare their coffee or do personal shopping for them, more men would be willing to jump into the secretarial pool. [12]There are plenty of men who have graduated from business schools or completed army training and are thus skilled in office work. [13]If the position would lose its stigma as "woman's work," more of them would turn to it as a possible job.

NO. OF ERRORS

If you have made any errors, correct them, listing any
misspelled words below. As this is the last selection in STEP 1,
you may chose any other essay and simply *copy* it, ignoring
any other instructions.

_____   _____   _____

Step 1

Writing Assignments: Proofreading

You are well on your way toward improved writing skills if you have trained yourself to *see* the words and punctuation on the page. Most of the errors writers tend to make are errors on the page. If they were reading their essays aloud, chances are that the listeners would be unaware of most of the errors.

If the errors, then, are in writing, get your eyes and hands used to the correct spelling of words and punctuation of sentences. If you become familiar with the appearance of words and grammatical symbols, you will be able to "check" your writing against an accurate picture in your mind.

1. Take the words you have copied incorrectly or the words that seem unfamiliar. Then write each of them carefully 15 or 20 times. Chances are that the word you have misspelled in copying is a word you have misspelled repeatedly in other writings. Each time you wrote it incorrectly, you "practiced" the wrong version. To develop the habit of spelling the word correctly, you should similarly practice writing it the way it is actually spelled. Think of this repetition as being similar to standing at the foul line and practicing foul shots, to hitting 200 balls across the net with your backhand, to plucking the guitar strings, to learning to drive a standard transmission. You want to be so familiar with the correct spelling that you will eventually be able to write the word that way automatically.

2. Proofread a classmate's essay after your instructor feels you are ready for STEP 2. Indicate it in the margin of the paper if you believe that there is an error in the line. Sign your name to the essay.

3. Proofread a newspaper article, paying particular attention to the way quotations are punctuated and words broken into syllables at the end of the line. Copy the sentences or the paragraph in which you find examples of quotation and syllabification, but check the syllables in your dictionary.

4. Locate the word you have misspelled or the word that seems unfamiliar in a book, newspaper, or magazine. Copy the entire sentence, underlining the particular word.

5. Have someone dictate the words below. They are often misspelled. Check your spelling by comparing your version to their spelling below.

a lot	environment	miniature	refuge
bejeweled	fallacious	occurred	secretary
business	impossible	perspective	symptom
capitalize	lightning	preferred	synonymous
erroneous	medieval	professional	tournament

Step 2

The Articles: *a* and *an*

This is one of the few times in the book when we would like you to trust your ears instead of your eyes. In order to use the indefinite articles *a* and *an* correctly, you must *listen* rather than look. The key is the first letter of the word that follows the article.

Use *a* before all of the *consonants* as well as before *u* when it sounds like "you."

a *b*oy	a *g*host	a *l*amb
a *c*at	a *h*ouse	a *m*ad owl
a *d*ate	a *j*olly man	a *n*ose
a *f*at man	a *k*id	a *p*ainter

a *q*uick fox	a *v*est
a *r*obe	a *w*izard
a *s*nowmobile	a *y*outh
a *t*op	a *z*ipper

also   a *u*seful article   a *u*nited nation   a *u*kelele

Use *an* before all of the *vowel sounds*, including the silent "h."

an *a*nimal   an *e*ffective leader   an *i*sland   an *o*gre   an *u*ncle
also   an hour   an honorable woman

LISTEN for the sound. You must HEAR a vowel to use *an*. You must HEAR a consonant to use *a*.

STEP 2 We would like you to make some changes in the essay below. These changes *may* affect the articles *a* and *an*. If necessary, change the *a* to *an* or the *an* to *a*. Change nothing else. Copy the rest of the essay and proofread.

STEP 2

In sentence 1 change *administrator* to *president*. (and *an* to *a*)
In sentence 2 change *handsome* to *attractive*.
In sentence 4 change *obese* to *corpulent*.
In sentence 10 change *aging* to *elderly*.
In sentence 13 change *substitute* to *alternate*.
In sentence 15 change *ancestry* to *descent*.

What Is a President Like?

---

[1]Many of us have preconceived notions of what an administrator of the United States is supposed to be like, but those preconceptions need not be so. [2]For example, we often think that the president should be a handsome, tall man, but not all of them have been; Lincoln was the tallest at 6 feet 4 inches, but he was far from handsome. [3]Madison was the shortest at 5 feet 4 inches. [4]William Howard Taft was an obese man at 352 pounds. [5]Washington seems to have had a startling appearance. [6]Not only did he have wooden false teeth, but his face was badly scarred by smallpox.

[7]Most presidents have been mature men. [8]The average age upon taking office has been 54 years, 3 months, and 14 days. [9]But Theodore Roosevelt was an athletic young man of 42, younger than any other. [10]The oldest, William Henry Harrison, was an aging man when he assumed office at 68; he caught pneumonia at the inauguration and died a month later.

[11]We tend to think a president should be willing to serve his country in the armed services and, true enough, Jackson, W. H. Harrison, Taylor, Pierce, Grant, and Eisenhower were professional soldiers. [12]But Grover Cleveland was a draft dodger in the Civil War. [13]He hired a substitute to serve in his place. [14]When Cleveland was ridiculed for this by his opponent for the presidency, James G. Blaine, it was discovered that Blaine had done the same thing.

[15]Most presidents have claimed an ancestry from the British Isles. [16]Only Van Buren and the two Roosevelts were of Dutch origin, and Eisenhower was of Swiss German background. [17]Perhaps we may sometime see a time when a president is female, young, black, and short.

As you proofread, underline any changes you have made. Correct any errors your instructor has located in your essay.

STEP 2   We are going to ask you to make a number of changes in the essay below. The changes you make *may* force you to replace *a* with *an* or *an* with *a*. The articles would be the only words affected. Copy everything else and proofread your copy carefully.

In sentence 3 change *unbiased* to *honest*.
In sentence 4 change *ideal* to *perfect*.
In sentence 7 change *puffy* to *inflated* and *protruding* to *jutting*.
In sentence 12 change *tiny* to *small*.
In sentence 13 change *moist* to *slightly wet*.

Eye Power

¹There are a number of steps a woman can take that would improve her use of eye shadow. ²All too often, according to makeup experts, this cosmetic is "abused."

³The first step toward more effective use of eye shadow is an unbiased evaluation of the woman's face, say the experts. ⁴The idea is to enhance what nature has put there rather than create some sort of an ideal look.

⁵The second step makeup artists urge the woman to take is to accept brown as a color for eye makeup. ⁶Experts feel that brown "shades and minimizes" more effectively than any other color. ⁷The shade helps make a puffy eyelid seem less swollen and a protruding brow less prominent. ⁸For deeply set eyes the experts recommend a lighter, beige-ivory color.

⁹The most important consideration for the woman, whether she wears blues, greens, or other colors, is the delicacy of the application. ¹⁰The touch of the brush must be light because a little looks best. ¹¹More is not better. ¹²A tiny amount, particularly in the case of a roll-on or crayon, is usually sufficient. ¹³A powdered shade is generally softer and more flattering, but does not have as much staying power as a moist shadow. ¹⁴For this reason, powders and shades applied with water should be refreshed in the course of the day.

¹⁵The right color, selected for the right reason, will improve anyone's appearance, makeup artists insist.

NO. OF ERRORS

As you proofread, underline any changes you have made. Correct any errors your instructor has located in your essay. For more work in articles, choose another selection in STEP 2. List corrected spelling words below.

_____   _____   _____

Step 2

The Articles a/an

Helpful Hints and Special Situations

Here are two special situations that the rules at the beginning of this STEP did not mention. We deliberately separated these exceptions from the general rule because we do not want rules and exceptions to be discussed at the same time. Still, we do want to prepare you for the situation when the unusual appears.

The basic principle remains. Use *a* before all consonant sounds. We mentioned one letter that sometimes *sounds* like a consonant, the *u*, as in *union*. (It sounds like *you*.)

Here is another vowel that sounds like a consonant: *o* as in *one, once, oneness*

a *one*-way street   a *once*-in-a-lifetime chance   a *one*-year contract

---

For the use of *an*, the basic rule is still the vowel *sound* of the first letter of the word that follows. This includes the silent *h*, as in an hour.

Here are some other rare cases of the invisible vowel sound:

an X-ray machine (we hear *ex*)   an "F" on the report card (we hear *eff*)

Be particularly careful with numbers: an 18-year-old (eighteen; also eight, eighty) How about ⅛? It could be either an *eighth* of an inch or a one-eighth-inch piece.

A and *an* are also called *indefinite articles*, whereas *the* is the *definite article*.

He is *a* man.   *A* car is expensive to maintain.
He is *the* man who robbed the   *The* car I sold was too expensive
store.   to keep.

Use *a* or *an* when you have no particular or definite person or item in mind.

STEP 2   We are going to ask you to make a number of changes in the essay below. These changes may force you to change the article (*a* or *an*) before the word. The articles would be the only words affected. Copy everything else.

In sentence 2 change *young* to *unknown*.
In sentence 2 change *experienced* to *veteran*.
In sentence 4 insert *single* before *major league*.
In sentence 5 change *steal* to *bargain*.
In sentence 7 change *foolish* to *absurd*.
In sentence 9 change *.387 average* to *average of .387*.
In sentence 12 change *All Star* to *MVP*.

Major League Mistakes

¹In the long history of baseball trades, certain deals become memorable as "stinkeroos."

²Back in 1900, the Cincinnati Reds traded a young pitcher named Christy Mathewson to the New York Giants for an experienced pitcher named Amos Rusie. ³Rusie, at twenty-eight, had won 20 or more games for eight consecutive seasons. ⁴By contrast, Mathewson was an inexperienced college kid without a major league victory. ⁵What seemed a steal for the Reds at the time is now considered to have been one of the more awful deals ever made. ⁶Rusie did not win a single game for the Reds, whereas Mathewson went on to win 373 for the Giants.

⁷Twenty-eight years later it was the Giants' turn to make a foolish trade. ⁸They sent Rogers Hornsby, "The Rajah," to Boston for Shanty Hogan and Jimmy Walsh. ⁹Hornsby led the league with a .387 average that season and batted over .300 for a half dozen additional seasons. ¹⁰Hogan and Walsh are remembered only as the players for whom Hornsby was traded.

¹¹More recently the Reds have been on both sides of memorable deals. ¹²They gave up too soon on Frank Robinson, an All Star for years after he was traded, but recouped when they picked up George Foster in another deal. ¹³Foster has become their leading home-run hitter whereas the Giants have had little use out of shortstop Frank Duffy and pitcher Vern Geishert, the two men they received for Foster in the 1971 deal.

NO. OF ERRORS

As you proofread, underline any changes you have made. Correct any errors your instructor has located in your essay. For more work in articles, choose another selection in STEP 2. List corrected spelling words below.

STEP 2   We are asking you to make some changes in the essay below. These changes may affect the articles (*a* and *an*). If you think it is necessary, make the changes in the articles. Copy everything else and proofread carefully.

In sentence 2 change *time* to *era*.
In sentence 3 change *bride* to *wife*.
In sentence 6 insert *envious* before *rival*.
In sentence 11 change *armament* to *weapon*.
In sentence 12 change *abbreviated* to *short*.

The Best Man

---

[1]The best man did not always look forward to his selection. [2]There was a time when his duties were quite dangerous.

[3]It was the best man's responsibility to help the bridegroom capture a bride. [4]A warrior thought it was beneath his dignity to woo a woman, but not undignified to kidnap one.

[5]The best man was also expected to extend his protection to the bride. [6]On the day of the wedding it was possible for a rival to appear and carry her off. [7]The best man had to be there to guarantee her safety. [8]Scandinavians used to hold weddings at night to prevent such intrusions. [9]The best man used to keep his lance close at hand during the ceremony. [10]With sockets for torches, the lance's function was twofold. [11]It was both an armament and a source of illumination for these midnight festivities.

[12]A marriage was likely to last a lifetime in those days, but the career of the best man was often an abbreviated one.

NO. OF ERRORS

As you proofread, underline any changes you have made. Correct any errors your instructor has located in your essay. For more work in articles, choose another selection in STEP 2. List corrected spelling words below.

_____   _____   _____

STEP 2   We are asking you to make a number of changes in the essay below. These changes may affect the articles (*a* and *an*). If necessary, change the *a* to *an* or the *an* to *a*. You need not make any other changes. Copy everything else and proofread carefully.

In sentence 1 change *old* to *classic*.
In sentence 2 omit *earphone*.
In sentence 7 change *simple* to *uncomplicated* and *service* to *repair*.
In sentence 9 change *unwilling* to *helpless*.

TV Jacks

---

¹If an old movie you have been waiting for is finally shown on the late, late show, you can enjoy it without waking up the rest of the household.

²First, see if your set is already equipped with an earphone jack. ³If it is, buy an adapter called "stereo jack for a ⅛-inch plug." ⁴It is a small investment, selling for under two dollars at most electronics dealers. ⁵Then plug in a set of earphones and you are "set" for private listening.

⁶If your set does not have a jack, you can buy one. ⁷A simple system can be wired by a service man for about forty dollars. ⁸More expensive transmitter and wireless sets are available, but they could run you ten times as much as a more simple system.

⁹In any case, the rest of the house no longer has to be an unwilling prisoner of your late viewing habits.

NO. OF ERRORS

As you proofread, underline any changes you have made. Correct any errors your instructor has located in your essay. For more work in articles, choose another selection in STEP 2. List corrected spelling words below.

---   ---   ---

STEP 2   We are asking you to make some changes in the essay below. These changes may force you to change the articles (from *an* to *a* or *a* to *an*). Make the changes that seem necessary. Copy everything else and proofread carefully.

In sentence 3 change *relative* to *aunt* and *foreign* to *Italian*.
In sentence 6 change *service* to *hospital*.
In sentence 9 change *established* to *school*.
In sentence 11 insert *accomplished* before *catcher*.
In sentence 15 change *outstanding* to *leading*.

Young O. J. Simpson

---

¹Despite his jokes on the subject, O. J. Simpson's real name is not "Orange Juice." ²He was born Orenthal James Simpson, July 9, 1947. ³He was named by a relative who thought "Orenthal" sounded like a name for a foreign movie star. ⁴This same aunt gave her own children familiar names like Stanley, Stewart, and Pamela.

⁵Simpson, his two sisters, and his brother were raised in San Francisco's predominantly black Potrero Hill section, near Chinatown. ⁶Their mother, a service employee, was separated from O. J.'s father. ⁷Young Orenthal led a rambling streetcorner existence, running with a gang and coming close to trouble with the law on several occasions before his energies found a positive outlet in athletics.

⁸Simpson's participation in sports began at Booker T. Washington Community Center and at a playground near his home. ⁹His fleetness of foot first began to show itself at Everett Junior High School, where he broke an established record for the sixty-yard dash. ¹⁰Later he went to Galileo High School, where most of the students were of Chinese descent. ¹¹He was a catcher on the baseball team until he broke his thumb. ¹²Because of his size (five feet ten, 160 pounds), Simpson was a tackle until the coach noticed his speed in running. ¹³He was moved to fullback, and in that position he ran to glory.

¹⁴At San Francisco City College he compiled the most sensational record of any running back in junior college history. ¹⁵He transferred to the University of Southern California, where he was the outstanding national player in his senior year. ¹⁶And in professional football he ranks as one of the most accomplished players of all time.

NO. OF ERRORS

As you proofread, underline any changes you have made. Correct any errors your instructor has located in your essay. For more work in articles, choose another selection in STEP 2. List corrected spelling words below.

_____   _____   _____

STEP 2   We would like you to make some changes in the essay below. These changes *may* affect the articles *a* and *an*. If necessary, change the *a* to *an* or the *an* to *a*. Change nothing else. Copy the rest of the essay and proofread.

In sentence 3 change *long time* to *extended period*.
In sentence 4 change *United States* to *American*.
In sentence 7 delete *sensitive* entirely.
In sentence 9 insert the word *expert* before *graphologist*.
In sentence 11 change *loquacious* to *talkative*.
In sentence 13 change *good* to *exceptional*.
In sentence 15 change *relaxed* to *easygoing*.

Handwriting Analysis

[1]The study of the ways in which people reveal their personality through their handwriting is called graphology. [2]Many people are only just now accepting graphology as a trustworthy means of measuring consciousness and self. [3]Europeans have studied graphology for a long time, and two Swiss universities, Basel and Bern, have departments devoted to the subject. [4]A United States college offering courses in graphology is the New School for Social Research in New York City. [5]Here are some of the elementary observations an introductory graphology student might learn.

[6]Heavy pressure and dark strokes indicate a robust sensualist with deep feelings. [7]Very light pen pressure reveals a sensitive idealist who is often impractical. [8]Even pressure reveals an acceptable depth of feeling, neither shallow nor long-lasting.

[9]Oval letters, *a, d, g,* and *o,* are the first a graphologist wants to inspect. [10]When oval letters are open at the top, they indicate a truthful person. [11]Wide-open ovals are used by a loquacious person who cannot keep a secret. [12]A secretive person prefers closed ovals; such an individual keeps an inside piece of information and knows when to keep his or her mouth shut. [13]An oval locked with a double loop is preferred by a liar with a good memory.

[14]The shape of letters in general counts next in significance. [15]Rounded letters are used by a relaxed, receptive person. [16]Such a person follows the path of least resistance and does not try to make waves. [17]Someone who prefers pointed letters is a domineering, competitive person and is likely to take himself or herself seriously.

[18]Other matters to consider are slant, capitalization, and end strokes.

NO. OF ERRORS

As you proofread, underline the changes you have made. Correct any errors your instructor has located in your essay. For more work in articles, choose another selection in STEP 2. List corrected spelling errors below.

Step 2

Writing Assignments: The Articles *a/an*

The sequence we suggest is from STEP to summary to independent writing assignments. If you have used the various grammar workbooks over the years, you know that often you can do the assignments in the text correctly yet find yourself making the error in your own writing.

To enable you to reach complete mastery of this STEP, we have devised a number of topics below that will enable you to practice using articles. Your teacher may ask you to organize the paragraphs in a particular way and suggest a length. All we ask you to do is pay attention to the use of the articles.

1. Give instructions on how to tune your car or an instrument, identifying the various tools you need in the process. (a wrench)
2. You observe individuals from all over the world enter the United Nations by way of a revolving door. Characterize them by their nationalities. (a Scot)
3. Mix a crazy salad, your own concoction, adding the various ingredients one by one. (*a* or *an* before *eucalyptus leaf?*)
4. If you could take only ten different items with you to a desert island, what would they be and why?
5. Name the things in your room that are there for your comfort or amusement as opposed to necessity. How essential are these "luxury" items to you?
6. What professions seem to you worth pursuing? (an accountant, a teacher)
7. What places do you like to go to on the weekend?
8. Name the positions on a sports team, and discuss what the job of each player at that position is.
9. Think of the last public situation you were in (on the bus, in a movie), and describe how people were behaving. Use an adjective as you name the people. (a tall man, an angry usher)
10. Your house is the scene for a party. How would various household animals react to the special situation?

A good writing habit is to write about specific people, places, or things rather than about any or all people, places, or things. However, for the sake of this assignment, do write about the general. For particular people or items, you would have to use the definite article *the*. For items or people in general, you would use the indefinite articles *a* or *an*. Write about what *a* (typical) cat might do in *a* house, during *a* loud party. For this assignment only, do not write about *the* black and white cat at *the* tall kid's house where *the* best party you have ever attended was.

Step 3

Pronoun Agreement and Reference (Plurals)

In this STEP you will be asked to rewrite short essays so that you will be writing about two or more people, things, or ideas. When you make the subject of a sentence plural, you also have to make other changes in the sentence. A very important change is with the verb in the sentence, but that will be taken up in STEP 4.

> A chimney sweeper I knew enjoyed his work because he found himself being kissed by brides for good luck.

Rewritten in the plural (about two or more chimney sweepers), the sentence would read:

> Chimney sweepers I knew enjoyed their work because they found themselves being kissed by brides for good luck.

1. The article *a* is dropped.
2. *sweeper* receives the *s* (indicating the plural).
3. *his* becomes *their*.
4. *he* becomes *they*.
5. *himself* becomes *themselves*.

The pronouns *he, his, himself* "refer" to the chimney sweeper and, because there is one chimney sweeper, the pronouns are also singular, "agreeing" with the subject to which they refer.

Similarly, when the subject under discussion becomes plural (chimney sweepers), the pronouns referring to the chimney sweepers also become plural—*they, their, themselves*—"agreeing" in number with the plural *chimney sweepers*.

Personal Pronouns

Nominative		Objective	
I and another →	we	me and another →	us
you and another →	you	you and another →	you
(Jill) she and another →⎫		her and another →⎫	
(Jack) he and another → ⎬ they		him and another → ⎬ them	
(the pail) it and another →⎭		it and another →⎭	

Notice that in the plural you would use the same terms (*they* or *them*) whether the singular person or pronoun is masculine (*Jack, he, him*), feminine (*Jill, she, her*) or neuter (*pail, it*). And, of course, "**you**" can be either plural or singular.

Students seem to have more difficulty with two other sets of pronouns, the reflexive and the possessive. As you read through the list below, please notice that there is *no apostrophe* in sight. The entire word, in the case of the possessive pronoun, shows possession. There is no need to attach the apostrophe *s* or to use an apostrophe to show possession.

Reflexive

(I)	myself and another	→	ourselves
(you)	yourself and another	→	yourselves
(she)	herself and another	→ ⎫	
(he)	himself and another	→ ⎬	themselves
(it)	itself and another	→ ⎭	

Possessive

(I)	my	→	our	(me)	mine	→	ours
(you)	your	→	your	(you)	yours	→	yours
(she)	her	→ ⎫		(her)	hers	→ ⎫	
(he)	his	→ ⎬	their	(him)	his	→ ⎬	theirs
(it)	its	→ ⎭		(it)	———	⎭	

Notice that none of these pronouns takes the apostrophe.

Stay with the same pronoun throughout a paragraph if you are speaking of the same person, place, or concept. Do not switch from "they" to "you" when you are writing about "people."

Using plural subjects and plural pronouns to refer to the subject helps eliminate the problem with sexism in language. If you are reluctant to use "he" when you mean "one" or "a person," you could use the plural "they." Of course, you would first have to make your subject plural. Write about many people instead of about one and you can use *they* or *them*.

STEP 3   Rewrite the short essay below so that you will be discussing many cowboys, not only Henry Beckwith. Instead of the sentence that now begins the second paragraph, substitute: *Many of these cowboys won their spurs in those thickets.* As you can see, the change from "cowboy" to "cowboys" forces you to make other changes in the essay, specifically in pronouns and articles. Make these changes. Copy everything else and proofread carefully. (Note that *cowboy's* in sentence 12 becomes *cowboys'.*)

A New Look at the Old West

---

¹In *Black Heroes in our Nation's History,* Phillip T. Drotning says that between three thousand and five thousand black cowboys rode the Western ranges after the Civil War. ²Hundreds of these black cowhands worked in Texas, either on ranches or on cattle trails. ³The most daring of these black men were those that searched the thickets of South Texas for stray cattle.

⁴One famous black cowboy who won his spurs in those thickets was Henry Beckwith. ⁵Little is known about him. ⁶He had probably been a runaway slave who had taken to the brush to avoid capture. ⁷When the Emancipation Proclamation freed him, he just stayed on, making a good living for himself hunting the cattle that had grown up wild during the four years of the Civil War.

⁸The black cowboy spent his days in thickets so dense that neither men nor cattle could see more than a few feet ahead. ⁹He slept on the ground, with only his horse blanket spread over sticks covering him. ¹⁰He sustained himself by drinking black coffee mixed with chili juice, jerked beef, and cornbread. ¹¹He rode mostly at night, trusting his sense of smell, his keen hearing, and pure instinct to lead him to the man-eating cattle he sought. ¹²The cowboy's night habits were such that the Mexican cowboys joked that he lived like a coyote.

¹³When he had rounded up enough of the longhorn cattle, he would drive them to one of the big factories for tallow and hide located just outside brush country. ¹⁴After spending a day in civilization, he would return to his beloved *brasada* (brush).

NO. OF ERRORS

As you proofread, underline the changes you have made. Correct any errors your instructor has located in your essay. For additional work in plurals (pronoun agreement and reference), choose another STEP 3 selection. List corrected spelling errors below.

STEP 3   In the essay below, change *mourner* to *mourners* and *widow* to *widows*. These changes will force you to make other alterations in the essay, specifically in the *pronouns* and *articles*. Make the changes you must, and copy everything else. In sentence 10 change *mourner's* to *mourners'*. Proofread carefully. Your first sentence should read: *European mourners wore black if they wished to express their grief.*

Mourning Colors

---

[1]A European mourner wore black if he* wished to express his grief. [2]A mourner of another culture chose to clothe himself in different colors if he wished to express his emotions.

[3]There are many instances of white, the color of hope, being used as a sign of mourning. [4]A female mourner in Sparta or Rome wore white during her mourning period. [5]Prior to 1498 a widow in England, France, or Spain would generally dress herself in white. [6]Mary, Queen of Scots, was called "the White Queen," because she mourned her husband, Lord Darnley, dressed in white.

[7]A mourner in ancient Egypt wore yellow. [8]A Burmese mourner dressed in saffron. [9]His yellow clothing was intended to recall the color of withering leaves. [10]Similarly, a Persian mourner's pale brown clothing attempted to remind the living of dying leaves. [11]A Syrian or Armenian mourner generally selected sky blue as a mourning color for himself. [12]His choice of color expressed his hope that the deceased had gone to the blue heaven.

[13]The color range of mourning even includes purple. [14]Because it was considered to be a "royal" color, Christian princes often mourned in purple. [15]To this day, on Good Friday, the cardinals, also known as "Princes of the Church," wear purple in mourning the death of Christ.

NO. OF ERRORS

As you proofread, underline any changes you have made. Correct any errors your instructor has located in your essay. For additional work in plurals (pronouns and possessives), choose another STEP 3 selection. List corrected spelling errors below.

---------------   ---------------   ---------------

*The generic *he* is idiomatic in English and is *not* to be interpreted as sexist.

Step 3

Pronoun Agreement and Reference (Plurals)

Helpful Hints and Special Situations

Words do not just *mean*. They also *do*. They have function, particularly in the way they interact with other words in a sentence. It is worth reviewing the list of pronouns in the introduction to this STEP.

Subject		Object
we	——	to us
you	——	to you
they	——	to them

When to use *we* and when to use *us?* When to use *they* and *them?* Your clue is the word *to*. The pronouns in the *object* group work with *to*. The pronouns in the *subject* group cannot function with *to*. Try other words, such as *for, of, on,* and others; and see which group works with them.

Possessive pronouns also fall into two groups. Knowing their formal names is less important than knowing how they function in sentences.

Modifiers

our hats	The hats are *ours*.
your bats	The bats are *yours*.
their cars	The cars are *theirs*.

The first group contains *modifiers*. The item owned or possessed follows the pronoun. The possessive pronouns in the second group are used when the person, place, or concept that is owned has already been named.

One difficulty with pronouns seems to occur when students move from proper nouns (capitalized, formal names) to pronouns.

Jack and Jill went up the hill.   They went up the hill.

"Jack and I went up the hill," said Jill.   "We went up the hill," said Jill.

Jack and Jill were with Hansel and Gretel.   Jack and Jill were with them.

STEP 3   In the essay below, give Bert B. Webber, Jr., a partner. This addition will mean that you will be talking about two people instead of one throughout the essay. Rewrite the entire essay, making the changes you must in pronouns and articles. In sentence 6 change *family's* to *families'*. Copy everything else and proofread carefully. Your first sentence should read: *For twenty years Bert B. Webber, Jr., and his partner, along with their crews, searched for sunken treasure.*

Treasure Hunt

---

¹For twenty years Bert B. Webber, Jr., along with his crews, searched for sunken treasure. ²The main object of his search was the treasure galleon *Concèpcion* that had sunk near the Dominican Republic in 1641, filled with gold and silver.

³He had prepared for the search by reading all the books he could find about sunken treasure, including *Treasure Island.* ⁴He had perfected his diving skills by shipping out on various expeditions. ⁵Although all of the expeditions had failed, he had not given up.

⁶Over the years he had dealt with his family's living expenses by doing odd jobs. ⁷He did welding and bricklaying, and he sold encyclopedias. ⁸Each year he spent only four months at home. ⁹His other eight months were spent aboard ships, searching for salvageable treasure.

¹⁰Finally, he secured a former British minesweeper to help in his search. ¹¹With this ship and a crew of sixteen he systematically surveyed a series of reefs in the Atlantic Ocean called Silver Shoals. ¹²Webber had convinced himself that the treasure of the *Concèpcion* was right beneath him somewhere. ¹³On November 28, 1978, he struck it rich. ¹⁴The value of the hoard inside the *Concèpcion* was estimated at $40 million.

NO. OF ERRORS

As you proofread, underline any changes you have made. Correct any errors your instructor has located in your essay. For additional work in plurals (pronouns and possessives), choose another STEP 3 selection. List corrected spelling errors below.

---   ---   ---

STEP 3   In the story below, remove the parentheses around *and his young son, Icarus* in sentence 4, and rewrite the story so that you are speaking about both Daedelus and Icarus. Because you will be writing about two people instead of one, you will have to change the pronouns and eliminate any articles. In sentence 5 change *prisoner* to *prisoners*; in sentence 10 change *builder's* to *builders'*. Copy everything else and proofread carefully.

The Flight

¹Daedelus of Athens was an architect and a sculptor. ²While he was at the court of Crete's King Minos, he received particular honors for his accomplishments. ³The most notable of these artistic works was Daedelus' design of the labyrinth that became the abode of the Minotaur, a monster half man and half bull. ⁴At last Daedelus (and his young son, Icarus) grew tired of Crete and decided to return to Athens.

⁵Prevented by King Minos from leaving, the prisoner resolved to escape by air. ⁶He knew that King Minos would guard only the land and sea. ⁷His plan was to collect the feathers birds had dropped along the mountainous coast and fashion wings for himself. ⁸He gathered the feathers and arranged them in order, putting the shorter feathers first. ⁹He bound them in the middle with linen threads and fastened the ends with wax. ¹⁰The builder's final task was to bend the feathers into a curve. ¹¹This was how he fashioned wings for his escape.

¹²He fitted his wings to his body, balanced himself for an instant, and then floated up into the sky, light as the birds that flew there. ¹³After lowering himself to earth, he made ready to leave. ¹⁴Daedelus warned his son to "steer a middle course" and avoid flying too close to the sun.

¹⁵The two then rose upon their wings, son closely following father. ¹⁶They had left Crete behind and seen other coasts recede, when Icarus, emboldened by the ease of their flight, darted toward the sun. ¹⁷Before he was even aware of it, the sun's rays melted the wax holding the feathers in place. ¹⁸His wings having dissolved, Icarus plunged into the sea. ¹⁹The sorrowful Daedelus journeyed on to Sicily.

NO. OF ERRORS

As you proofread, underline any changes you have made. Correct any errors your instructor has located in your essay. For additional work in plurals (pronouns and possessives), choose another STEP 3 selection. List corrected spelling errors below.

STEP 3   In the essay below, the work on radium is attributed to Marie Curie. Remove the parentheses around *and her husband, Pierre* in the first sentence, and rewrite the essay so that you will be describing their work as a joint venture. Because you will be writing about two people, you will have to change the pronouns that refer to them to the plural. Pay close attention to articles. In sentence 6 change *scientist's* to *scientists'*. Copy everything else and proofread carefully.

The Discovery of Radium

---

¹In 1898, in a small laboratory in Paris, Marie Curie (and her husband, Pierre) stumbled upon an element for which she had not been looking. ²Today that element, radium, is a major weapon in fighting cancer.

³She had been working on the radioactivity of uranium when she noticed that her electroscope was registering a current for no apparent reason. ⁴She found the source of the current to be the ore itself, pitchblende, not the uranium that the ore contained. ⁵She continued to analyze the ore, separating the pitchblende into its constituents. ⁶The scientist's final results showed the presence of two new, highly radioactive elements, radium and barium.

⁷Three years later, working by herself, Marie Curie successfully isolated the pure element, radium. ⁸The continuous dissolution of this element produces alpha, beta, and gamma rays. ⁹The alpha and beta particles are the ones used to attack malignant growths deep inside the body.

¹⁰In honor of the Curies' discovery, when a new element was produced during research on the atomic bomb, its name became "curium."

NO. OF ERRORS

As you proofread, underline any changes you have made. Correct any errors your instructor has located in your essay. For additional work in plurals (pronouns and possessives), choose another STEP 3 selection. List corrected spelling errors below.

_____   _____   _____

Step 3

Writing Assignments: Pronoun Agreement and Reference (Plurals)

The assignments below should all be written in the past tense. Writing the essays in the past tense eliminates most complications with subject-verb agreement.

While you are working on some of these assignments, remind yourself that you are writing in the plural and should be using *plural pronouns* when you are referring to plural subjects.

In these assignments below, name your subject early; then try to use pronouns to refer to that subject for the rest of your essay.

1. Think of a famous team or group in an entertainment field—The Beatles, The Rolling Stones, the Bee Gees, Rowan and Martin, Mork and Mindy, The Fondas, The Bunkers—and tell how you liked them during a performance.

2. Describe the exploits of some famous team in history: Lewis and Clark, The Curies, Teddy Roosevelt and the Rough Riders, the astronauts, Romeo and Juliet, Koufax and Drysdale, Mantle and Maris.

3. What rights *did* landlords have in the past? Did apartment dwellers have more rights or fewer?

4. Describe the behavior of a group of animals that you once observed.

5. What sort of obligations did parents have toward their children?

6. Compare the pitching staffs of two teams that participated in a past World Series.

7. Describe some experience that you and a sibling or a close friend shared.

8. If a friend has recently established a relationship with someone, how did that affect your friendship?

Step 4

Subject-Verb Agreement and Possessives (Plurals)

Step 4 continues Step 3. Once again you are being asked to rewrite short essays so that you will be writing about many people, places, or ideas rather than about one. When you rewrote essays from the singular to the plural in STEP 3, you had to change the pronouns to their plural forms to make them "agree" with the plural subjects. In STEP 4 you must continue to make the pronouns plural (and drop the articles). In addition, in STEP 4 you will also have to change the verbs, making them agree with the subjects.

Singular	Plural
Carin Flood worked as a physical therapist but was unhappy with what *she was* doing. Then she read of openings for chimney sweepers. Now *she is* making less money but enjoying herself tremendously. As a fringe benefit, *she gets* to kiss newlyweds who believe that kisses from a chimney sweeper bring good luck.	Carin Flood and her brother worked as physical therapists but were unhappy with what *they were* doing. Then they read of openings for chimney sweepers. Now *they are* making less money but enjoying themselves tremendously. As a fringe benefit, *they get* to kiss newlyweds who believe that kisses from chimney sweepers bring good luck.

The passages illustrate the changes. Notice that in addition to making the pronouns plural and dropping the article (STEP 3), you must also make the verbs agree with the plural subject.

Notice that, in the last sentence in each paragraph, *kisses bring* good luck. Whether the words between *kisses* and *bring* are *a chimney sweeper* or *chimney sweepers*, the verb *bring* has to agree with the subject *kisses*.

(I walk)	——	we walk	As you can see, making the verb
(you walk)	——	you walk	"agree" calls for a change only in
(he walks)	——	they walk	the third person. *He, she*, and *it*
(she walks)	——	they walk	change to *they;* and, as a result, the
(it walks)	——	they walk	verb becomes *walk* instead of *walks*.

The forms of the verb *to be* vary in the singular (I *am*, you *are*, he/she/it *is*), but in the plural there is only one form: *are*.

> We *are* happy.
> You *are* happy.
> They *are* happy.

When the plural is formed by adding *s* or *es* to the subject, the verb can be made to agree quite easily. You need simply remember that there is no *s* at the end of the verb. It is as if the noun "took" that *s*.

A street☐ in my neighborhood lacks lighting.   A city☐ grows daily.
Many streets in my neighborhood lack☐ lighting.   Cities grow☐ daily.

The "Hints and Situations" section contains a discussion of less frequent situations.

To form the possessive *s* in the case of plurals, follow the three-step procedure below:

1. Indicate the plural.
2. Indicate possession by adding *'s*.
3. If the word ends in *s*, eliminate the second *s*.

Singular	1. Form plural	2. Add possessive ('s)	3. Eliminate the second *s*	Result
body	bodies	bodies's	bodies's	bodies'
jogger	joggers	joggers's	joggers's	joggers'
wolf	wolves	wolves's	wolves's	wolves'
child	children	children's	only one *s*	children's
woman	women	women's	only one *s*	women's

Agreement becomes an issue in sentences that contain "complements." The term means that a later part of a sentence contains a noun "equal" to the subject of the sentence.

A happy man is a wealthy man.   Happy men *are* wealthy men.
A house is not a home.   Some houses *are* not homes.
A horse is not a smart animal.   Horses *are* not smart animals.

STEP 4   Rewrite the essay below so that you will be discussing many women instead of just Helen Keane. Begin the second paragraph with *Many of these women are housewives and grandmothers* instead of the sentence there now. Then continue to write about *many women* throughout the essay. Remember to make pronouns and verbs agree with your new, plural subject. Make the changes you must. Copy everything else and proofread carefully.

The Ladies of Smell

---

[1]Every few weeks or so, a few women gather in the offices of the Odor Sciences Center of the Illinois Institute of Technology Research Institute. [2]They sit and chat until their names are called. [3]Then, one by one, they walk into a room next door and inhale deeply from plastic nozzles.

[4]One of these women is Helen Keane, housewife and grandmother. [5]She is a veteran sniffer. [6]She is known by friends and neighbors as the "smelly lady" of Park Forest. [7]She is so named because she smells odors for the Research Institute. [8]Over the years she has stuck her nose into smells from underarm deodorants, sewer sludge, and rendering plants. [9]For her work she earns three dollars an hour.

[10]The Research Institute hired her because it needs the special ability that human noses have of being able to recognize and quantify 50,000 different smells. [11]Although machines are used to tabulate and analyze the tester's responses, no machine is available that is even one-tenth as sensitive as the nose of a human being. [12]This is where the "nosey" grandmother comes in. [13]First, the institute takes a substance and runs it through an instrument that breaks the substance into its compounds. [14]For example, perspiration is broken into all its smell-producing components. [15]Then a tester is brought in. [16]She sniffs the different components and tries to indicate which of them actually creates the distinctive smell of body odor. [17]The Park Forest grandmother answers questions about the strength and uniqueness of the smells. [18]For her, tobacco, cooking oil, coffee, genital odors, perfumes, and paint thinner smells are all in a day's work.

[19]The institute uses the information to help a deodorant company pinpoint from which of 100 compounds sweat is composed so that it can try to counteract it with its product. [20]Your next pleasant fragrance might have come by way of a grandmother's sense of smell.

NO. OF ERRORS

As you proofread, underline the changes you have made. Correct any errors your instructor has found. For additional work in subject-verb agreement and possessives (plurals), choose another selection from STEP 4. Correct spelling errors below.

---   ---   ---

STEP 4   In the essay below, change *neighbor* to *neighbors* and *enemy* to *enemies*. These changes will force you to make other changes in the essay because verbs must "agree" with their subjects. Make these changes. Remember that you will be writing about many neighbors and enemies, not just one. Copy everything else and proofread carefully. Note that when a noun becomes plural in number, it drops the articles *a, an* or *the).*

You Are Not a Blankety Blank

---

[1]The old saying "Sticks and stones may break my bones but words will never hurt me" is far from true. [2]If your neighbor calls you names that expose you to public contempt, you can take him to court on a charge of libel. [3]If he is not satisfied with saying those words but decides to print them in the newspapers or on display signs, you can take him to court and charge him with libel.

[4]Written defamation or libel is considered by the courts to be more harmful because your enemy's offensive opinions of you are in a permanent form. [5]If he accuses you in a television broadcast, you may also charge him with libel. [6]Though his words are not in a permanent form, he is reaching many people and is, therefore, very damaging of your reputation. [7]In general, however, your enemy's spoken words of defamation are considered slanderous rather than libelous. [8]If he thus thinks that your house is filthy or your lawn a disgrace to the neighborhood, your enemy is better off saying it than printing it. [9]No matter which of the two he does, if he does it with malicious intent, you can charge him with defamation.

[10]The best defense against a charge of slander or libel is the truth. [11]If your neighbor can prove that his statements are true, you can do nothing. [12]If they are not true, on the other hand, you can show him that the words he threw at you instead of stones can fly back and break his bones.

NO. OF ERRORS

As you proofread, underline any changes you have made. Correct any errors your instructor has located in your essay. For additional work in plural subject-verb agreement, choose another STEP 4 selection. Other work in plurals is in STEP 3. Correct any misspelled words below.

---   ---   ---

Step 4

Subject-Verb Agreement and Possessives (Plurals)

Helpful Hints and Special Situations

As nouns move from the singular to the plural, they generally add an *s* or *es* to indicate their plural state.

a dish→many dishes   a car→many cars   a house→many houses

In some cases, additional changes have to be made, most of which are familiar to you.

a wolf→many wolves   a knife→many knives   a city→many cities

Other nouns indicate plurals without using the *s* or *es*.

a child→child*ren*   a man→m*en*   a woman→wom*en*
one criterion→many criteria   one medium→many media

Still other nouns show no change at all.

one fish→many fish   one sheep→many sheep

The most frequent error in subject-verb agreement in the plural is with compounds or double subjects.

A Mercedes and a pickup truck are parked in the driveway.

You may feel uncomfortable writing " . . . . truck are . . ." in the middle of the sentence, but you can clearly see that the sentence is talking about two items, not one. The plural *are* is thus the correct verb.

If the sentence above is reversed, with the verb placed before the subject or subjects, you would still have to use *are*. Because the situation is an unfamiliar one, students sometimes get confused.

There are a Mercedes and a pickup truck in the driveway.

Again, there are unmistakably two items in the driveway; use *are*. In general, be careful with sentences that begin with *There are* or *There is*.

When the subject and the verb are near each other, it is not difficult to make them agree. The difficulties arise when other words come between the subject and verb and when that intervening group of words is different in number from the subject.

The cost of renting apartments is high. (The *cost* is high, not apartments.)
The woman in the jogging shoes is my sister. (The subject is *woman*, not shoes.)

An effective way of solving this problem is to locate the verb and ask *who* or *what*, then substitute a pronoun.

1. What *is* high?	1. Who is my sister?
2. the cost	2. the woman
3. the cost → it	3. the woman → she
4. singular	4. singular

The owners of the blue bus live in it.
    They   live

The possessive *s* sounds awkward at times in the plural. In speech we tend to avoid using it (after all, it cannot be heard), and we use the *prepositional phrase* instead.

Singular	Plural	Prepositional Phrase
the wolf's features	wolves' features	the features of wolves
an adolescent's problems	adolescents' problems	the problems of adolescents
the child's class	the children's class	the class of the children

The final item in each row probably sounds more comfortable or idiomatic than the item just before. Use the prepositional phrase if you like, although you should know how to use the plural possessive. In the case of the third item, the possessive is actually used more frequently by writers and speakers than the prepositional phrase.

It is worth remembering that, while working on STEP 3, you did not need to be concerned with subject-verb agreement because the essays were written in the past tense (*was* and *were* are exceptions). When you are writing your own essays, you might consider using that tense to help eliminate agreement difficulties. Of course, the tense must be appropriate, as you will discover in subsequent STEPs.

STEP 4

In the passages below, change *pig* to *pigs* each time the word occurs. This change to the plural will force you to make other changes in the essay, specifically with pronouns (STEP 3) and verbs. Remember that there has to be agreement between subject and verb throughout the essay. Make the changes you must and copy everything else. Your first sentence should read: *Of all barnyard animals, pigs have had the worst publicity.* (*Has* changed to *have,* "agreeing" with *pigs.* Note that the article *the* is dropped in the plural.)

Pigs Are Not Hogs

---

[1]Of all barnyard animals, the pig has had the worst publicity. [2]Almost all popular notions about it are inaccurate.

[3]Most people believe that a pig's lack of cleanliness is a matter of choice. [4]In fact, a pig is scrupulously clean if it is given the opportunity. [5]It prefers clean sleeping quarters and rarely needs housebreaking if it is kept indoors. [6]As for wallowing, the pig does it only to cool off. [7]It wallows in mud only if no clean water is available.

[8]Another fallacy concerns the eating habits of a pig. [9]Although "piggishness" means the willingness to eat anything, a pig is actually picky about its food. [10]It does not like tomatoes, cucumbers, and orange peels. [11]It does have a particular liking for items it considers delicacies, such as cabbages, cantaloupes, and acorns.

[12]In Ireland there are instances of a pig kept as a household pet. [13]If it becomes devoted to people, it follows them around like a faithful dog. [14]The time has come to end the slander about this often delightful animal.

NO. OF ERRORS

As you proofread, underline any changes you have made. Correct any errors your instructor has located in your essay. For additional work in plural subject-verb agreement, choose another STEP 4 selection. Other work in plurals is in STEP 3. Correct any misspelled words below.

_____   _____   _____

STEP 4   In the short essay that follows, change *child* to *children* and *baby* to *babies* each time those words appear. As usual, this change will force you to make other changes in the essay. Remember that you will be writing about many children and babies, not just one. Pay particular attention to the verbs in the essay. Your first sentence should read: *Before children understand the meaning of words, they learn the message of sounds.* (Note changes from the original sentence.)

Speech Development

---

¹Before a child understands the meaning of words, she learns the message of sounds.

²From the time of her birth, a baby makes sounds to signal her happiness or dissatisfaction. ³She cries to express pain; she coos to indicate pleasure. ⁴Sometimes she makes sounds for the sheer joy of hearing herself.

⁵By the third month, her parents' voices can influence their child's responses. ⁶If the parents make approving sounds, the baby's cooing will increase in frequency. ⁷If, on the other hand, the parents do not respond to the child's crying, they will actually teach her to cry less often.

⁸When the child is nine months old, she listens to songs and stories very carefully. ⁹Although the words do not have any meaning for her, the sound of the telling is something she does understand. ¹⁰The tone of the parents' voices saying, "Happily ever after," will reassure the child although she has no idea what any of the words mean.

NO. OF ERRORS

As you proofread, underline any changes you have made. Correct any errors your instructor has located in your essay. For additional work in plural subject-verb agreement, choose another STEP 4 selection. Other work in plurals is in STEP 3. Correct any misspelled words below.

_____   _____   _____

STEP 4   In the essay below, change *stork* to *storks* each time the word appears. Because of that change you will have to make other alterations in each sentence. You will have to make the verb agree with the subject. Make the changes you must, but copy everything else and proofread carefully. Remember that you will be writing about many storks instead of one. Your first sentence should begin: *The story that storks deliver babies . . .* (You should not change "stork" in sentence 5.)

Storks

---

¹The story that a stork delivers babies is an old and a charming one, even if it is unsound biology.

²There are several reasons for associating the stork with the delivery of babies. ³The stork is usually a tender bird, toward both its young and old. ⁴According to legend, a stork's responsibility was to look after aged, blind, and weak parents. ⁵The very word "stork" in English may come from a root word meaning "strong natural affection." ⁶People in northern Europe like to have a stork nest on their houses and thus put wagon wheels on their roofs to help the bird get started.

⁷Another reason to associate the stork with babies is that it migrates and frequently stays away from its nest for as much as nine months. ⁸German peasants used to believe that the migrating stork went to Egypt, where it would become a man. ⁹In fact, the stork does fly as far as Africa, as modern studies have shown.

¹⁰Another of the stork's associations with the delivery of babies came from the need to explain the confinement of the new mother. ¹¹Dutch, German, and Scandinavian mothers would say that a stork had bitten them on the legs when it brought the babies, in spite of the reputation for gentility that was the bird's.

NO. OF ERRORS

As you proofread, underline any changes you have made. Correct any errors your instructor has located in your essay. For additional work in plural subject-verb agreement, choose another STEP 4 selection. Other work in plurals is in STEP 3. Correct any misspelled words below.

---   ---   ---

Step 4

Writing Assignments: Subject-Verb Agreement and Possessives (Plurals)

While working on the assignments below, remind yourself constantly that you are using a plural subject that you must match with plural pronouns. Also make sure that the verb and subject agree. When you need to form possessives, remember to indicate number first, then possession. At times the word you have formed may not seem idiomatic. For example, "photographers' pictures" looks unfamiliar and sounds awkward. "The pictures of the photographers" seems more idiomatic. For the sake of this assignment, you should try to indicate possession with the apostrophe rather than the prepositional phrase. Once you have learned the correct use of the apostrophe, you should use the more idiomatic construction in your writings.

Use at least three possessive forms in each of the assignments.

1. Describe how a person behaves when he or she is alone in a restaurant. Compare this to the behavior of people who are with others in a restaurant.
2. Compare the rights of landlords to apartment dwellers' rights.
3. How do people in various parts of the country react when a crisis threatens or occurs? Try to illustrate the generalizations by specific examples.
4. How do neighbors affect people's lives?
5. Discuss the ways in which brothers or sisters can make life easier or more difficult for other children in a family.
6. Who has advantages in the family? The oldest, the youngest, or the middle child? Use the plural to discuss this, but give personal examples whenever you can.
7. Can restaurants replace home cooking?
8. How do pets influence their owners? From another point of view, what do pets reveal about the personality of their owners?
9. What are parents' responsibilities toward their children after the children reach age 18?
10. Are modern ballplayers more talented than ballplayers were in the fifties and sixties?

Step 5

Pronoun Agreement, Reference, and Possessives (Singulars)

STEP 5 is the opposite of STEP 3. In STEP 5 you will be asked to rewrite short essays so that you will be discussing one person, place, or concept at a time instead of many. In making the subject of a sentence singular, you will have to make other changes in the sentence. Making the subject singular has a particularly important effect on the verb. That effect will be discussed in STEP 6.

> Many ballerinas twirled on their toes. They seemed aware only of themselves although thousands of people watched them intently.

If you had to rewrite this so that it discusses only one ballerina, you would get:

> A (or *The*) ballerina☐ twirled on *her* toes. *She* seemed aware only of *herself* although thousands of people watched *her* intensely.

1. The indefinite (*a* or *an*) or the definite (*the*) article is added.
2. The plural indicator (*s*) is dropped from *ballerinas*.
3. The plural possessive pronoun *their* becomes the singular *her*.
4. The plural nominative pronoun *they* becomes the singular *she*.
5. The plural reflexive pronoun *themselves* becomes the singular *herself*.
6. The plural objective pronoun *them* becomes the singular *her*.

Here is a reverse of the pronoun lists that can be found in the introduction to STEP 3, on pages 26–27. Notice the pairings.

Personal				Reflexive	
Nominative		**Objective**			
Plural	Singular	Plural	Singular	Plural	Singular
we	I	us	me	ourselves	myself
you	you	you	you	yourselves	yourself
they	he	them	him	themselves	himself
they	she	them	her	themselves	herself
they	it	them	it	themselves	itself
Possessive					
our	my	ours	mine		
your	your	yours	yours		
their	his	theirs	his		
their	her	theirs	hers		
their	its	their	—		

For *the possessive s* in the case of singulars,

1. Add apostrophe *s* to show possession. (*'s*)
2. You *may* eliminate the second *s*.

Singular	+ Possessive	Eliminate second *s*	Result
body	body's		body's
wolf	wolf's		wolf's
boss	boss's	boss's	boss' *or* boss's
Jones	Jones's	Jones's	Jones' *or* Jones's
Moses	Moses's	Moses's	Moses' *or* Moses's

When you are changing possessive nouns from the plural to the singular, do not forget that invisible *s*.

the joggers' stamina	is really *the joggers'* [s] *stamina*	–singular *jogger's*
the animals' lair	is really *the animals'* [s] *lair*	–singular *animal's*
the girls' gym	is really *the girls'* [s] *gym*	–singular *girl's*

STEP 5   In the essay below, change *trees* to *tree* each time the word appears. Because you will be writing about one tree instead of many, you will have to change the pronouns that refer to *tree* from the plural to the singular. You will also have to add articles *a, an* or *the*). Pay particular attention to words that have the possessive (*'s* or *'*). Copy everything else and proofread.

The Christmas Tree

---

¹Pagans used Christmas trees in their celebration of life. ²The main features of this ceremony were green foliage and lit candles. ³On December 22, the time of the winter solstice, nature seems dead. ⁴Pagans used the decorated trees in a magical rite that sought to ensure the return of vegetation. ⁵The trees' green branches were reminders of nature alive. ⁶The evergreen trees also figured in the winter celebrations of other peoples. ⁷To the Norse, they symbolized immortality. ⁸The Romans used them as decorations in the home and temple during the Saturnalia, a season of merrymaking and good will.

¹⁰Christmas trees as we know them today originated in Germany. ¹¹According to one story, the English St. Boniface chopped down an oak sacred to the city of Geismar and had to plant a fir tree to pacify the angry citizens. ¹²The event, the story goes, occurred on Christmas Eve. ¹³According to another story, Martin Luther, the Protestant reformer, used a Christmas tree to describe the evening sky. ¹⁴Words failed him, forcing Luther to cut small fir trees from his garden, fill their branches with candles, and let them illustrate by themselves the glories of the sky.

¹⁵From Germany the Christmas trees' popularity spread around the world. ¹⁶The English, however, did not seem very interested. ¹⁷The first time Christmas trees appeared in England was during a children's party at Queen Caroline's court in 1821. ¹⁸Charles Dickens thought the trees to be toys. ¹⁹Then, in 1841, the Prince Consort decided to surprise his young son and provide himself with a reminder of his German home. ²⁰He had Christmas trees brought into Windsor Castle. ²¹After this royal example, the trees' lights soon illuminated every British home, making them the most visible sign of Christmas.

NO. OF ERRORS

As you proofread, underline any changes you have made. Correct any errors your instructor has located in your essay. For additional work in singulars (pronouns and possessives), select another STEP 5 selection. For work in articles, select a STEP 2 selection. Correct any spelling errors below.

_____   _____   _____

STEP 5   In the essay below, change *housewives* to *housewife*. This means you will be writing about one housewife only. As a result, you will have to change all the pronouns that refer to the housewife to the singular, as well as add articles. Pay particular attention to words that have the possessive (*'s* or *'*). Copy everything else and proofread. Your first sentence should read: *According to a 1978 study by a life insurance company, a housewife deserved more pay than she received for her labor.*

The Underpaid Housewife

[1]According to a 1978 study by a life insurance company, housewives deserved more pay than they received for their labor.

[2]The study found that housewives worked about 100 hours per week in the household. [3]At the minimum wage rate those hours were worth nearly $12,000. [4]Housewives, however, performed the functions of twelve different professions, and at the 1978 pay scale for these professions they deserved as much as $18,000 for their work. [5]As the housewives surveyed received no pay at all for their work, they certainly undervalued themselves.

[6]Housewives spent half of their hours in the nursery. [7]They should have received $118 for that. [8]At the rate of $2.65 per hour, that is how much a nursemaid would have made. [9]The housewives' other "lower paying" jobs included doing the laundry and the dishes. [10]They merited $46 a week for those services.

[11]Their pay scale should have been higher for other work they performed. [12]When they kept house and cooked, they did for free services for which a housekeeper and cook charged $4.00 per hour in 1978. [13]As chauffeurs, maintenance workers, seamstresses, and practical nurses, they had the right to expect $5.00 per hour. [14]The total per housewife came to 99.6 hours of work per week, and $18,282 in deserved compensation. [15]The study emphasized that those were cold figures that did not place monetary value on love and devotion. [16]Housewives' contributions cried out for recognition.

NO. OF ERRORS

As you proofread, underline any changes you have made. Correct any errors your instructor has located in your essay. For additional work in singulars (pronouns and possessives), select another STEP 5 selection. For work in articles, select a STEP 2 selection. Correct any spelling errors below.

_____   _____   _____

Step 5

Pronoun Agreement, Reference, and Possessives (Singulars)

Helpful Hints and Special Situations

As nouns move from plurals to singulars, they generally surrender the *s* that had indicated their plural state.

many houses→a house□

Some nouns, however, undergo additional changes as they move from plural to singular.

many wolves→one wolf (*v* to *f*, in addition to the loss of plural *es*)
many bodies→one body (*i* to *y*, in addition to the loss of plural *es*)

Still another group of nouns change differently, for their plural indicator was neither *s* nor *es*.

many women→one woman many children→one child
many media→one medium many criteria→one criterion

Be careful with sentences beginning, "There is . . ." A sentence that begins with "There is" should be pointing at only one item.

One difficulty with pronoun agreement occurs when students move from proper nouns (capitalized, formal names) to pronouns.

Jack went up the hill. He went up the hill

Jill went up the hill. She went up the hill.

Benji the rat went up the hill. It (or He) went up the hill.

The plural demonstrative pronoun *these* is, in the singular, *this*.
The plural demonstrative pronoun *those* is, in the singular, *that*.

these old men→this old man those old women→that old woman

Do not forget to make "complements" agree with the singular subject.

Lizards make good pets. → A lizard makes *a* good pet.
They were late arrivals. → He was a late arrival.

STEP 5   In the essay below, change all references to *Bonnie and Clyde* to *Bonnie Parker* alone, and focus all the discussion on her alone. Therefore, all references to *the couple* or *they* should be changed to *she*. Change other pronouns, possessives, and nouns accordingly. Copy everything else and proofread carefully. Your first sentence should read: *Bonnie Parker was the female half of the most famous man-woman criminal duo in American history.* Underline movie titles for italics.

American Robin Hoods

---

[1]Bonnie Parker and Clyde Barrow were the most famous man-woman criminal duo in American history. [2]During the 1930s, Bonnie and Clyde robbed banks in Texas, Louisiana, Oklahoma, and Arkansas. [3]Sometimes they shared what they stole with poor and unemployed people. [4]The couple gave the most money to the poor of the Ouachita Mountains in southwestern Oklahoma. [5]Hearing of their actions, some people began to think of them as Robin Hood figures. [6]And, true enough, they kept little of their loot for themselves. [7]Before long, Bonnie and Clyde could hear themselves celebrated in popular songs. [8]They liked to sing them along with the car radio as they drove from bank to bank.

[9]The real romance of their legend did not begin until their execution in Arcadia, Louisiana, May 24, 1934. [10]Still under thirty, their young bodies caught several rounds of bullets from sheriffs' patrols and the state police. [11]Their death shocked even the people who had feared and hated them. [12]Since then many books have been written about them. [13]More importantly, many movies were made about their lives. [14]Some of these movies have been *They Live by Night* (1948), *The Bonnie Parker Story* (1958), *Thieves Like Us* (1973), and, most influentially, *Bonnie and Clyde* (1967). [15]People who remember the real Bonnie and Clyde object to the glamorized portrayal of their lives. [16]And there are still people in the mountains who think of them as ruthless killers instead of as Robin Hoods.

NO. OF ERRORS

As you proofread, underline the changes you have made. Correct any errors your instructor has located in your essay. For additional work in singulars (pronouns and possessives), select another STEP 5 essay. For work in articles, choose a STEP 2 selection. Correct any spelling errors below.

---   ---   ---

STEP 5   In the essay below, change *gangs* to *gang* in the first sentence, and talk about only *one gang* throughout the essay. Use the pronoun *it* to refer to the gang, and make sure other pronouns that refer to the gang are also in the singular. Pay particular attention to words that have the possessive *s* (*'s*) or just the possessive (*'*). Copy everything else and proofread carefully.

Beating the Odds

---

¹Interpol, the international police organization, admitted it was investigating international gangs of "gambling thieves." ²The daring bands of robbers apparently collected about seven million dollars by rigging roulette wheels in European, South American, and African casinos. ³Among the casinos they hit is the famous Monte Carlo gaming house in Monaco.

⁴The gangs' method, according to Interpol, was to loosen the screws that hold in place the tiny walls between the numbers of the roulette wheel. ⁵When the gangs' members loosened these screws, they increased the elasticity of the walls. ⁶The greater elasticity made it more likely that the ball would fall into those slots that the gangs had played.

⁷Another trick the gangs worked effectively involved inserting slivers of rubber beneath undesirable slots. ⁸By placing the slivers, they caused the ball to bounce away from those numbers toward numbers they had played. ⁹Although neither method guaranteed their success, both methods helped increase the odds in their favor.

¹⁰Interpol feels that gambling gangs had been successful in the past. ¹¹It feels that the present groups had been working the casino circuit for at least three years, enriching themselves considerably in the process.

NO. OF ERRORS

As you proofread, underline any changes you have made. Correct any errors your instructor has located in your essay. For additional work in singulars (pronouns and possessives), select another STEP 5 selection. For work in articles, select a STEP 2 selection. Correct any spelling errors below.

---------------------   ---------------------   ---------------------

STEP 5   In the essay below, change *Aries men, Taurean men, Virgoan women,* and *Pisces women* to the singular; write about *an Aries man, a Taurean man, a Virgoan woman,* and *a Pisces woman* throughout the essay. These changes mean that you will have to make the pronouns that refer to these individuals singular as well. You will also have to use articles. Pay particular attention to words that have the possessive indicator (*'*). Copy everything else and proofread carefully.

Love and the Stars

---

¹Do men and women born under different signs of the zodiac behave differently in love? ²One astrologer is convinced differences exist, basing her beliefs on intuition and personal observation.

³Aries men that she has observed plunged blindly into love. ⁴Their sign is the Ram, and, like a ram, they jumped headlong and heart first. ⁵When their romances ended, Aries did not give up. ⁶Determinedly they pursued their beloved, hoping to "rekindle the flame." ⁷They cared little about themselves while they were in love. ⁸With their romance over, they found themselves completely forlorn. ⁹By contrast, Taurean men the astrologer has known controlled themselves while involved in romance. ¹⁰They rarely pursued a loved one intensely. ¹¹They preferred to be pursued instead. ¹²The Taureans' personality was basically passive. ¹³They cared for themselves too much to be destroyed when their romance ended.

¹⁴The astrologer has observed differences among Virgoan and Pisces women she has known. ¹⁵She knew of Virgoans who had left husbands for lovers, facing the disapproval of the world defiantly. ¹⁶Only true love mattered to them. ¹⁷When they discovered their love life to be imperfect, they ended it. ¹⁸They did not fool themselves into substituting security for love. ¹⁹The Virgoans' pet hate, in love and friendship, was hypocrisy. ²⁰As far as the astrologer is concerned, Virgoan women contrasted most sharply with Pisces women. ²¹Pisces women she has known did not leave their husbands. ²²They simply convinced themselves that their beloved was the most perfect person in the world and their love a true love. ²³Their sign is the Fish. ²⁴Like a fish, Pisces women can swim in both directions, adapting to conflicts that would send Virgoans screaming.

NO. OF ERRORS

As you proofread, underline any changes you have made. Correct any errors your instructor has located in your essay. For additional work in singulars, select another STEP 5 selection. For work in articles, select a STEP 2 essay. List any unfamiliar words and corrected spelling errors below.

Step 5

Writing Assignments: Pronoun Agreement, Reference, and Possessives (Singulars)

The topics listed below are designed to help you practice singulars. Write them in the past tense to help eliminate difficulties with subject-verb agreement, which is covered in STEP 6. In writing on these assignments, remember to use the singular subject whenever possible and also the apostrophe s ('s) to show possession.

1. Name some of the people with whom you worked once. Describe what each person did. (Jim's job, the buyer's job)
2. Try to remember some of your classmates in an elementary grade. Name some of them, and identify the most outstanding feature of each.
3. Describe a car you or your parents once had, using the apostrophe s ('s) for its various features. (the car's hood, its color)
4. Describe a pet that you had, using its generic name (dog, cat, alligator), as well as its given name. Use "it" as the pronoun.
5. What were some of the foods you and your friends liked? Use "it" as the pronoun when you name the food.
6. Describe the actions of someone who served you once, in a store, restaurant, or office. Use "he" or "she" after your first identification. Include some possessives.
7. Observe signs in your neighborhood that use the possessive s incorrectly. Write them down correctly.
8. Many stores and companies that advertise tend to use the plural pronouns when they speak of themselves. "Come to Midas; they will take good care of your muffler." This is not correct. The singular "it" should be used. It is not used because it sounds impersonal, and "he" or "she" makes little sense. Write down some of these incorrect uses, correcting them in the process.

Step 6

Subject-Verb Agreement (Singulars)

STEP 6 continues STEP 5. Once again you are being asked to rewrite short essays so that you will be writing about one person, place, or idea rather than many. In STEP 5, when you did this, you had to make pronouns agree with the singular subject. In STEP 6 you will continue to make pronouns agree, but you will also have to make the verbs agree. As STEP 4 has shown you, subjects and verbs must agree in number. In this STEP you will be practicing making singular verbs agree with singular subjects.

Plural	
Indian men *learn* to fish with their bare hands. Otherwise *they catch* fish in weirs, traps, gigs, and dip nets. *They* also use spears and poisons. *They have* been successful in poisoning fish in a slow-moving stream by using powdered dove weed.	*The* (or *An*) Indian man *learns* to fish with his bare hands. Otherwise *he catches* fish in weirs, traps, gigs, and dip nets. *He* also *uses* spears and poisons. *He has* been successful in poisoning fish in a slow-moving stream by using powdered dove weed.

The passage illustrates the changes. Notice that, in addition to making the pronouns singular and adding the article, you also have to make the nouns singular and make the verb agree.

Making the verb agree with the subject is difficult only when you need to write about the third-person singular—*he, she* or *it*. In all other situations, the verb remains the same as it is in the plural.

we/you/they walk → I walk, you walk, BUT he walk*s*, she walk*s*, it walk*s*

Similarly with the verb to *be*.

we/you/they are → you are, BUT I am, AND he is, she is, it is

To make the singular verb agree with the singular subject *in the third person*, you need only remember to add an *s* or *es* to the verb. Usually, you can "take" this *s* from the plural noun.

Indians_fish with their bare hands. They wear□ colorful clothes.
The Indian fishes with his bare hands. She wears colorful clothes.

STEP 6   In the essay below, substitute *wolf* for *wolves*. This substitution will oblige you to make other changes in words that must agree with *wolf*. When speaking of what a specific wolf might do, you should write *the wolf*. If you are speaking of any individual wolf, you should write *a wolf*. Similarly, if you speak of wolves collectively you should write *the wolf* as in the sentence "The wolf has been misunderstood." But English idiom prefers that you use the indefinite article in sentences like "It is difficult to trap *a wolf*." Copy everything else and proofread carefully. (Do not disturb the title in sentence 5.)

The Wolf

---

¹Wolves exert a powerful influence over the human imagination. ²They take your stare and turn it back at you. ³Wolves have been despised, mythologized, feared, and admired by human beings. ⁴Few animals have been so misunderstood as wolves. ⁵A book by the naturalist Barry Holstun Lopez, *Of Wolves and Men* (New York: Scribner's, 1978), tries to clarify our perceptions about them.

⁶Wolves' bad literary reputation begins as early as Aesop's fables and continues through Dante, Little Red Riding Hood, and Jack London. ⁷Wolves are not always seen this way, however. ⁸In the mythologies of many native North American peoples, wolves are portrayed as beloved brothers of many heroes. ⁹The Pomo Indians of California give wolves prominence in their myths. ¹⁰The Tlingit people of Alaska name one portion of their society after the wolf.

¹¹Considering wolves' grim literary reputation, Lopez finds their social life astonishingly engaging. ¹²Wolves run in packs that are really extended families of five to eight members. ¹³The pack may be led by a female, who is often a swifter hunter than the male and is always a strong influence on the pack's decisions. ¹⁴Wolves in a pack spend eight to ten of every 24 hours in hunting over as much as 100 square miles.

¹⁵Wolves are the most socially evolved of all canines. ¹⁶They have a high degree of communal organization and keenly developed methods of communication, of which the eerie howl that may carry six miles in still arctic air is best known. ¹⁷Biologists have formulated wolves' vocabulary of facial gestures as "licking attention," "antagonistic pucker," "intimidating stare," and so on.

¹⁸Lopez does not argue that they are cuddly, however. ¹⁹Wolves' grace and stamina are that of fiercely efficient hunters. ²⁰They are admired by hunting societies but abhorred, with some justification, by agricultural ones.

NO. OF ERRORS

As you proofread, underline any changes you have made. Correct any errors your instructor has found. Correct spelling errors below.

_____   _____   _____

STEP 6   In the essay below, substitute *road* for *roads*. This substitution will oblige you to make other changes as well; make those other changes that you have to. The first sentence in paragraph 5 should begin: "Only one Irish road . . . " Copy everything else and proofread carefully. (Note the use of articles, *a, an,* or *the,* in the singular.)

Driving in Ireland

---

¹A North American driver has a difficult time adjusting to Irish roads. ²To begin with, traffic goes on the left side of them instead of the right. ³A driver has to continue to control his or her instincts at every corner, traffic circle, or rotary to make sure he or she does not revert to driving on the right.

⁴Because there are fewer cars in Ireland, Irish roads are built to carry less traffic. ⁵They are narrower, especially in rural areas. ⁶Country roads often have hedges running along their sides, sometimes just a few inches from the edge of the pavement. ⁷In some counties, like Galway and Kerry, the roads have stone fences instead of hedges. ⁸This makes a driver's margin for error extremely narrow.

⁹Roads with heavy traffic have four lanes, two going each way. ¹⁰But, unlike the practice in the United States, the two center lanes are for fast, through traffic, whereas the two outer lanes are for slower traffic. ¹¹On such roads, the faster traffic does not have to pass slower traffic. ¹²Instead, slower and local traffic are expected to take the roads' slower lanes.

¹³Until about 1970, the Irish government did not give roads route numbers; there seemed no need to. ¹⁴Roads running out of one town take the name of the next town. ¹⁵A road running out of Limerick toward Tipperary is called "the Tipperary Road" until it gets closer to Tipperary, when it becomes "the Limerick Road." ¹⁶This is an easy system for natives, but tourists cannot find their way across the island without knowing what lies beyond Tipperary.

¹⁷Not many Irish roads compare with the typical North American superhighway or interstate route. ¹⁸The Irish equivalent is called a "dual carriageway." ¹⁹So far the only one runs southwest out of Dublin to a little town in Kildare called Naas. ²⁰With the increasing cost of fuel and the presence of good public transportation, there may not be a need to build another.

NO. OF ERRORS

As you proofread, underline any changes you have made. Correct any errors your instructor has found. Correct spelling errors below.

---   ---   ---

Step 6

Subject-Verb Agreement (Singulars)

Helpful Hints and Special Situations

Most writers have no difficulties with subject-verb agreement when the two are right next to each other. Difficulties occur when other words come between the subject and the verb.

The advice I got from my friends was helpful.

To determine the subject of the sentence, locate the verb and ask *who* or *what*. In the sentence above, the answer to "What was helpful?" is "the advice." Match "advice" with "was."

The man driving the blue car with the shiny hubcaps is my uncle.

Who is my uncle? The man. The man is.

Although you should not use contractions in formal essays or letters of application, you should be aware of the "rule of *s*" in the third-person singular when you add the negative contraction to the end of a verb.

Positive	Negative	Negative Contraction
I do	I do not	I don't
you do	you do not	you don't
he does	he does not	he doesn't
she does	she does not	she doesn't
it does	it does not	it doesn't

Take special care with words that seem to be plurals but that function as singulars:

physics, measles, news, economics, linguistics, civics

Another group contains words that indicate only one item but function as plurals:

glasses, scissors, pants, trousers

Because writers are becoming more aware of the bias in using "he" to refer to "one," they have begun to substitute *he/she, he or she,* even *s/he* for *he.* Speakers tend to veer away from the awkward alternatives altogether and slip into "they." That is incorrect, of course. Use *he* or *she* or even one of the choices above, but do make sure you retain the singular.

The words below often confuse students. Note that they take the singular.

everyone is	nobody is	no one is
each is	another is	nothing is
everybody is	anybody is	someone is
somebody is	neither is	everything is

STEP 6   In the essay below, substitute *the body* for *our bodies*. This substitution will force you to make other changes. Make those changes that you have to. Copy everything else and proofread carefully.

Familiar Oddities

---

¹The lump in the throat, goose bumps, and blushing are ways in which our bodies react to emotions. ²Although we can explain *how* our bodies produce these symptoms, we do not always know *why* they produce them. ³In some cases, it is not known how the emotions trigger the reactions.

⁴The lump in the throat is our bodies' reaction to fear and anxiety. ⁵The emotions produce an involuntary tensing of the throat muscles, interfering with swallowing. ⁶Saliva accumulates and thickens. ⁷We thus literally have a "lump" in the throat.

⁸Our bodies produce goose bumps in reaction to feelings of fear and stress. ⁹The bumps are raised by tiny muscles that lift the hair on the arms and the back of the neck. ¹⁰This is part of our bodies' effort to look ferocious, a reaction to anxiety that our bodies retain from caveman days.

¹¹Blushing occurs when blood fills tiny capillaries near the skin's surface. ¹²We thus know how the familiar redness develops. ¹³What we do not know is why feelings of embarrassment should trigger this particular response in our bodies.

NO. OF ERRORS

As you proofread, underline any changes you have made. Correct any errors your instructor has found. For additional work in singular subject-verb agreement, choose another STEP 6 selection. Other work in singulars can be found in STEP 5. Correct spelling errors below.

_____   _____   _____

STEP 6   In the short essay below, change *joggers* to *a jogger* each time
the word appears. Making that change will force you to make
other alterations in the essay. Make only the changes you must.
You must get the subject and the verb to agree in number.
Copy everything else. Proofread carefully. Remember that you
will be writing about one jogger, not many. Your first sentence
should say: *Why does a jogger decide to run?* (Note: joggers\
a jogger.)

Reasons for Running

---

¹Why do joggers decide to run? ²Male joggers' answers differ considerably from female joggers' responses.

³Male joggers often say that they begin to run out of fear. ⁴They are
frightened of dying from a coronary and feel jogging might insure them
against a heart attack. ⁵Once they are running, they continue to run because they feel they have something to prove or because they want to
be the very best at what they are doing.

⁶Female joggers, by contrast, seem less driven. ⁷Their reasons for
running are less anxious. ⁸They simply want to feel more fit, more free,
and more graceful. ⁹Perhaps because they are more relaxed about running, they seem to enjoy themselves more. ¹⁰Female joggers rarely have
that grim and pained look on their faces that male joggers' faces so
often show.

NO. OF ERRORS

As you proofread, underline any changes you have made.
Correct any errors your instructor has found. For additional work
in singular subject-verb agreement, choose another STEP 6
selection. Other work in singulars can be found in STEP 5.
Correct spelling errors below.

_____   _____   _____

STEP 6   In the short essay that follows, substitute *alien* for *aliens,* and write about one person throughout the essay. This change means that you will have to make the verbs as well as pronouns "agree" with the singular *alien.* Pay close attention to articles and the possessive ('). Copy everything else and proofread carefully. Your first sentence should read: *Before an alien becomes an American citizen, she must meet residency requirements.* (In this case, the alien is female.)

Citizenship

---

[1]Before aliens become American citizens, they must meet residency requirements.

[2]The usual length of residency they must meet before they can apply is five years. [3]After living in the United States for that period of time, aliens become eligible for "naturalization." [4]If they meet the additional requirements of good character and adherence to the Constitution, their application for citizenship is granted.

[5]Aliens' quickest route to citizenship is through marriage. [6]If they marry American citizens and reside in the United States for just three years, they become eligible for naturalization. [7]If they marry American citizens stationed abroad, their application is acceptable even if they have "no prior residency in the United States," according to Alice K. Helm, in *The Family Advisor.*

[8]Helm reminds aliens applying for citizenship that their acceptance by the United States is their gift, not their right.

NO. OF ERRORS

As you proofread, underline any changes you have made. Correct any errors your instructor has found. For additional work in singular subject-verb agreement, choose another STEP 6 selection. Other work in singulars can be found in STEP 5. Correct spelling errors below.

Step 6

Writing Assignments:
Subject-Verb Agreement (Singulars)

In writing the assignments below, follow your instructor's advice as to length and organization. Pay special attention to subject-verb agreement, and use the possessive s ('s).

1. Describe the type of foods offered in some of the quick-food restaurants. Discuss those restaurants that use the apostrophe in their trademark. (McDonald's, Pudgie's)
2. Compare the outstanding players on a number of teams, identifying each athlete by his city or team. (Boston's Jim Rice, the Pirates' Dave Parker)
3. Describe the table manners of various members of your family. Use the apostrophe.
4. Does a man behave differently when he is alone in a restaurant or when he is with others? How about a woman alone or with others?
5. What are some of the physical and psychological qualities of a person you consider a hero or heroine?
6. Discuss some of the things you do that indicate your independence from others in your age group or grade.
7. Rewrite any sentences in your own essay that your instructor has corrected for subject-verb errors.

The Verb

Whatever else it does, the verb also tells you about the *time* of the action. The verb is the word in the sentence that tells you *when* the action is taking place.

Could writers and speakers manage without the verb as an indicator of time? Some languages do, and many speakers of English get around it as well.

They dance. When? Some speakers might answer: *I dance yesterday.* Without altering the verb (*dance*), these speakers would indicate time by adding "yesterday," a special "time" word. Similarly, if some speakers wished to indicate future time, they might say: *They dance tomorrow.* To indicate present time, they might say: *They dance today.* or *They dance now.* In each of these cases, the speakers leave the verb undisturbed in its *base* or *infinitive* form and indicate time by adding a special word.

Speakers of standard English do not do this. English is an inflected language; it indicates time by altering the verb rather than by adding a special time word to the sentence.

I dance (yesterday) is indicated by adding *-ed:* I danc*ed*. (regular verb)
I sing (yesterday) is indicated by alterátion: I s*a*ng. (irregular verb)
I dance (tomorrow) is indicated by adding *will:* I will dance.
I dance (today) is indicated by leaving the verb undisturbed.
He dance (today) is indicated by adding *-s:* He dance*s*.

The various *times* in English will be discussed in STEPs 7–11. You should be aware, however, of this important function of verbs as indicators of time. Verbs indicate time by changing from the base form or by adding an auxiliary or helping verb. The base or infinitive form is the simplest form of the verb.

As you manipulate or change the verbs in subsequent STEPs, you should begin by returning verbs to their infinitive form. They are found in dictionaries under this simple form

Infinitives: to + base form: to dance   to sing   to sleep   to eat   to type

You can always locate the subject of the sentence if you locate the word that shows time and ask "Who?" or "What?"

Step 7

The Present Tense

In this STEP you will have to rewrite essays so that the tense or time of the action will be the present. If you listen to the way you generally use this tense you will notice that you tend to use it to indicate an action or activity that you do usually or habitually. For this reason, the present tense is also called *the habitual* tense. This tense is also used to indicate a condition or state of being that is always true or always exists.

I eat pancakes for breakfast.	(my usual breakfast)
He is a happy person.	(his general state of being)
The sky is blue.	(a general condition)
I type my essays.	(a habitual action)
He likes ice cream.	(usually)
E is equal to mc^2.	(a scientific truth)

The "Helpful Hints" section later in this STEP will discuss other situations where the present tense is used.

In all of the sentences above, the verbs indicate some habitual action or some usual condition. No actual action is going on. In a sense, the present tense is used to indicate that the action or activity is not taking place at any particular or specific time.

When you use this sense, keep the base or simplest part of the verb. The only change you ever need make is in the third-person singular (*he, she, it*). With *he, she,* or *it*, add the *s* to the base. (He likes ice cream.) This is the work you completed in STEP 6.

Sentences in the essays that follow often contain two parts. One part can stand by itself. It has a subject and a verb. This is an *independent clause*. In an independent clause or *main clause*, the verb changes when time changes. Another group of related words also contains a verb and its subject, but it cannot stand by itself. This is a *subordinate* or *dependent* clause. It "depends" on the independent clause, and it is "subordinate" to that independent or main clause. The job of a dependent or subordinate clause is to explain, modify, or add to the main clause. The time or *tense* of this clause does not necessarily change when the tense of the main clause changes.

I will tell you about the house that burned. ("will" indicates the future)
I told you about the house that burned. ("told" indicates the past)

Notice that the dependent clause (*the house that burned*) is not affected by the change in the tense of the main or independent clause.

STEP 7   Rewrite the essay below by changing the past tense to the present or habitual tense. Do not copy the first sentence but substitute instead this sentence: *I prefer the original version of King Kong to the recent color version.* You will be indicating that the film is always happening because it is still available for rental and can be shown at any time. Change only what you must to indicate the present. Copy everything else. Proofread carefully.

The Original Version of *King Kong*

¹In 1933 Hollywood released one of its most enduring classics, the original version of *King Kong*. ²This black and white *King Kong* began with a daredevil movie producer, Carl Denham, sailing for an uncharted island he believed to contain some kind of mysterious native god or monster. ³With him Denham took some business associates and a beautiful girl, Ann Darrow (played by Fay Wray).

⁴On the island, the film party broke up a sensational native ceremonial dance, after which the chief of the island decided he wanted the blonde Ann Darrow as a "bride for Kong." ⁵Later that night tribesmen stole Ann from the company's yacht and offered her as a sacrifice to the great Kong. ⁶And, sure enough, King Kong did come through a gap in the great log fence and take Ann back into the jungle with him.

⁷The country beyond the fence was a primitive throwback inhabited by a brontosaurus, an allosaurus, and other monsters, chief among them Kong. ⁸Although Kong made short work of the rival beasties, he didn't hurt Ann; instead, he wanted to love her. ⁹But Jack Driscoll, a man from the ship's crew who loved Ann, came to her rescue. ¹⁰The producer Denham was more interested in capturing Kong and taking him back to civilization.

¹¹Once captured, the huge beast was taken to New York City, where he became a freak attraction at Madison Square Garden. ¹²Eventually, he broke loose and left a wake of death and destruction in the city as he recaptured Ann and sought a refuge atop the Empire State Building.

¹³A squadron of biplanes attacked Kong by circling the building and firing machine guns at him. ¹⁴Kong tried to fight them off while holding Ann in his hand. ¹⁵Finally, he was killed. ¹⁶Ann went to the arms of Jack Driscoll.

¹⁷I always wished it might come out differently.

NO. OF ERRORS

As you proofread, underline any changes you have made. Correct misspelled words below.

_____   _____   _____

STEP 7   The essay below is written as if the camel had become an
extinct animal. All its attributes and actions are given in the past
tense. Because the camel is not extinct, rewrite the essay to
indicate that its qualities are still true. Such general or scientific
truths are written in the *present tense*. Rewrite the essay in the
present tense, paying special attention to subject-verb
agreement. Change only the verbs. Copy everything else and
proofread. Your first sentence should read: *The camel is
justifiably called the ship of the desert.* (*was* changes to *is*)

Sailing on Sand

¹The camel was justifiably called the ship of the desert. ²It was well
equipped by nature to survive where other animals still die from lack of
food and water. ³The camel not only survived, it also transported people
and merchandise across the seas of sand.

⁴The camel's most important feature was, of course, its famous
hump. ⁵The animal stored both food and water for its journey in that hump.
⁶Like an empty storage bag, the camel's hump hung loosely before it was
filled. ⁷It developed its firm shape as it filled with food. ⁸While it prepared
for a trip, a camel ate continously, storing the food in the form of fat inside
the hump. ⁹When the hump was full, it held as much as one hundred
pounds of fat.

¹⁰In addition to stockpiling food, a camel also loaded up on water.
¹¹Gallons were stored in little pouches that lined the wall of its stomach.
¹²While the camel traveled, it fed itself by drawing from both its hump
and its stomach walls. ¹³If other sustenance was available, the camel
ate that, resorting to its storehouse only when it had to. ¹⁴By the end of
its journey, the empty hump hung loosely.

¹⁵There were other features that aided a camel's arduous journey
across the desert. ¹⁶Its bushy eyebrows and long eyelashes protected
its eyes, and long hairs in its ears kept the sand from blowing inside.

NO. OF ERRORS

As you proofread, underline the changes you have made.
Correct any errors your instructor has found. For more work in
the use of the present tense, choose another STEP 7 selection.
Work in the subject-verb agreement can be found in STEP 4
(plurals) and STEP 6 (singulars). List below unusual spelling
words or corrected spelling errors.

_____   _____   _____

Step 7

The Present Tense

Helpful Hints
and Special Situations

The verb *to be* is very useful but also highly irregular. Here it is in the present tense:

to be (infinitive)

I am	we are	
you are	you are	
he is		
she is	they are	
it is		

The two more frequently used forms of *to be* are *is* and *are*. They appear frequently in contractions, considerably complicating our sense of the apostrophe. Develop the habit of writing out these two words. This will help eliminate many problems in spelling and usage.

Remember that when you are using the present tense, you must make sure that the subject and verb in a sentence agree. Specifically, this means being careful in the third-person singular (*he, she, it/Jack, Jill, the pail*). Use the "rule of *s*"; add the *s* to the base verb.

Be consistent in your use of this tense. As long as you are speaking about the same *time*, use the same tense. Remember, however, that the tense of subordinate clauses does not *have* to be altered, and should not be, in many situations.

She has to stand on the spot where the tree had fallen. (The verb "has" is in the present; "had fallen" is in the past perfect tense.)

PLOT SUMMARIES are rendered in the present tense, even though the book or movie is old and the characters (as well as the author or director) may be dead. This use of the tense is the *historical present*. It suggests that as people read or view the story, they are, in a sense, keeping it alive.

In *The Deer Hunter*, three young men *go* off to war immediately after one of them *gets* married.

Similarly, use the present tense in describing the author's activities as they relate to the writing of the story.

Hawthorne *suggests* that Robin is a foolish young man.
He *shows* Robin behaving the way naïve young men generally behave.
He *has* Robin arrive at a strange city in the evening.

STEP 7   Rewrite the essay below by changing the past tense into the habitual tense. You will be indicating that the punishments of Sisyphus and Tantalus happen constantly. Keep in mind STEP 4 and STEP 6, which showed the connection between the subject and the verb. Change only what you must to indicate the habitual tense. Copy everything else. Proofread carefully.

Sisyphus and Tantalus

---

¹The Greek myths of Sisyphus and Tantalus tell the story of two mortals who were favored by the gods but who fell into evil ways and were punished for eternity.

²Sisyphus, "the craftiest of all mortals," received his punishment in the underworld. ³He was sentenced to roll a great block of stone up a hill, straining constantly against the weight. ⁴When he reached the top, his load escaped from him and plunged back to the plain below. ⁵He had to begin his labor again until he doubled over in anguish and sweat flowed from his limbs.

⁶Tantalus' punishment was worse. ⁷He had to stand in Hades in the middle of a lake whose waters came to his chin. ⁸His torment was that the waters came no further. ⁹He could not drink. ¹⁰When he bent down toward the water, it receded. ¹¹At the same time he had to suffer from hunger. ¹²There were beautiful fruit trees on the shore, their branches hanging over him. ¹³But the moment he reached for the fruit, a strong wind pushed the branches from his grasp. ¹⁴One remnant of Tantalus' agony is the modern word "tantalize," meaning "to tease or torment."

NO. OF ERRORS

As you proofread, underline any changes you have made. Correct any errors your instructor has found. Choose another STEP 7 selection for more work in the present tense. Work in subject-verb agreement can be found in STEP 4 and STEP 6. Correct misspelled words below.

_____   _____   _____

STEP 7 · The story below tells about a woman's behavior on one occasion. In order to indicate that she behaves this way all the time, you have to rewrite the story, changing the past tense to the *present* or *habitual* tense. Change only those words that you must, paying attention to subject-verb agreement (STEPS 4 and 6). Proofread carefully.

A Rose by Another Name?

[1]A well-known feminist reacted angrily when someone addressed her by her husband's name. [2]"Would you answer to your wife's name?" she demanded.

[3]She argued that birthnames are "psychic possessions." more important than laws or traditions. [4]As for laws, she knew of none requiring a woman to change her name after marriage. [5]"I, for one, would rather fight than switch," she declared.

[6]Obviously, she felt it was time to bring to an end the outdated idea that a woman is part of her husband's property. [7]In fact, France, Israel, and Sweden guarantee a woman's right to retain her birthname. [8]English common law, the basis of most U.S. laws, also allows a woman this right.

NO. OF ERRORS

As you proofread, underline any changes you have made. Correct any errors your instructor has found. Choose another STEP 7 selection for more work in the present tense. Work in subject-verb agreement can be found in STEP 4 and STEP 6. Correct misspelled words below.

_____   _____   _____

STEP 7   The story below tells of the past actions of a particular group of people. Beginning with the second paragraph, rewrite the story to indicate that these activities are typical of any group of people that comes to live at the village. Use the *present* or *habitual tense* to indicate this habitual behavior. Change only the verbs, and remember to take subject-verb agreement into consideration. Begin the *second* paragraph with: *Whenever people come to live at the compound* . . . (Do not change sentence 10.)

Roughing It in the Iron Age

¹Can people today, used to the comforts of the Technological Age, survive the living conditions of the Iron Age? ²In an attempt to answer this question, a Danish group built twelve Iron Age dwellings and invited families to live in the prehistoric village.

³The people who first came to live at the compound wore rough sackcloth during their stay. ⁴They lived in drafty mud huts with clay walls and thatched, straw roofs. ⁵The open fires filled the rooms with more smoke than heat; many of the participants soon yearned for comfortable clothes and central heating.

⁶As part of their daily activities, the volunteers harvested grain with flint sickles and plowed the land with primitive plowshares. ⁷Cloth dyeing was done with vegetable dyes, and pottery was baked in primitive kilns. ⁸A wild boar, one of the many nearly extinct animals that are essential to the village's economy, grazed outside.

⁹The organizers of this venture hoped to re-create a place where ancient arts and crafts could be studied before they disappeared forever. ¹⁰Although the past has been successfully re-created, the average group lasts only one week.

NO. OF ERRORS

As you proofread, underline any changes you have made. Correct any errors your instructor has found. Choose another STEP 7 selection for more work in the present tense. Work in subject-verb agreement can be found in STEP 4 and STEP 6. Correct misspelled words below.

_____   _____   _____

STEP 7   The essay below discusses the findings of a 1978 survey. Because the facts it contains are still valid today, rewrite the essay to indicate this. You can accomplish this by changing the *time* or *tense* of the sentences from the past to the *present* or *habitual* tense. Change only those words that you must. Copy everything else and proofread. Your first sentence should read: *When companies look for advertising trademarks, they often select dogs.* Note the changes from *looked* to *look* and *selected* to *select*. (Do not change sentence 8.)

Dogs as Insignias

---

[1]When companies looked for advertising trademarks, they often selected dogs. [2]People seemed to love these animals above all others.

[3]RCA's symbol, as a result, was Nipper, a fox terrier. [4]The company's trademark showed the dog listening to "his master's voice" as it emerged from a Gramophone.

[5]Other dogs that represented products included a pair of terriers that stood for a brand of Scotch whisky, a bulldog for Mack trucks, and a greyhound for the bus line of the same name. [6]There was also that team of a Boston terrier and a basset hound that symbolized a brand of shoes.

[7]In choosing dogs to represent their corporate images, companies were continuing an old tradition. [8]Dogs were featured throughout history on ancient signboards, knights' crests, and signet rings.

NO. OF ERRORS

As you proofread, underline any changes you have made. Correct any errors your instructor has found. Choose another STEP 7 selection for more work in the present tense. Work in subject-verb agreement can be found in STEP 4 and STEP 6. Correct misspelled words below.

---------------   ---------------   ---------------

STEP 7   The information below is given in the *past tense,* as it might be recollected by a traveler remembering a trip to South America. Rewrite the entire essay in the present tense to emphasize the habitual nature of the events. After all, the piranha still exists, and all the events related here could be happening right now. Change only the verbs, and pay special attention to subject-verb agreement. Copy everything else and proofread. Your first sentence should read: *In the waters of southern Brazil and Paraguay lies the most ferocious creature on the face of the earth, the deadly piranha.*

Killer Fish

¹In the waters of southern Brazil and Paraguay lay the most ferocious creature on the face of the earth, the deadly piranha (pronounced "pir-AHN-ya"). ²With a silver and brown-speckled body, it looked harmless enough, but its size did not fool anyone. ³A school of these flesh-eaters stripped a man's skeleton clean in a matter of minutes.

⁴The piranha's jaws were lined with teeth as sharp as razor blades. ⁵Each tooth was shaped like a small triangle, and a row of them resembled the points of a buzz saw blade. ⁶The Indians of South America used individual teeth as tips for their arrows.

⁷Armed with these lethal dentures, the piranha did not hesitate to attack any living creature, no matter how large. ⁸One piranha was bad enough, but they attacked their victims in schools of a hundred or more. ⁹And no animal of any size could withstand their relentless assault. ¹⁰Surprisingly, piranhas did not attack the feet of cows crossing a stream. ¹¹But as soon as one cow scraped her foot on a sharp stone and lost a drop of blood, the piranhas descended and ripped the cow's feet until the unfortunate creature keeled over. ¹²Once the cow fell, it was only a matter of minutes before the blood-crazed piranhas tore every bit of flesh from her bones.

¹³The piranhas' insatiable appetite made them easy fish to catch. ¹⁴They went for almost any bait. ¹⁵But when other piranhas in a school saw that one of their brothers was hooked, they picked his bones clean too. ¹⁶It took a nimble fisherman to find a piranha in one piece at the end of his line.

NO. OF ERRORS

As you proofread, underline the changes you have made. Correct any errors your instructor has found. For more work choose another STEP 7 selection. List below unusual spelling words or corrected spelling errors.

_____   _____   _____

STEP 7

Writing Assignments: The Present Tense

Be careful with subject-verb agreement while you are working on the assignments in this STEP. For explanation and work in subject-verb agreement, see STEP 4 (plurals) and STEP 6 (singulars).

Choose the topic below that interests you. Follow your instructor's suggestions as to the organization and length of the essay. You must, however, use the *present* or *habitual* tense as much as possible.

Your topic and your approach are your own. We would like to guide you only in your use of the tense. Use the *present* or *habitual* tense for the topics below.

1. Write a summary of the plot of a movie or TV show you have seen recently. (What happens?)
2. Describe the kind of service you like or dislike in a restaurant.
3. Choose a concept from one of your other courses—psychology, economics, biology, or physics—and explain it. (What is "paranoia," for example, or "free enterprise" or "mitosis" or a "simple machine"?)
4. Transcribe an inning or a sequence of first downs.
5. Explain why you think a particular team or individual is the "best" there is.
6. Describe how or why something works: the carburetor, poker, time zones, hail, tape recording, weaving, telephones, guitar, and so on.
7. What is your favorite time of day, and what do you generally do during that time?

STEP 8

The Progressive Tenses

The way to indicate that an action is ongoing or continuous is to use the *progressive* form of the verb. If the action or activity is continuous right now (in the "present"), you would use the *present progressive*. If the action or activity was continuous in the past, you would use the *past progressive*. The progressive form of the verb is called the *present participle*.

To form the *present progressive:* use *am, is* or *are* + verb + *ing*

I read science fiction (habitual)—I *am* reading science fiction.
He skis at Aspen. (habitual—He *is* skiing at Aspen.
They fly kites. (habitual)—They *are* flying kites.

To form the *past progressive:* use *was* or *were* + verb + *ing*

I *was* reading science fiction.
He *was* skiing at Aspen.
They *were* flying kites.

When the sentence already contains *is* or *are, was* or *were*, you must use the verb *to be*, specifically, in its progressive form, *being*. *Being* is the present participle of *be*.

I am a difficult person.	→ I am *being* a difficult person.
I was told to behave.	→ I was *being* told to behave.
She is a strong leader.	→ She is *being* a strong leader.
She was honored.	→ She was *being* honored.
They are placed on display.	→ They are *being* placed on display.
They were dusted.	→ They were *being* dusted.

Remember to use *is* and *was* with singular nouns and to use *are* and *were* with plurals.

Once again, subordinate or dependent clauses do not necessarily have the same tense as the independent or main clause.

independent clause   dependent clause

I am telling you that she was already here.

[present progressive]   [past]

STEP 8

The Present Progressive

Helpful Hints and Special Situations

When you are adding the *ing* to verbs, you may have to drop a letter from the base verb. If the verb ends in a silent *e*, drop the *e* before attaching *ing*.

shake + ing   is shaking   take + ing   is taking

bake + ing   is baking   wake + ing   is waking

Notice that the progressive form of the verb *to be—being—*is a combination of *be + ing*. Use *being* in situations where it seems to make no sense to attach the *ing* to the verb.

The lion was hunted down. (past)→The lion was being hunted down.

If you try attaching *ing* to *hunted*, you get: The lion was hunting down. Clearly that is not what you intended to say.

Some writers use the word *getting* instead of *being*. The word will be understood, but its use should be restricted to informal situations, such as casual conversation, for example.

He is being paid too much money.   He is getting paid too much money.

Do be careful with this word, however, for it cannot always replace *being*.

Remember to return irregular verbs to their base form before adding *ing*.

The outfielder caught the ball.   The outfielder is catching the ball.
caught (past tense—catch (base)→catching (base + *ing*)

STEP 8   In the short essay below, the sentences are written in the
present tense. With the exception of sentences 3, 5 and 10,
which express general truths, the activity in the other sentences
is ongoing. Because they are occurring right now, many writers
would find it more appropriate to write the essay using the
present progressive tense. This means using *is* or *are* with the
-ing form of the verb. Rewrite the essay in this tense (except for
sentences 3, 5 and 10). Begin the first sentence with: *Right now
energy experts are hoping to find alternatives . . .* Change only
the words you must.

Heat from Beneath the Earth

[1]Energy experts hope to find alternatives to our present depend-
ence on oil and other fossil fuels. [2]They look especially for sources of
energy that will not run out. [3]One of the least-known and most promising
of these is geothermal energy or, more simply, the earth's heat.

[4]Geologists drill wells along the shorelines of the east and west
coasts of the United States to find subterranean cones of hot pluton.
[5]This energy source heats water to a considerable temperature, often
higher than the boiling point. [6]Brought to the surface, this heat replaces
the need for dwindling supplies of existing fuels. [7]Presently, geothermal
energy heats greenhouses and apartment buildings in California.

[8]A history of earthquakes and volcanic activity makes exploration
work easier on the West Coast; hot pluton comes closer to the surface
on its own. [9]Recent discoveries of subsurface cracks in East Coast bed-
rock encourage drilling in the energy-hungry Northeast, too. [10]Geothermal
wells in the East run deeper than those in the West. [11]Nonetheless, they
become economic with the rising cost of existing fuels despite heavy
drilling expenses.

[12]Virginia Polytechnic Institute maintains a mile-deep well in North
Carolina that yields water at about 140°F. [13]In Ocean City, Maryland, an
old gas exploration well 1.5 miles deep gives forth water at temperatures of 215°F.

[14]Because of little exploration in the past, the government's geothermal program grows steadily. [15]Currently $137.7 million is spent on
research, but that figure should double in the next few years.

NO. OF ERRORS

As you proofread, underline changes you have made. Correct
any errors your instructor has found. Choose another STEP 8
selection for work in the progressive tenses. Work in subject-
work agreement can be found in STEP 4 (plurals) and STEP 6
(singulars). Correct misspelled words below.

_____   _____   _____

STEP 8   The essay below is written in the present tense. Because the events are ongoing—in progress—rewrite the essay, using *the present progressive* tense. You can indicate this tense by inserting *is* or *are* before each verb and adding *-ing* to the base verb. Otherwise, copy the essay and proofread carefully. Your first sentence should begin: *As the world's great cities are dying* . . . (Do not change sentences 2, 9, and 17.)

The Fate of Cities

---

[1]As the world's great cities die, other cities around the world emerge to replace the old metropolises. [2]The new centers of population expect to avoid the fate of New York, London, Paris, and Rome by seeking solutions to the problems that continually destroy these former jewels.

[3]A city like New York loses its power as it loses its people. [4]The city's population diminishes by the day, and its influence along with it. [5]People who move take their tax dollars with them, further reducing revenues and employment opportunities. [6]At the same time, the cost of services increases, stretching the city's financial resources even thinner. [7]Although New York, as well as the other great cities, continues to attract tourists, it is fast approaching the saturation point beyond which it is incapable of providing for its own citizens.

[8]While these cities decline, other cities grow relentlessly. [9]Mexico City, Tokyo, São Paulo, Rio de Janeiro, and Cairo—all Third World cities—are rapidly becoming the premium urban centers of the world. [10]These cities gain population quickly; as many as 360 people settle in Cairo each day. [11]At the same time, living conditions in these cities deteriorate. [12]A whiff of fresh air gets to be as difficult to find as a job. [13]In Mexico City, for example, visibility drops steadily, from seven miles in 1950 to less than three miles today.

[14]What keeps these new giants from suffering the fate of the old titans? [15]Mexico City hopes that new oil revenues will help. [16]Jakarta and Manila, two emerging giants, are taken under the care of their countries' first ladies. [17]Indonesia's Mrs. Suharto and the Philippines' Mrs. Marcos are devoting themselves to the restoration of their capitals.

NO. OF ERRORS

As you proofread, underline changes you have made. Correct any errors your instructor has found. Choose another STEP 8 selection for work in the progressive tenses. Work in subject-work agreement can be found in STEP 4 (plurals) and STEP 6 (singulars.) Correct misspelled words below.

---   ---   ---

STEP 8   Rewrite the essay below to indicate that the process being
                described is going on right now. Once again, you will have to
                manipulate the word that carries information about time. You
                will also have to add *is* or *are*. Copy everything else and
                proofread. Your first sentence should read: *California and*
                Mexico are moving closer to each other daily; geographically,
                that is. (Do not disturb sentence 9.)

California Is Slipping

---

¹California and Mexico move closer to each other daily; geograph-
ically, that is. ²As Southern California's terrain gets compressed, it slides
four inches closer to Mexico each year. ³Scientists have difficulties explaining the phenomenon.

⁴In the first place, the compression moves in a north-south direction. ⁵Yet the land plate that drifts under the area and much of the Pacific Ocean creates northwest land slippage.

⁶Scientists also find it puzzling that there is no ground swell or
buildup of land. ⁷A compression should pile up the landscape northeast
of Los Angeles by as much as three inches a year.

⁸That drifting land plate, by the way, travels at a fairly slow speed
compared to the cars on the highways. ⁹It has been taking the coastal
side of the San Andreas fault 30 million years to move 125 miles northwest in relation to the continental side of the fault.

NO. OF ERRORS

As you proofread, underline changes you have made.
Correct any errors your instructor has found. Choose another
STEP 8 essay for work in the progressive tenses. Work in subject-
work agreement can be found in STEP 4 (plurals) and STEP 6
(singulars). Correct misspelled words below.

_____   _____   _____

STEP 8   The essay below is written in the *present tense*. Change all the main verbs to the *progressive present*, to reflect that the development of large, power-generating windmills is something that is happening *right now*. Copy everything else without change. Your first sentence should read: *Great changes are happening in the way we think about windmills.*

Some Windmills Are Giants

¹Great changes happen in the way we think about windmills. ²City governments, corporations, and backyard tinkerers, assisted by the Department of Energy (DOE), build gigantic new windmills to help solve our power needs. ³No longer mere attractions for tourists in Holland, the new windmills run to 150 feet in height with 200 foot blade spans.

⁴The DOE and associated federal agencies spend $60 million a year on windmill research. ⁵Government-sponsored windmills work in New Mexico, Rhode Island, Puerto Rico, and now North Carolina. ⁶On some projects the DOE cooperates with the research laboratories of large corporations like General Electric and Boeing.

⁷Right now a windmill in Boone, North Carolina, locally called "The Monster," generates 2,000 kilowatts an hour. ⁸This electricity satisfies the needs of about 500 homes. ⁹Although wind power is free and inexhaustible, the windmill presents the people of Boone with some problems. ¹⁰Because of high installation costs for the windmill (about $5.8 million), electricity from it costs six to eight cents a kilowatt hour versus 3.75 cents for current, conventional power.

¹¹Another problem with the windmills appears at a Rhode Island installation. ¹²The heavy metal blades of that power generator interfere with local television signals. ¹³As a result, the DOE spends an additional $700,000 to provide residents with a cable television system.

¹⁴All the same, expectations for wind-generated electricity run high. ¹⁵The new Boeing Mod II windmill furnishes power at no more than eight cents per kilowatt hour. ¹⁶Plans develop for fiberglass blades, which are lighter and reduce television interference. ¹⁷DOE experts anticipate seeing fully 2 percent of U.S. electricity needs met by windmills in the year 2000, for which we shall require 30,000 windmills.

NO. OF ERRORS

As you proofread, underline the changes you have made. Correct any errors your instructor has found. Choose another STEP 8 for any work in the progressives. Work in subject-verb agreement can be found in STEP 4 (plurals) and STEP 6 (singulars). Correct misspelled words below.

STEP 8

The Past Progressive

Helpful Hints and Special Situations

The helping verb in the past progressive is the past tense of the verb *to be*. It is *was* in the singular, *were* in the plural. Note that *you* takes *were* in both the singular and plural.

Singular	Plural
I was trying to win.	We were trying to win.
You WERE trying to win.	You were trying to win.
He was trying to win.	
She was trying to win.	They were trying to win.
It was trying to win.	

The word "lie" is often confused with another word. Try to associate this word with two others.

lie	sit	rise
I am lying down.	I am sitting down.	I am rising.

Now the past progressive:

I was lying down.   I was sitting down.   I was rising.

The other word cannot be used in this same situation. It needs something else for the "I" to hold in hand.

The progressive form can also be used with other tenses; the helping verbs *will*, *has*, and *have* substitute for *is/are* and *was/were*. These tenses will be discussed in STEP 10 (the future tense) and STEP 11 (the perfect tenses).

It has been called to your attention repeatedly that subordinate clauses are not necessarily in the same tense as the main clause. Although this is true, a writer should be careful to make the tense in the subordinate clause relate logically to the tense in the main clause.

I told her that I was pleased with her essay. (not "I am pleased")

STEP 8   The story below is written in the *past tense*. Rewrite it to emphasize the continuing nature of the events. Notice that the events in the first paragraph (and parts of the others) are all occurring at the same time. The *past progressive* is thus a particularly appropriate tense to use. Insert *was* or *were* before each verb, and add *-ing* to the *base* part of the verb. (Leave sentences 7, 10, 11, 12, and 13 undisturbed.) Your first sentence should read: *The Yankees were trailing by a run.*

The Infield Fly Rule

---

¹The Yankees trailed by a run. ²Randolph stood near second. ³White waited off first. ⁴The Baltimore first baseman guarded the hole between first and second. ⁵Munson was careful with a count of two strikes against him. ⁶The fans leaned forward, waiting for the pitch.

⁷Munson swung. ⁸As the ball went straight up, high above the pitcher's head, the umpires yelled, "Infield fly," and the runners moved to stand on their bases.

⁹To the amazement of everyone, the catcher let the ball hit the ground. ¹⁰Then he threw it to second. ¹¹One out. ¹²The second baseman fired to first. ¹³Double play?

¹⁴No. ¹⁵To the Yankees' relief, only Munson, the batter, was called out. ¹⁶The infield fly rule was used once again to protect the helpless runners.

NO. OF ERRORS

As you proofread, underline changes you have made. Correct any errors your instructor has found. Choose another STEP 8 essay for work in the progressive tenses. Work in subject-work agreement can be found in STEP 4 (plurals) and STEP 6 (singulars). Correct misspelled words below.

_____   _____   _____

STEP 8   The essay below is written mostly in the *present progressive* tense. The speaker is John T. Daniels, who witnessed and photographed the events of December 17, 1903, when Orville and Wilbur Wright first flew an engine-driven vehicle. The telling below is done as the events *are taking* place. Most of the sentences use the progressive to emphasize the ongoing nature of the events. Rewrite the essay so that it tells of the events after they had been completed. Use the past—*was* and *were*—but keep the progressive form in the sentences where it occurs. Copy everything else and proofread. Begin with: *It was the first flight. Orville was lying down. . . .*

The Wright Flights:
John T. Daniels, Eyewitness

---

¹It is the first flight. ²Orville is lying down on the lower wing and grasping the lever. ³The motor is coughing. ⁴The propellers are beginning to turn. ⁵The Wright Flyer is beginning to move slowly into the strong wind. ⁶Wilbur is running alongside, steadying the wing. ⁷The craft is rising into the air. ⁸It is aloft! ⁹It is a very exciting sight. ¹⁰I am hoping that the camera is not missing any of it.

¹¹The five of us on the ground are counting the seconds. ¹²We are all wondering how Orville is feeling. ¹³He is surely filled with exhilaration.

¹⁴The Wright Flyer is landing. ¹⁵It covered 120 feet during the 12 seconds of its flight. ¹⁶We are considering the flight a success, but we are hoping the brothers would try again.

¹⁷The second and third flights were not successful. ¹⁸During the fourth, Wilbur is at the controls. ¹⁹The Flyer is in the air again. ²⁰We are counting the seconds anxiously. ²²It is a historic day, no question about it. ²³The Flyer is landing after 59 seconds in the sky. ²⁴It is 852 feet from where I am taking the photographs.

NO. OF ERRORS

As you proofread, underline the changes you have made. Correct any errors your instructor has located in your essay. For additional work in the past progressive tense, choose another selection in STEP 8. Correct any spelling errors below. Note the form of *to lie* in the second sentence.

_____   _____   _____

STEP 8   The following essay is written in the *past* tense. Change it to the *past progressive* to show what people in China were doing until modernization came.

Chinese civilization is extremely old, and, over most of its history, it was isolated from most of the rest of the world. For these reasons the Chinese traditionally did things differently from people in cultures elsewhere—at least they did until modernization began under Dr. Sun Yat-sen in 1912. As you rewrite the essay in the past progressive, you should reflect the idea that these customs were current for many years, up through the time of modernization. The first sentence you must rewrite, sentence 2, should read this way: *To greet a friend or new associate, they were shaking their own hand, not his.* Do not change sentences 1, 3, 8, and 13. Proofread carefully.

Old Chinese Customs

---

¹One could see how differently the Chinese viewed themselves at introductions. ²To greet a friend or new associate, they shook their own hand, not his. ³Differences were greater in the household. ⁴To build a new house, they constructed the roof first. ⁵They used paper in their windows instead of glass. ⁶After bathing, they dried themselves with a wet towel. ⁷They drank hot beverages to cool themselves. ⁸Yet some of these customs seemed like a good idea. ⁹They placed the saucer over a cup of tea to keep it warm, not under it.

¹⁰Their isolation from the world gave them an entirely different sense of direction. ¹¹Their compasses pointed south, not north. ¹²They described Burma, for example, as being "westsouth" instead of "southwest."

¹³Mail from Western countries, such as America, was difficult to deliver, and not just because of the difference in alphabets. ¹⁴They put their surnames first, not last. ¹⁵They addressed letters in the following manner: "Colorado, Denver, Street Main 108, Wang, John, Mr."

¹⁶They read books from the back to the front, and they put their footnotes at the top of the page.

¹⁷Most disturbingly of all, they insisted their hearts were on the right side of the body, not on the left as in the bodies of foreigners.

NO. OF ERRORS

As you proofread, underline the changes you have made. Correct any errors your instructor has located in your essay. For additional work in the past progressive choose another selection in STEP 8. Correct any spelling errors below.

---   ---   ---

STEP 8

Writing Assignments: The Progressive Tenses

The virture of the progressive tense, whether present or past, is that it enables you to describe ongoing events. The topics attempt to steer you into using the progressive tense because it seems most suitable.

The Present Progressive

1. Describe what is happening right now in an international trouble spot.
2. You are at a party, watching two people meeting for the first time. Describe the scene.
3. What is happening to your attitude about certain things as you are growing older?
4. What is occurring to your body while you are sleeping?
5. What are other members of your family doing while you are writing this essay?

The Past Progressive

6. What were you doing at a significant moment in the recent past?
   a. During the 1979 solar eclipse.
   b. While some important election was taking place.
   c. While Bicentennial celebrations were going on.
   d. When you heard the news about the death of some well-known figure.
   e. When you heard important news about some member of your family.
7. Ask one of your parents for the information and recount what he or she was doing when he or she was at the same stage in life where you are now.
8. Find out what someone else was doing (or, if you remember, describe your own moment) during
   a. The first moon landing.
   b. The Kennedy assassinations.
   c. The Martin Luther King assassination.
   d. The Nixon resignation.
   e. The Watergate hearings.

Step 9

The Past Tense

In this STEP you will have to rewrite essays in the *past tense*. That means you will have to change the verb in each sentence so that it indicates that the event or action took place in the past.

Most verbs are regular. Regular verbs indicate the past by adding *ed* to the base. (Notice that the "silent e" drops.)

love + *ed* → loved
dance + *ed* → danced
walk + *ed* → walked

Irregular verbs indicate the past in a variety of ways. Some change completely; some remain unchanged. The past tense of irregular verbs must be learned individually. Learn the forms as you come across the verbs. Above all, learn them in context.

break → broke
go → went
lay → laid
catch → caught

The following are examples of verbs that do not change in the past:

set → When I was a child, I   hit → After the batter hit the
   often set the table.   ball, he ran to first base.

Here is a chart of the forms of a regular verb. Alongside is an irregular verb in all forms and persons. Notice that the past tense does not change in the plural or singular for the third or first person. It is always the same.

A Regular Verb		An Irregular Verb	
Present Tense	Past Tense	Present Tense	Past Tense
I dance.	I danced.	I slide.	I slid.
You dance.	You danced.	You slide.	You slid.
He dances.	He danced.	He slides.	He slid.
She dances.	She danced.	She slides.	She slid.
It dances.	It danced.	It slides.	It slid.
We dance.	We danced.	We slide.	We slid.
You dance.	You danced.	You slide.	You slid.
They dance.	They danced.	They slide.	They slid.

There is one notable exception to the statement that the past tense is not affected by singulars and plurals. The verb *to be* in the past tense is affected by number (singular or plural).

Use *was* with a singular subject.   Use *were* with a plural subject.
He *was* pleased with the news.   They *were* fine athletes.

STEP 9　Notice that the first paragraph of the essay below is told in the past tense. Rewrite the rest of the essay in that tense. You can indicate the past by manipulating the verbs. (You might want to refer back to the discussion of showing time at the beginning of this section.) Change only the verbs. Copy everything else and proofread carefully.

Teddy Bear

¹In 1978 we marked the seventy-fifth anniversary of three events. ²It was 75 years earlier that the Wright brothers' first flight occurred and when the first World Series was played. ³It was also in 1903 that Teddy Bear was born, making 1978 his seventy-fifth birthday. ⁴Actually, his story began in 1902.

⁵In 1902, President Roosevelt is in Mississippi trying to settle a boundary dispute. ⁶The dispute settled, he goes hunting. ⁷When his hunting party's dogs corner a thin, lame bear, Teddy releases the animal. ⁸Back in Washington, Charles Berryman portrays the president in a cartoon that shows him sparing the trapped animal. ⁹The caption, "Drawing the line," is taken to refer both to Teddy's merciful act and to his defiance of racists during the boundary argument. ¹⁰Soon after, the Roosevelt Bear begins to appear on toys, postcards, books, and buttons. ¹¹There is no mention yet of "Teddy Bear."

¹²In 1903, Morris Michtom, a Russian Jewish immigrant, designs two toy bears for the windows of his candy store in Brooklyn. ¹³When someone offers to buy the stuffed animals, he gets the idea of asking President Roosevelt if he could name the bears after him. ¹⁴Teddy gives his consent. ¹⁵Teddy Bear is born.

¹⁶In 1938, Morris Michtom dies. ¹⁷At his death he is the head of the multimillion dollar Ideal Toy Corporation. ¹⁸Ideal is producing 100,000 teddy bears a year at the time of its founder's death.

NO. OF ERRORS

As you proofread, underline changes you have made. Correct any errors your instructor has found. Choose another selection in STEP 9 for work in the past tense. Correct misspelled words below.

_____   _____   _____

STEP 9   If people living at the time were asked about their president's interest in sports, they would have responded using the present tense. Because you are writing about presidential interests in the past, you must rewrite this essay in the *past tense*. What this means, of course, is that you will have to change the verbs to make them indicate the past. Change only the verbs. Copy everything else and proofread. Notice that many of the sentences are already *in the past*. (Leave the dates out.)

Presidents and Sports

---

¹President Garfield, according to some accounts, used to amuse himself by writing Greek with one hand and, at the same time, Latin with the other. ²Other presidents, however, were more athletic.

³An interest in horses was one thing a number of presidents had in common. (1771) ⁴President Washington spends a great deal of his time riding horses. ⁵He also enjoys attending races. (1806) ⁶President Jackson both breeds and races horses; he wins a famous race riding Truxton, his bay stallion. (1870) ⁷Ulysses S. Grant's passion is horsemanship. ⁸He is well known for his acrobatic feats on horseback. (1905) ⁹Teddy Roosevelt is referred to as "the cowboy" for his skills on horseback.

¹⁰Football was another sport in which presidents, particularly in the twentieth century, shared an interest. (1895) ¹¹Herbert Hoover, as an undergraduate at Stanford, manages the school's football team. (1910) ¹²Playing halfback on the West Point football team, Dwight D. Eisenhower injures his knee while tackling the great Jim Thorpe. (1938) ¹³A football injury to his back ends John F. Kennedy's football career at Harvard; he continues playing touch football. (1972) ¹⁴A bench warmer at Whittier College, President Nixon retains a keen interest in football. ¹⁵He suggests a play for Miami in the Super Bowl. ¹⁶The play does not gain any yardage. (1975) ¹⁷Gerald Ford is the best football player ever to occupy the White House. ¹⁸He is the only president to play in the College All Star game while an undergraduate and the only one who receives an offer to play pro ball.

¹⁹One other presidential sport was wrestling. ²⁰At least it was President Lincoln's sport. ²¹While he was a clerk in Illinois, he won a wrestling match that was attended from as far as fifty miles away. ²²Most of the spectators bet against him.

NO. OF ERRORS

As you proofread, underline changes you have made. Correct any errors your instructor has found. Choose another selection in STEP 9 for work in the past tense. Correct misspelled words below.

_____   _____   _____

Step 9

The Past Tense

Helpful Hints and Special Situations

When *ed* is added to the base form of the verb, the silent *e* drops from the end of the verb.

dance + ed → danced   skate + ed → skated   flare + ed → flared

Some texts will tell you that the past tense in the cases above is formed by simply adding *d* instead of *ed*. In fact, it is *ed* that is being added. It might not appear very significant which *e* is eliminated, but, in fact, it is quite important. The principle that is at work is the same as the one that dictated that *ing* endings force the silent *e* to drop. The ending is so important that it remains intact. It is the silent *e* that falls. This is even more obvious in case of an ending (suffix) such as *able*. When added to a word that ends in silent *e*, it is the inner vowel, the *e*, that drops.

love + able → lovable   like + able → likable   live + able → livable

---

A number of words appear very frequently as helping verbs. You should be familiar with them in both the present tense and the past tense.

has *and* have	→	had
does *and* do	→	did
can	→	could
shall	→	should
will	→	would

It is important to remember that sentences often contain a main or independent clause and a subordinate or dependent clause. When you are changing the tense of a sentence, you may have to change the tense of only the main verb. The verb in the subordinate clause may remain untouched.

I am telling you that he is a trustworthy person.   (*am telling* is present progressive)
I told you that he is a trustworthy person.   (*told* is in the past)

Although the tense of the main verb changed from the present progressive to the past, the tense of the verb in the dependent clause remains untouched. Of course, if you say, *I told you that he was a trustworthy person*, you would also be correct.

STEP 9   The essay below describes celestial events for the month of January in 1979. We would like you to rewrite this essay, making it clear that these are events of the past. Make the changes that clearly indicate this historical past. Do not change anything else. Proofread carefully. Your first sentence should read: *Astronomers promised an interesting sky in January.* (Notice the change from *promise* to *promised.*)

Celestial Events for 1979

---

[1]Astronomers promise an interesting sky in January. [2]They expect a "splendid young moon" but urge viewers to look for the "spectacular show" of the evening stars.

[3]The moon's show begins on New Year's Eve, when it is a young crescent. [4]On the thirteenth of the month it is full. [5]On the fourteenth, just past full, it moves south of Jupiter. [6]During the night it slips slowly to the left of the planet. [7]On this date it is at its "apogee," farthest from the earth. [8]From January 15 to January 17 the moon moves past Saturn. [9]"Perigee," nearest earth, occurs on January 28.

[10]The "really big show," however, is in the morning sky. [11]It is there that Mars, Jupiter, and Saturn perform. [12]Mars enters the sky on the twentieth. [13]On the twenty-fourth, Jupiter becomes an evening star. [14]It is visible as a very brilliant object in Cancer. [15]Between January 20 and 24 all the planets are morning stars, with Venus and Jupiter the brightest and second brightest objects in the sky and with Saturn visible to the lower right of Regulus.

[16]There will be an eclipse of the sun by the moon near the end of February.

NO. OF ERRORS

As you proofread, underline changes you have made. Correct any errors your instructor has found. Choose another selection in STEP 9 for work in the past tense. Correct misspelled words below.

_____   _____   _____

STEP 9   Imagine that your discussion refers to events that took place back in 1970. To indicate this historical past, you must change those words that inform your reader about time. Make those changes, but copy everything else and proofread. Your first sentence should say: *By 1970, fermentation, the process by which the juice of the grape turns into wine, was no longer a matter of chance.* (Notice that the time change was indicated by changing *is* to *was.*)

Grape Juice to Wine

¹Fermentation, the process by which the juice of the grape turns into wine, is no longer a matter of chance.

²An important first step in standardization is the development of "dehydrated pure wine yeast." ³No longer does the wine maker have to depend on the unpredictable behavior of wild yeasts. ⁴Those simple, one-celled plants found naturally in the bloom of the skin of the grape used to control fermentation. ⁵With the development of dehydrated yeast, the wine maker selects yeast strains with desirable characteristics. ⁶He or she thus guarantees predictable excellence year after year.

⁷The other factor that has been brought under control is the amount of heat produced during fermentation. ⁸The process itself creates too much heat, injuring the yeast at 90°F and killing it altogether at 100°F. ⁹Newly developed cooling methods keep the fermenting liquid at ideal temperatures and add to the delicacy of the wine.

NO. OF ERRORS

As you proofread, underline changes you have made. Correct any errors your instructor has found. Choose another selection in STEP 9 for work in the past tense. Correct misspelled words below.

_____   _____   _____

STEP 9   The essay below discusses a satellite project named *Landsat II.* Since the essay was written, *Landsat III* was launched, replacing *Landsat II.* That launch makes everything about *Landsat II* a thing of the past. Rewrite the essay to indicate that the statements about *Landsat II* were true *back in 1975.* Your second sentence should read: *By that reckoning, the worth of* Landsat II *was immeasurable.* Remember that each verb should indicate *the past.* Change only the verbs. Copy everything else and proofread.

An Eye in the Sky

---

¹"A picture is worth a thousand words," said an anonymous philosopher. ²By that reckoning, the worth of *Landsat II* is immeasurable. ³Each picture the satellite sends back to Earth is the equivalent of one thousand conventional photographs. ⁴One of the most significant applications of these photographs has been in the evaluation of agriculture and food resources. ⁵*Landsat* provides information that enables planners to determine Earth's ability to sustain human existence.

⁶*Landsat's* images display climate, weather, and soil content data. ⁷A program called LACIE uses this data to estimate what volume of crops could be grown in a particular area and how fast they were likely to grow. ⁸On the basis of such estimates, scientists can predict how much food will be available for consumption, and how much fresh water, timber, oil, and minerals can be used without depletion.

⁹Because *Landsat's* "eyes" can see wavelengths such as X rays and reflected energy, they are useful in many other ways. ¹⁰Geologists use *Landsat's* sensors to locate scarce mineral deposits. ¹¹Navigators use *Landsat* to update maps. ¹²The satellite's eyes are always open, and they can note shifting sand bars and new channels as soon as some storm makes those changes.

NO. OF ERRORS

As you proofread, underline changes you have made. Correct any errors your instructor has found. Choose another selection in STEP 9 for work in the past tense. Correct misspelled words below.

_____   _____   _____

STEP 9   The selection below describes the emergence of new games. Let us assume that these games have come and gone, that they were in style back in 1977 and 1978 but are no longer around today. To indicate this, you must change those words in the sentences that carry information about time. Change the time into the past. Otherwise copy the selection and proofread carefully. Your first sentence should read: *In the late seventies there were new games in town that participants neither won nor lost.* (Note the changes from *are* to *were*, *win* to *won*, and *lose* to *lost*.)

Noncompetitive Games

¹There are new games in town that participants neither win nor lose. ²All they do is play. ³With these games what counts is how you play. ⁴The emphasis is on cooperation rather than competition.

⁵In "Total Basketball," for example, officials do not keep separate scores for each team. ⁶Instead they keep a single, combined score, for both teams. ⁷Creators of the game feel that players on both sides enjoy themselves more with competitiveness removed.

⁸Other noncompetitive games are Earthball and People Pass. ⁹In the first of these, a crowd spends hours trying to keep a large globe made of canvas bouncing in the air. ¹⁰In the second, a person is passed overhead by the others in the game, with each of the participants eventually getting a ride.

¹¹Like more traditional games, these two new games also require well-conditioned bodies and alert minds. ¹²The inventors of the games feel, however, that Earthball and the other noncompetitive games have the additional virtue of teaching people to work with each other instead of against one another. ¹³With the focus on the joy of playing, there are no suffering losers either.

NO. OF ERRORS

As you proofread, underline changes you have made. Correct any errors your instructor has found. Choose another selection in STEP 9 for work in the past tense. Correct misspelled words below.

_____   _____   _____

STEP 9   The essay below describes the longest known swim as it would have been reported by a radio sports commentator of the time, in the present tense. As these events actually took place in 1940, you should rewrite the essay putting all the verbs in the past tense. You may, if you like, include the reported times given in parentheses here as part of your revised sentences. Your first sentence should read: *On July 25 at 7:22 A.M. John Sigmund, a 30-year-old St. Louis butcher, set out on one of the most adventuresome swims ever attempted.* Do not change anything else. Proofread carefully.

Longest-Distance Swimmer

¹(July 25. 7:22 A.M.) John Sigmund, a 30-year-old St. Louis butcher, sets out on one of the most adventuresome swims ever attempted. ²He lowers himself into the Mississippi River after weeks of thorough preparation. ³Sigmund is accompanied by his lovely wife, Catherine, who rides in a cabin cruiser. ⁴At intervals, Catherine furnishes her husband with his only sustenance, high-energy candy bars.

⁵(July 25. 7:30 P.M.) The Mississippi River is so muddy that Sigmund cannot see floating objects. ⁶Because of the poor visibility, Sigmund injures his leg on an unseen, submerged log.

⁷(July 26. 2:05 A.M.) The waves of a passing barge wash against Sigmund and push him against the cabin cruiser, nearly knocking him unconscious. ⁸But after almost nineteen hours in the water, Sigmund shows no signs of flagging strength.

⁹(July 27. 9:30 A.M.) With Sigmund in the water more than two days and two nights, enthusiastic crowds gather at Caruthersville, his announced goal, the last Missouri City on the river, 292 miles from his starting point.

¹⁰(July 28. 4:30 P.M.) In the most discouraging episode of the swim, Sigmund wanders three miles off course when he mistakenly enters one of the Mississippi's tributaries. ¹¹Without the continual encouragement and prodding of his wife, Sigmund would fall asleep in the water.

¹²(July 28. 11:58 P.M.) Hundreds of bystanders cheer in Caruthersville, Missouri, as John Sigmund is pulled from the water 89 hours after he entered it. ¹³He cannot acknowledge the crowd's acclaim, however. ¹⁴Unable either to walk or to talk, he is carried off by friends.

¹⁵(July 29. 10:45 A.M.) Amazingly, Sigmund appears to be fully recovered and ready to return to work in his butcher shop. ¹⁶What ill-effects he sustains, a sun-blistered face, wobbly legs, and aching muscles, are already on the mend. ¹⁷But Sigmund does not think he would like to swim back to St. Louis.

NO. OF ERRORS

As you proofread, underline the changes you have made. Correct misspelled words below.

Step 9

Writing Assignments: The Past Tense

Your instructor will make suggestions about the length and organization of these writing assignments. The topics should give you a context for using the past tense. Proofread carefully, looking words up in the dictionary if you are not sure of their spelling or past tense form. The Appendix to this text contains a list of some of the more difficult verb forms.

1. Give the details of the best or worst meal you have ever had.
2. Describe a particularly pleasant or frightening event in your childhood. Write about it from your present age, looking back.
3. Interview one of your parents, and write a biography of him or her up to the time you were born.
4. How did the most recent winner of the World Series, Super Bowl, or other championship game achieve that victory?
5. Retell an event in history that interests you.
6. Write about a person in America's past or in the past of the native country whom you find interesting or heroic.
7. Find out about one of your ancestors, and tell an anecdote about the person.
8. Describe a significant moment—wedding, birth, funeral, graduation—in your family history that you had attended.
9. If you have a possession you value greatly, tell about the circumstances of getting it.

Remember to use the simple past in writing these essays. You will discover that the past tense helps you focus on events. Instead of speaking in general terms about things that happen, you will be writing about one specific or particular event. You can also relax, somewhat, about subject-verb agreement. Other than *was/were*, the past tense of *to be*, other verbs remain unchanged in both the plural and singular.

Step 10

The Future Tense

In STEP 10 you will be asked to change verbs written in one tense to the future tense. To indicate the future tense, you must return the verb to its base form and place *will* (sometimes *shall*) in front of it. *Will* is called the auxiliary verb.

Past	Future
General Foods Corporation reduced the amount of maple syrup in its Log Cabin brand to 3 percent. Some other companies eliminated the maple content altogether.	General Foods Corporation *will reduce* the amount of maple syrup in its Log Cabin brand from 3 to 2 percent. Some other companies *will eliminate* the maple content altogether.

This tense is used to indicate the time of a coming event. It is the tense used for prediction. Some writers avoid using *will* and substitute *going to*, as in:

Some companies are going to eliminate the maple content altogether.

The verb *to be*, which takes the forms *is/are* in the present and *was/were* in the past, is *be* in the future.

John Travolta is a star. → He will be a star for many more years.

If you disagreed with the above statement, you would write: *He will not be a star for many more years.* Notice that *not* comes between *will* and the verb.

Here is a chart of a verb in the future tense in all persons and forms:

to love

I
You
He
She   will
It   love.
We
You
They

The future tense is not affected by a change in the subject from the singular to the plural. You need not be concerned about subject-verb agreement when your sentence is in the future tense. However, because subordinate clauses use different tenses sometimes, make sure that there is subject-verb agreement in them.

STEP 10   The essay below discusses the utopian vision of the future found in the science fiction novel *Triton* by Samuel R. Delany, published in 1976.

All the writing in the essay is from the point of view of someone living in 2112 A.D., and therefore the verbs are either present or present progressive. Rewrite the essay so that it becomes a prediction of the future. To do this, you must insert *will* and change the verb back to its base form. Make what other changes you must and proofread.

Delany's Vision

---

¹In the year 2112 A.D., people from earth are settling Mars and the satellites of Jupiter, Saturn, Uranus, and Neptune. ²Triton, the largest moon of Neptune, is also the center of human civilization among the outer moons of the solar system. ³Life on Triton is a curious mixture of an uncontrolled existence and an ever-present bureaucracy. ⁴Human beings live in an area protected from the alien environment by a force shield and artificial gravity. ⁵Although governed by an elected board, the people of Triton generally follow unstructured lives based on mutual cooperation. ⁶Money is obsolete. ⁷People have automatic credit from the state for basic food, shelter, and transportation. ⁸Everyone goes on welfare at one time or another, but never for very long. ⁹There is no poverty and no possibility of economic disability, and there are no ghettos.

¹⁰The city does have a section where no laws apply, to release any social frustrations that might build up among the populace.

¹¹Body decorations are worn by both men and women. ¹²Fashions are nonexistent. ¹³Body covering ranges from complete nudity, with or without decoration and body paint, to elaborate costumes.

¹⁴Distinctions between the sexes are blurred on Triton. ¹⁵Names like Gene, Sam, or Bron may be used by either sex. ¹⁶Sex change operations, complete in every respect, with psychological counseling to match, can transform men or women into their opposite numbers in six hours' time.

¹⁷Despite a certain looseness in the social fabric, the bureaucracy still operates. ¹⁸Citizens are assigned 22-digit identification numbers and are routinely surveyed by machines. ¹⁹The government has ten hours of videotaped information on every member of society. ²⁰According to Delany's book, the citizens of Triton prefer their life to that on earth—and eventually they destroy the planet that colonized them.

NO. OF ERRORS

As you proofread, underline any changes you have made. Correct any errors your instructor has found in your essay. Choose another selection in STEP 10 for work in the future tense. List below any unfamiliar words or any corrected spelling errors.

STEP 10   The story below discusses the feelings of teen-age girls back in the seventies. It is, therefore, about *past time* and thus written in the *past tense*. Rewrite the story so that it becomes a prediction about the way teen-age girls *will* feel in the 1980s. To do this, you must insert *will* and change the verb back to its *base* form. In addition, *was* or *were* change to *be*. Change the title to: *What Will Girls Like?* Your first sentence should read: *Teen-age girls of the eighties will differ little from their counterparts in the sixties.*

What Girls Like

¹Teen-age girls of the seventies differed little from their counterparts in the sixties. ²A large majority of them dated boys over their parents' objections, but as many as 92 percent expected to get married eventually. ³Also similar were the two generations' taste in boys.

⁴Teen-age girls preferred boys with personality rather than muscle power. ⁵More than 80 percent of the girls felt that a pleasant personality was the most desirable trait in a boy. ⁶A sense of humor was also in great demand. ⁷Continuing a recent trend, 75 percent of the girls showed interest in boys who showed emotion. ⁸Although looks mattered to 60 percent of the girls, the older the girl, the less of a difference looks made.

⁹The girls were just as definite about qualities that made them reject boys. ¹⁰The list was headed by heavy drinking, swearing, and use of drugs. ¹¹Poor manners and disrespectful behavior were also frowned upon by the girls. ¹²Nine out of ten girls dismissed the possibility that the captain of the football team deserved special consideration, and eight out of ten thought that a boy's finances were unimportant.

¹³The general trend, thus, was away from macho and toward more sensitive and considerate boys.

NO. OF ERRORS

As you proofread, underline any changes you have made. Correct any errors your instructor has found in your essay. Choose another selection in STEP 10 for work in the future tense. List below any unfamiliar words and any corrected spelling errors.

Step 10

The Future Tense

Helpful Hints and Special Situations

Many speakers use other indicators for the future tense. In formal essays for a college class, you should use *will*. Look for these other indicators, however, because they are clues for the time of sentences. In informal situations these indicators are acceptable.

going to	I am going to hold my breath.
about to	He is about to jump into the pool.
can	I can go home soon. (a possible action)

As with other tenses, a change in the tense of the main verb in the future tense does not necessitate a change in the tense of the subordinate or dependent clause. In addition, the future tense often needs only one indicator, even in independent clause.

Past	Future
On Christmas I sang, danced, and made merry.	On Christmas I will sing, dance, and make merry.

Although each of the verbs in the past carries a past indicator, a single *will* suffices in the future tense.

Although *will* generally comes immediately before the verb, the negative—*not*—comes between *will* and the verb, and so do the words *always, sometimes, never,* and *also*.

Witch doctors make housecalls and will also accept checks.
They will not always guarantee their work.

Won't is a contraction of *will not*. Avoid the contraction in essays for class.

The future indicator—*will*—is a useful tool for locating the verb in a sentence. Insert *will* in a sentence (try to make it the future). The word that *will* fits in front of is the verb.

Dr. Lauer, a noted psychologist, urges people to become aware of the effects of their lies on themselves and others in order to keep lying under control.

Will fits only before *urges* or *urge*, in the sentence, locating the verb. Other words—*become, keep, lying*—may seem to be time indicators to the confused reader.

Future time also contains a progressive. It is used to express some activity that will be ongoing or in progress in the future.

In September the Yankees and Red Sox *will be fighting* for the pennant.
I *will be trying* to get a ticket for the World Series.
The science fiction film *will be playing* all next week.

. As you can see, the *future progressive* is formed with: will + be + *ing* form of verb.

Step 10   The essay below discusses population trends in the United States as of 1977. Change 1977 to 1987 throughout the essay and rewrite the essay in the *future tense*. You will now be predicting what the trend in population *will be* in 1987. Remember, the future tense of *was* and *were* is *will be*. Do not change sentences 5 and 9.

Graying America

¹According to the Census Bureau, as of 1977 the United States had an "aging" population.

²By 1977, the median age in this country was around thirty years. ³This means that there were as many people over 30 as there were under. ⁴If one expected to mistrust anyone over 30, one had to mistrust half the population in the United States. ⁵And this midpoint in ages will continue to rise.

⁶By 1977 there were also significant changes in the distribution of ages. ⁷Whereas the 5 and under population declined by about 11 percent, the elderly, 65 and up, increased by 17.6 percent. ⁸The 25–34 age grew by 8 million or 31.8 percent.

⁹In terms of the labor force, the trend toward an older population means that by the year 2030 there will be only three active workers for each retired person, a considerable decline from the ratio of ten active workers per retired person that exists today.

NO. OF ERRORS

As you proofread, underline any changes you have made. Correct any errors your instructor has found in your essay. Choose another selection in STEP 10 for work in the future tense. List below any unfamiliar words or any spelling errors.

———————————   ———————————   ———————————

STEP 10   The article below contains descriptions by manufacturers of their various products. Because these are products available today, the manufacturers describe the way these products are right now. We would like you to rewrite the selection, substituting a date ten years from today whenever the word *today* appears. With this future date in mind, we ask you to rewrite the article, making the statements into predictions. In other words, the manufacturers will be describing the way their products *will* perform when they become available in

_____.
(date ten years from today)

As before, indicating the future will force you to change some of the words in the essay. Make those changes; then proofread carefully. Your first sentence will read: *"Savings" is the main idea on the minds of manufacturers as they advertise products that will be available ten years from now.*

Marketplace News

---

[1]"Savings" is the main idea on the minds of manufacturers as they advertise products that are available *today*.

[2]A squatter device, ready *today*, is a back saver, according to Mr. T. Industries, its manufacturer. [3]This equipment enables gardeners, hunters, fishermen, and others who work on their feet to sit down whenever they wish. [4]It weighs only two pounds and is belted around the waist. [5]When standing becomes too tiresome, the wearers of this device will be able to squat and rest on the wooden seat they will carry strapped to themselves.

[6]A shower control by B and D of Brooklyn is presented as a resource saving device. [7]According to the firm, this new product reduces the flow of water a person uses during a shower from six gallons per minute to only three. [8]There are additional savings in time and money. [9]The device takes only a minute to install and does not require the services of a plumber.

[10]A third product out *today* promises to save its user from bad luck. [11]The product is a glassless mirror. [12]According to the manufacturer, it reflects without distortion, is attractive and lightweight, and, most important, is unbreakable. [13]No seven years of bad luck possible with this mirror!

NO. OF ERRORS

As you proofread, underline changes you have made. Correct any errors your instructor has found in your essay. Choose another selection in STEP 10 for work in the future tense. Correct any misspelled words below.

_____   _____   _____

STEP 10   Rewrite the following selection based on the familiar nursery rhyme so that you will be predicting everything that will happen to Old Mother Hubbard and her dog. You will need to add the word *will* and make some alterations in the words that carry information about time. Copy everything else and proofread carefully. Your first sentence should read: *Old Mother Hubbard will go to the cupboard to fetch her poor dog a bone.*

Old Mother Hubbard

---

¹Old Mother Hubbard goes to the cupboard to fetch her poor dog a bone. ²But when she gets there, the cupboard is bare, and so her poor dog gets none.

³She goes to the baker's to buy him some bread. ⁴When she gets back, the poor dog is dead.

⁵She runs to the undertaker's to buy him a coffin. ⁶But when she comes back, the poor dog is laughing.

⁷She takes a clean dish to get him some tripe. ⁸By the time she returns, he is smoking a pipe.

⁹She walks to the alehouse to get him some beer. ¹⁰When she comes home, he sits in her chair.

¹¹She goes to the tavern for white wine and red. ¹²When she gets back, the dog stands on his head.

¹³The dame makes a curtsy; the dog makes a bow. ¹⁴The dame says, "Your servant." ¹⁵The dog answers, "Bow-wow."

NO. OF ERRORS

As you proofread, underline changes you have made. Correct any errors your instructor has found in your essay. Choose another selection in STEP 10 for work in the future tense. Correct any misspelled words below.

_____ _____ _____

Step 10

Writing Assignments:
The Future Tense

The only way you can be sure that you have mastered a particular STEP is by writing an essay in which you make no errors of the type you have studied. The assignments that follow are designed to guide you into using the future tense. As usual, your instructor may give you additional suggestions about your organizational scheme. Do pay close attention to the *future time* in these essays.

1. What will your day be like ten years from now? Consider a workday or a day of leisure.
2. Predict the appearance of the cars of the future.
3. Which teams do you think will win their divisions or leagues next year? (You might try picking the national College Football Champion or the winner of the NCAA.)
4. What will be the state of marriage ten years in the future?
5. What qualities will a hero of the future have to have?
6. What are some of your resolutions for the coming year?
7. Along with so many seers, why not foretell what the coming year will hold for a famous person?
8. Of the songs currently on radio, which will become a top seller and how will it affect its listeners?
9. What kind of a parent do you think you will make? If you already are a parent, are there things you will do differently if you have another child?
10. Compare the place (state, city, neighborhood, or house) where you live now to the place where you think you will live eventually. (One paragraph would be written in the present tense; the other, in the future tense.)

Note this last assignment in particular. It will not happen often that you will have to write an entire essay using the future tense. Do remember, however, to use the future indicator in sentences that discuss that period of time.

Step 11

The Perfect Tenses

In addition to using the simple past tense to indicate the past time, you can use the *present perfect* and the *past perfect* tenses.

The *present perfect* seems to express an action that occurred at some indefinite time in the past, continues into the present (the time of narration), and may even extend into the future. Generally, however, the tense is "perfect" or complete in the present, even though it also occurred in the past.

	THE PRESENT RIGHT NOW	
somewhere back here the lake froze	The Past	I AM STARTING TO SKATE
		I AM TALKING
		The Future

The lake has frozen by now, and I am starting to skate.
Present Perfect

To form the *present perfect*, use *has* (with third-person singular subjects) or *have* (with all other subjects) and the past participle form of the verb. Because irregular verbs have irregular past participles, you must learn them individually, although you are probably familiar with most of them. The Appendix lists many of the irregular forms.

Infinitive	Present	Past	Present Perfect
All regular verbs: to walk	he walks we walk	he walked we walked	he has walked we have walked
One irregular verb: to eat	he eats we eat	he ate we ate	he has eaten we have eaten

The *past perfect* is used when an event in the past occurred before some other event in the past. The past perfect distinguishes between these two past times. "Perfect" means whole, finished, complete. The simple past indicates an event in the past. The *past perfect* moves even further back, to an event before.

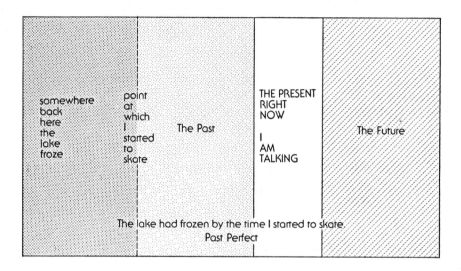

To form the *past perfect*, use *had* (with both singular and plural subjects), and the past participle form of the verb. Again, irregular verbs have irregular past participles. Consult the dictionary or Appendix 2 if you are not sure of the correct form.

Infinitive	Present	Past	Present Perfect	Past Perfect
All regular verbs: to walk	he walks we walk	he walked we walked	he has walked we have walked	he had walked we had walked
One irregular verb: to eat	he eats we eat	he ate we ate	he has eaten we have eaten	he had eaten we had eaten

Step 11

The Present Perfect

Helpful Hints and Special Situations

When a sentence contains two or more independent clauses, you need to use the auxiliary *has* or *have* only once. You do, however, have to use the past participle form for all the verbs

> I have pleaded and I have shouted, but I have succeeded with neither.

The sentence can be written as:

> I have pleaded and shouted but succeeded with neither.

If, however, the time of one of the independent clause is different from the time of the other, it has to be indicated clearly.

> I have been pleading and shouting, but nothing succeeds for me.

And as has been true with other verbs, the present perfect does not have to be used throughout a sentence, even if the sentence consists of an independent clause and a dependent clause.

present   present perfect

↓   ↓

Although nothing *works,* I *have continued* to plead and shout anyway.

dependent clause   independent clause

The past participle of the verb *to be* is *been.* In this STEP, if you must rewrite from the present tense to the present perfect, you must rewrite *is/are* as *been,* using it with *has* (for third-person singular subjects) and with *have* (for all other subjects).

Present	Present Perfect
The drilling venture *is* a success.	→ The drilling venture *has been* a success.
Snow storms *are* rare in June.	→ Snow storms *have been* rare in June.

The present perfect can also be combined with the progressive.

Present	Present Perfect Progressive
I am using a qualified dentist.	→ I *have been using* a qualified dentist.
We are trying to sleep.	→ We *have been trying* to sleep.
Snow White is living with the dwarfs.	→ Snow White *has been living* with the dwarfs.

Notice that *is/are* change to *been*, the past participle of *to be*, and combine with *has/have* + *ing* form of the verb.

The auxiliaries *has* and *have* are sometimes difficult to notice because they "disappear" into contractions. When you write out contractions, make sure that you are spelling out the auxiliaries.

He's been found innocent. → He *has* been found innocent.
They've bought a horse. → They *have* bought a horse.

Negative contractions also contain the auxiliaries. Be sure to write them out.

It hasn't rained for forty days. → It *has* not rained for forty days.
They haven't signed the contract. → They *have* not signed the contract.

The differences between the present tense and the present perfect are sometimes very subtle. One interesting distinction is the way in which the present perfect can be used for description. The present tense does not work in that situation.

John Doe is in jail. (This is a statement of fact; he is there now.)

John Doe has been in jail. (The reference is to an indefinite time in the past. Although it may have taken place a very long time ago, the fact of his stay in jail lingers. Some linguists see this more as a characterization or description of John Doe than as a statement of fact.)

STEP 11   The short report below is written mostly in the past tense, for it discusses the events of the past year. The opening paragraph is in the *present tense* because it deals with a situation that is a general truth. We would like you to rewrite the report, beginning with the second paragraph. Change the opening of that paragraph to: *Since the beginning of its operation.* You will now be describing events that took place in the indefinite past and also continue into the present. To indicate this *time,* use the *present perfect tense.* Add *has* or *have* before each main verb and make sure the verb is in its past participle form. Copy everything else and proofread. (Do not change sentences 14 and 15.)

Chutzpah Phone Service

---

[1]*Chutzpah* is the Yiddish word for audacity or nerve, as in, "Boy, you've got a lot of nerve doing that!" [2]*Chutzpah* is also the name of a nationwide franchise that originated in Philadelphia. [3]It is a service that delivers messages for people who do not have the nerve to deliver them themselves.

[4]In 1978, the first year of its operation, the Philadelphia Chutzpah Service did both domestic and "foreign" work. [5]The "foreign" or outside work consisted of delivering messages to celebrities. [6]It transmitted messages to Mike Schmidt, the Phillies' slugger, between innings, and to Barry Manilow, the performer, in his dressing room after performances. [7]Its more domestic work included acting as the "go-between" for several courting couples. [8]In some of those cases it was the service that presented the marriage proposal. [9]Other people used the service to quit work, fire employees, or ask for raises. [10]The most popular request was to call the boss and report that the individual was too ill to go to work.

[11]The rate for branches outside Philadelphia was fairly reasonable. [12]The two women who run the Syracuse franchise were charging five dollars for a simple phone message and slightly more for delivering a gift. [13]Charges for pie-throwing ranged upward from twenty-five dollars, and assignments were not accepted without the customer's guarantee that the delivery person "would not be sued or punched."

[14]Such items as "Chutzpahgrams" and "Chutzpah Gift Certificates" have also begun to appear. [15]*Chutzpah* seems to have arrived.

NO. OF ERRORS

As you proofread, underline the changes you have made. Correct any errors your instructor has located. Choose another STEP 11 selection for work in the *present perfect tense.* Subject-verb agreement is discussed in STEP 4 (plurals) and STEP 6 (singulars). Correct any misspelled words below.

STEP 11   The essay below discusses some research you completed last year. Pretend your research has been reopened. To indicate that an action you began in the past extends into the present, you would use the *present perfect* tense. Insert *have* or *has* before the *main verbs* in the essay and, if necessary, change the verb. Copy everything else and proofread. Your first sentence should read: *My research has revealed a number of errors in popular accounts of Paul Revere's ride.*

Revere's Short Ride

---

[1]My research revealed a number of errors in popular accounts of Paul Revere's ride.

[2]I discovered that Revere was not the only horseman riding to warn the patriots that British troops were on the move. [3]I found that William Dawes was also riding to Lexington, dispatched there by Dr. Joseph Warren, the president of the Massachusetts provincial congress.

[4]Additional research revealed that the famous lanterns, "One if by land and two if by sea," were signals to another group of patriots waiting on the Charlestown shore. [5]Work by other researchers showed that Revere needed to wait for those lights. [6]I found his own account in which he stated that he already knew the British would be moving by sea.

[7]Finally, although popular accounts told of Revere's arrival in Concord at the end of his ride, in fact he never reached the town. [8]Research showed him being intercepted by British scouts, questioned, and released, well short of Concord.

NO. OF ERRORS

As you proofread, underline the changes you have made. Correct any errors your instructor has located. Choose another STEP 11 essay for work in the *present perfect tense.* Subject-verb agreement is discussed in STEP 4 (plurals) and STEP 6 (singulars). Correct any misspelled words below.

STEP 11   With the exception of sentences 5 and 6, the essay below is written in the past. It describes events of the past year. Rewrite the essay so that you would be using *the present perfect* (*has* or *have* with the *perfect* form of the verb). You must use this *time* when you change the opening words and the final words of the essay to: *Each December 31 since 1972*, and the third paragraph to: *But since 1972*. You will now be talking about something that is true in the present yet also reaches back to an event in the past. Sentences 5 and 6 should not be changed. Use the present perfect in all the other sentences.

The Slow Earth

---

¹*Last December 31* the ball atop the tower at 1 Times Square fell to announce the New Year one second later than the year before. ²The time lag occurred because the world's official timekeepers added a second to the previous year.

³What was responsible for this unpublicized extension of time? ⁴Our planet itself was at fault. ⁵A year is the amount of time it takes the earth to complete a revolution around the sun. ⁶A revolution has always taken 31,536,000 seconds.

⁷But *last year* time was also measured by the vibrations of atoms in the famous cesium clock at the National Bureau of Standards. ⁸And this clock (a more stable measuring device than the solar clock based on the earth's rotation) showed an extra second. ⁹In other words, it is taking our planet one more second than before to complete its trip around the sun. ¹⁰It slowed down by a full second for the year.

¹¹Because people live by the solar clock, the two systems were synchronized on *December 31*.

NO. OF ERRORS

As you proofread, underline the changes you have made. Correct any errors your instructor has located. Choose another STEP 11 selection for work in the *present perfect tense*. Subject-verb agreement is discussed in STEP 4 (plurals) and STEP 6 (singulars). Correct any misspelled words below.

---   ---   ---

Step 11

The Past Perfect

Helpful Hints
and Special Situations

The past perfect is a useful tense in that it distinguishes between two events in the past, making clear which came first.

1522   Magellan's *Vittoria* sailed into Sanlúcar in September, 1522. It carried proof that the world was indeed round. Unfortunately, Magellan himself was not there to enjoy the welcome.

1521   He *had died* the previous year in the Philippines.

Because the last sentence moves to a time before the past tense of 1522, its time is indicated by the *past perfect*.

Notice, however, that if the above little story had been told in the order in which the events had happened, there would have been no need to use the past perfect.

Magellan died in the Philippines in 1551. His ship, the *Vittoria,* sailed into Sanlúcar in September, 1522. It carried proof that the world was indeed round. Unfortunately, Magellan himself was not there to enjoy the welcome.

Because there is no jump back into a time before the past, the simple past can be used throughout.

Even when there is a need to indicate a past event completed before another event in the past, the past perfect will be used very briefly. Many writers use the past perfect only to signal a shift in time. Once they have made it clear to the reader than this shift has taken place, they revert to using the simple past once again. Fiction writers do this quite frequently. They indicate a "flashback" with the past perfect, then continue the episode in the simple past.

The selections that you will be working on in this section ask you to use the past perfect whenever possible in order to have you become familiar with its use. Once you are comfortable with it, you will be able to manipulate it more easily.

The past participle of *to be* is *been.* In changing past tense verbs to the past perfect, *was/were* become *been.* Combined with *had,* you have the past perfect.

She was happy. ——Before she heard the bad news, she *had been* happy.

Use *been* when you want to write in the past perfect progressive.

Before she returned triumphant, Snow White *had been living* with the dwarfs.
The Beatles were finally noticed after they *had been playing* in relative anonymity in Liverpool.

The past participle is used with both the present and the past perfect. The past participle of regular verbs is the same as the past tense. Irregular verbs vary. Consult the dictionary or Appendix for forms if you are not sure.

STEP 11   The short essay below is written mostly in the simple past. It discusses events that took place in the past. Rewrite the essay to indicate that these inventors have ceased their work. They have died or abandoned their efforts. To indicate that an action was completed prior to a past action, you must use the *past perfect* tense. Add the following sentence to the first paragraph: *The wild-eyed inventors immortalized below have finally stopped knocking on the door of the U.S. Patent Office, but not before they had offered some incredible devices for consideration.* Then rewrite the rest of the essay in the past perfect. Notice that the dependent clause in the new sentence is in the past perfect. Put *had* before each main verb and change the verb into its perfect form.

Back to the Drawing Board

¹For every successful inventor like Benjamin Franklin or Thomas A. Edison, there is a Gyro Gearloose, a madcap inventor whose ideas prove impractical.

²One such inventor applied for a patent on huge elastic suspenders. ³He wanted to use the contraption as a fire escape. ⁴With the suspenders under his arms, he leaped from a burning hotel room. ⁵He landed safely. ⁶Unfortunately, the elastic in the suspenders yanked him right back into the fiery chamber.

⁷A team of inventors developed an alarm clock for heavy sleepers. ⁸The two designed the clock to hang on the wall above the sleeper and drop a hammer on his head to wake him. ⁹Needless to say, the "knock-clock" did not catch on.

¹⁰Other inventions proved profitable to their inventors, but for the wrong reasons. ¹¹Con men or charlatans assembled devices, devising them to bilk the naïve buyer. ¹²These machines included a dollar-making box, a self-adjusting diagnostic apparatus that analyzed a drop of rooster blood and proclaimed it was the blood of an alcoholic, and a magic pill that was supposed to transform ordinary water into gasoline.

NO. OF ERRORS

As you proofread, underline any changes you are making. Correct any errors your instructor might have found in your essay. For additional work in the *past perfect*, choose another essay in STEP 11. List below any unusual words or any corrected spelling errors.

_____   _____   _____

STEP 11   The essay below describes a period between 1969 and 1979, when television's picture of women was found to be inaccurate. Let us assume that this has changed, that in 1980 television corrected its misrepresentation of women. That event, written in the *past tense*, would force you to change the time of the essay to the *past perfect*. In other words, the events described are completed or "perfect" in a time before the 1980 correction. To change the time into the *past perfect*, change each *has* or *have* to *had*. Copy everything else and proofread. Your first sentence should say: *Before television corrected its misrepresentation, its portrait of women had been inaccurate*.

TV Women vs. Real Women

¹Television's portrait of women has been inaccurate. ²According to a 1979 study by the U.S. Commission on Civil Rights, the life of women in the real world has been quite different, since 1969, from the kind of life portrayed in television world.

³Some of the most glaring inaccuracies have appeared in television's version of the census. ⁴Whereas in the real world women make up more than half of the nation's population, in television world women have represented only 30 percent of the inhabitants. ⁵Similarly, though less than a quarter of all females are in their twenties, television has suggested that nearly half fall into the 20-to-25 age bracket.

⁶Television has not counted the number of working women in this country very precisely either. ⁷Although more than 40 percent of American women work full-time and more than 50 percent are in the work force, television has shown only about 20 percent of them at work. ⁸The rest have been made into students or not given any occupation at all.

⁹Although television has thus concealed how women live, it has revealed more than sufficiently how they look. ¹⁰According to the study, television has usually dressed young women in skimpy outfits and emphasized their physical qualities. ¹¹When it has chosen to combine style and profession by putting women in uniform as law enforcement agents, it has "balanced" the generosity by putting twice that number of women in prison garb.

NO. OF ERRORS

As you proofread, underline the changes you have made. Correct any errors your instructor has found in your essay. For additional work of this type, select another essay in STEP 11 that deals with the *past perfect*. Correct any spelling errors below.

_____   _____   _____

STEP 11   The essay below is written in the *past tense*. Several sentences in the essay should be changed to the *past perfect tense* because they tell of an episode in Elvis Presley's life that was not known until after his death. Predicates in main clauses may be changed into the *past perfect* by adding the helping verb *had* to the past participle. Sentence 5, the first you must change, should read: *As revealed shortly after his death in August, 1977, Elvis Presley once had offered his services as a spy to the FBI.* You need not change sentences 1, 2, 3, 4, 6, and 9. Copy everything else and proofread carefully.

Elvis Presley: Spy

¹During his career, Elvis Presley deliberately projected an anti-establishment image. ²Parents worried about the morality of allowing their children to attend Presley concerts. ³Clergymen and editorial writers denounced him. ⁴Little did these groups realize that Presley actually longed for acceptance by established institutions and denounced many of the same influences they did.

⁵As revealed shortly after his death in August, 1977, Elvis Presley once offered his services as a spy to the FBI. ⁶While visiting President Nixon at an undisclosed date in 1970, Presley visited FBI offices. ⁷Before arriving, he wrote the FBI to say that the then agency head J. Edgar Hoover was "the greatest living American." ⁸His letter also suggested that the "filthy and unkempt appearances and suggestive music" of the Beatles were responsible for many of the problems the United States was having with young people.

⁹Although no official record of the FBI visit has been released, Assistant Director Thomas Bishop later recollected Presley's 1970 words. ¹⁰The singer swore that the Smothers Brothers and Jane Fonda would have to answer in the hereafter for having denounced United States involvement in Vietnam and for poisoning young minds. ¹¹As Bishop remembered, Presley gave reasons why he would make a good spy. ¹²He sang in different urban centers already and would not be suspected. ¹³Even before his decision to come to the FBI, he was periodically approached by people in and out of the entertainment industry and asked to attach his name to questionable activities that were not in the best interests of the country. ¹⁴If accepted as an agent, he wanted to have the code name of "Col. Joe Burrows of Memphis."

¹⁵According to a surviving interoffice memo in Bishop's files, the Washington leadership denied Presley's request to meet with J. Edgar Hoover. ¹⁶As we may infer from the language of the memo, the FBI was unsure about trusting a singer who wore his hair down to his shoulders and who dressed in all sorts of exotic clothing.

As you proofread, underline the changes you have made.

NO. OF ERRORS

STEP 11   The essay below is written in the *past tense*. Most of the sentences should be changed to the *past perfect tense* because they tell of events completed before a fixed time and recollected in the past. Predicates in main clauses may be changed by adding the helping verb *had* to the past participle. Sentence 2, the first you must change, should read: *Son of an Irish adventurer and a Chilean mother, Bernardo O'Higgins had been converted to the cause of national independence while out of the country receiving his education.* In sentence 3 the predicate is: ". . . *army had gained* . . ." You need not change sentences 1, 5, 10, and 15. Copy everything else and proofread carefully.

O'Higgins's Army

---

¹One of the most unlikely battles of Latin American independence was fought in Chile by a patriot general with the improbable name of Bernardo O'Higgins. ²Son of an Irish adventurer and a Chilean mother, Bernardo O'Higgins was converted to the cause of national independence while he was out of the country receiving his education. ³After four years of fighting in 1814, his small, underequipped army gained few victories. ⁴Yet before the end of October of that year, O'Higgins had charged through a line of Spanish regulars to escape to the hills so that he might regroup for later battles. ⁵Spanish officers tried to reconstruct how he had escaped them.

⁶O'Higgins gathered his ragged troops outside the city of Santiago in a small farming village named Rancagua. ⁷In a previous day's fighting, O'Higgins lost many man and was himself wounded. ⁸Worse, the Spanish army, with an abundance of supplies and equipment, surrounded him. ⁹But the Chilean patriot thought of a plan, if only enough animals could be collected.

¹⁰Animals? ¹¹He ordered his men to round up as many mules, cows, sheep, and dogs as possible. ¹²Before long, the Chilean soldiers emptied barns, stables, and pastures of their livestock. ¹³And by the morning of October 2, 1814, the Chilean soldiers mustered all the animals before General O'Higgins. ¹⁴With this unusual method of conscription or draft, O'Higgins assembled a winning army.

¹⁵Once his last herd of animals had been assembled, O'Higgins was lifted to his horse. ¹⁶Even before he cracked his whip, the frightened animals began running. ¹⁷Within minutes it was clear they stampeded. ¹⁸The Spanish troops, all cleaned and polished, never saw such a thundering horde. ¹⁹To the later dismay of the Spanish colonial viceroy of Chile, the regulars broke and ran. ²⁰And as the dispatches noted, O'Higgins and his men galloped through the Spanish lines to escape and fight another day.

As you proofread, underline the changes you have made.

NO. OF ERRORS   _____   _____   _____

Step 11

Writing Assignments: The Perfect Tenses

THE PRESENT PERFECT   Use the present perfect for the essays. Remember that the singular (in the third person) uses *has*. All other persons use *have*.

1. What skill or knowledge that you are proud of *have* you *developed* over the years?
2. Describe how your hairstyle *has changed* over the last few years.
3. What *has* some outstanding athlete *accomplished* thus far in his or her career?
4. Who or what *has influenced* you most since you have been in college?
5. If there was a specific goal you had set for yourself when you were small, how close *have* you *come* to achieving it?
6. What have been some of the roles in which a favorite TV or movie star has appeared?
7. (present perfect progressive) How *have* styles *been changing* in the last few years? Consider (a) clothing, (b) hair (c) music, (d) furniture, and (e) cars.
8. (present perfect progressive) Consider a person you have known well for a few years. *Has* that person *been changing* in any way?

It is unlikely that your entire essay will use the same tense throughout. Even in the essays you have worked with, which have been designed to use the present perfect almost exclusively, there are sentences that are written in different tenses. Still, try to use the tense indicated above, paying careful attention to events that belong in different "time zones."

THE PAST PERFECT   Use the past perfect for the assignments below. The past perfect consists of *had* + the past participle for both singulars and plurals.

1. Choose any of the assignments you had worked on for the *present perfect* and rewrite it in the past perfect. Remember to write an opening sentence in the simple past that would force the rest of the essay into the past perfect.
2. Someone agreed to do you a favor. What *had* that person *said* or *done* prior to agreeing?

3. Begin by stating that you won the lottery last week. What had your life been like before that?
4. In 1979 students chose to study "practical" subjects. What *had* they *studied* before?
5. In the middle of the fifteenth century, Gutenberg made printing practical by inventing movable type. How *had* people *kept* records before then?
6. You have returned from a trip. What had been some of the places you had seen? What had been some of the things you had done?
7. Describe how you felt on your seventeenth birthday. Then discuss how you *had felt* about those same things before.

Remember to establish a past time with your opening
sentence. Then return to a time before for the past perfect.

Step 12

Indirect Quotation/Reported Speech

In STEP 12 you will be given passages containing the exact words that various writers have used. You will be asked to rewrite those direct quotations into "reported speech" or indirect quotations. In other words, rather than repeating the exact words of speakers, you will be reporting what they had said.

Fred: "You can use my car."

You might report what Fred had said if someone asked, thus:

Fred said that I can use his car.

But because the moment when Fred spoke to you has passed, you would be more precise if you indicated the *past tense* of his statement.

Fred said that I could use his car.

Here is a list of the various steps you must take in order to convert the exact words of a speaker (direct quotation) to reported speech (indirect quotation).

direct quotation ⟶ reported speech
Romeo (to Juliet): "I love you."→Romeo told Juliet that he loved her.

1. Remove quotation marks.
2. Add *told* (or *said to*).
3. Add *that* (an important clue for reported speech).
4. Change first person (*I*) to third person (*he*), and change second person (*you*) to third person (*her*).
5. Change present tense (*love*) to past tense (*loved*).

Here are the changes in the case of a question:

direct quotation ⟶ reported speech
Fiddler (to his wife): "Do you ⟶ Fiddler asked his wife if she
love me?"   loved him.

1. Remove quotation marks.
2. Add *asked* (the question mark becomes a word).
3. Add *if* (introduces a question, as does *whether*).
4. Change second person (*you*) to third person (*she*), and change first person (me) to third person (*him*).
5. Change present *tense* (love) to past tense (*loved*).

STEP 13 will discuss punctuation in situations when you would like to retain all or part of a speaker's words. The exercises that follow will help you practice converting direct quotations to indirect quotations or reported speech.

You should be aware of two additional details as you are changing direct quotations to indirect quotations. When dealing with a question, you may have to change the order of the words in the sentence. The subject and verb may switch positions.

"Is that the teacher?" ⟶ He asked if that were the teacher.

Notice that *is*, after becoming *were*, moved after *that*, from before *that*. Similarly, "Would you help me?" becomes: *She asked if I would help her*. *Would* moves after *I* (which had changed from *you* in the quotation).

The other movement in the sentence you should be aware of has to do with the position of the phrase "he said." If the phrase appears at the end of the quotation, it has to be moved to the beginning of the indirect quotation or reported speech.

"Come here," he said. ⟶ He told the man to come there.

And that sentence illustrates still another change. "Here" in a direct quotation may sometimes change to *there* in the reported speech.

An ease in changing direct quotations to reported speech will eventually enable you to summarize your source material, making your writing more economical by leaving out information that is irrelevant in various situations. If you were doing research on World War II, you might read this in General Bullroar's memoirs:

"Yes, I knew the men of the Fighting 169th very well. All fine men. Good fighters. I visited them at the front lines in the Sicilian campaign. What guts they had."

In your paper you might report on General Bullroar's words by writing: *He wrote that he had known from personal experience how bravely the men of the 169th fought in the Sicilian campaign.*

Accuracy is, of course, extremely important in reporting. The next STEP will thus show you how to combine such indirect quotations with the exact words of the author, should you need to use the exact words of the original.

STEP 12   The selection below contains the actual words of the speakers. Let us assume that you are a reporter who has listened to the discussion. You go home and report what it was that you heard. You decide to change the direct quotations into indirect quotations. In other words, you will report what was said without reproducing the exact words of the speakers. Begin a new paragraph with sentences 2, 8, and 10. Sentence 2 should read: *One of the Santas asked if they could eat.*

Instructions to Santas

---

¹Colonel Tim Costello, an official of Volunteers of America, discussed with his sidewalk Santas what they should or should not do as they ring their bells for Christmas contributions.

²"Can we eat?" asked one of the Santas.

³"Please don't," replied Colonel Costello. ⁴"You should not eat, smoke, or drink while you're on duty. ⁵In fact, avoid eating garlic, onions, or heavily spiced foods before coming to work."

⁶"What do we do if children ask for something impossible?" another of the red-suited Santas wanted to know.

⁷Colonel Costello responded, "Don't make unreasonable promises, but do send them away hopeful."

⁸Noticing the posture of one of the Santas, the colonel said, "Please don't lean on your chimney. ⁹It's important that you look alert and ring your bell with zest."

¹⁰Before sending them on their way, Colonel Costello gave the volunteers a final bit of advice. ¹¹"If children ask you why there are so many Santas around, tell them you are all Santa's helpers."

NO. OF ERRORS

Correct any errors your instructor has found. For additional work in using indirect quotations, choose another selection in STEP 12. Work in the past tense can be found in STEP 9; and in pronouns, in STEP 3 (plurals) and STEP 5 (singulars). Correct any misspelled words below.

---   ---   ---

STEP 12   The short essay below contains the words of various actors as movie-goers recall them. These bits of dialogue are set off by quotation marks. Rewrite the essay, changing each of those quoted statements into indirect, reported speech. Copy everything else and proofread carefully.

Me Tarzan and
Say It Again, Sam

¹Although old movies are constantly being reshown on television and in college film series, we are often unsure about the dialogue spoken in them. ²Sometimes we remember correctly, but more often we do not. ³For example, W. C. Fields never said, "Any man who hates dogs and babies can't be all bad." ⁴Instead, that line was made up by a journalist who thought Fields should have said it. ⁵Further, Fields did not request that the epitaph on his tombstone say, "On the whole, I'd rather be in Philadelphia." ⁶He may have disliked his home town, but his tombstone carries no epitaph at all.

⁷Two other characters who are usually misquoted are Humphrey Bogart in *Casablanca* (1943) and Johnny Weissmuller in the title role of *Tarzan the Ape Man* (1932). ⁸Bogart never said, "Play it again, Sam," though he did tell his friend to play the piano at different points in the film. ⁹Similarly, Weissmuller did not say he was Tarzan or that Maureen O'Sullivan was Jane. ¹⁰He merely pointed at himself and uttered the name Tarzan three times; later he pointed at Miss O'Sullivan and said the name Jane three times.

¹¹Memory has served moviegoers better with Groucho Marx and Bela Lugosi. ¹²In *Duck Soup* (1932), Groucho really did say, "We are fighting for this woman's honor—which is more than she ever did." ¹³And in *Dracula* (1932), Bela Lugosi actually says, "I never drink wine," with a hesitation before "wine" to suggest he drank something else.

¹⁴Finally, Greta Garbo did say, "I want to be alone," in *Grand Hotel* (1932), but she pronounced the "w" correctly. ¹⁵If we seem to have remembered that bit of dialogue correctly, it may be because she seems to have been repeating it ever since.

NO. OF ERRORS

Correct any errors your instructor has found. For additional work in using indirect quotations, choose another selection in STEP 12. Work in the past tense can be found in STEP 9; and in pronouns, in STEP 3 (plurals) and STEP 5 (singulars). Correct any misspelled words below.

Step 12

Indirect Quotation/Reported Speech

Helpful Hints and Special Situations

When you move from the exact words of a speaker to your report of his or her words, you must make clear that you are presenting someone else's words. You can do this by adding the words: *he* said, *she* said, *Mr. Jones* said, *Ms. Jones* said, *Professor Hardy* asked. You would be more informative if you characterized the act of speaking: he or she *argued, protested, pointed out, responded, denounced, suggested, insisted,* and so on.

The quoted statement is introduced with *said that* in reported speech.

The quoted question can be introduced with *asked if,* as well as a variety of other expressions, depending on what is being asked: *questioned how, wondered why, inquired when, queried where,* even *wanted to know* and *demanded what.*

In other words, punctuation that *shows* information in direct quotations is converted to words that *state* the same information.

exclamation point (!) = exclaimed, shouted, commanded
question mark (?)   = asked if, wondered why, inquired where, considered whether
"Yes."   = agreed, assented, would, could, did, has, have had, does
"No."   = disagreed, negated, would not, could not, did not, has not, have not, had not, does not

---

If the direct quotation is already in the past tense, you must sometimes use the past perfect. You will remember that the past perfect indicates an action completed before a past action. Because you introduce the reported speech with "said," which is in the past tense, the quotation in the past tense moves into the past perfect.

Direct Quotation
Asking her husband for a divorce, the woman said, "I loved you once."

Indirect Quotation
Asking her husband for a divorce, the woman said that she *had loved* him once.

STEP 12   In the essay below change all quotations, beginning with the second paragraph, into indirect quotations (reported speech). You will not be reproducing the exact words of the speakers. You will be *reporting* what those people said. Copy everything else and proofread carefully. Remember that you will be removing quotation marks and adding *that*, as well as making other changes.

Poets on Investment

¹There is something about making and losing money that turns ordinary men into philosophers. ²The world of banking has had a great many aphorisms and adages directed toward it. ³The originators of some of these bits of folk wisdom are unknown. ⁴One anonymous bit of·advice goes, "If you get too greedy, you end up needy." ⁵Sounds judicious, but it is contradicted by the words of another unidentified philosopher who suggested, "Let your profits run."

⁶Many famous literary figures, stung by investments gone wrong, have expressed their feelings about the world of finance. ⁷Mark Twain commented, "October is one of the dangerous months in which to speculate in stocks. ⁸The other dangerous months are November, December, January, February, March, April, May, June, July, August, and September." ⁹Robert Frost said, "A bank is a place where they lend you an umbrella in fair weather and ask for it back when it begins to rain." ¹⁰Ogden Nash seems to have shared Frost's feelings that banks were "fair weather" friends. ¹¹He declared, "The one rule banks have is never to lend money to people unless they do not need it."

¹²George Bernard Shaw and Ludwig von Mises directed their comments at financial experts rather than at institutions. ¹³Shaw said, "If all the economists in the world were laid end to end, they still would not reach a conclusion." ¹⁴Mises commented, "Government is the only agency that can take a useful commodity like paper, slap some ink on it, and make it totally worthless."

¹⁵In all fairness to bankers and banking, a statement about pronouncements, usually attributed to Oliver Wendell Holmes, should be mentioned. ¹⁶"All generalizations," Holmes said, "are false, including this one."

NO. OF ERRORS

Correct any errors your instructor has found. For additional work in using indirect quotations, choose another selection in STEP 12. Work in the past tense can be found in STEP 9; and in pronouns, in STEP 3 (plurals) and STEP 5 (singulars). Correct any misspelled words below.

_____   _____   _____

STEP 12 The selection below contains the exact words of the seven dwarfs. Rewrite their questions so that you will be reporting what they asked without using their exact words. Notice that you do not need the word *that* to introduce the indirect quotation when it is a question. Do use *that* with the other quotations. Copy everything else and proofread carefully.

The Dwarfs Return

---

¹When it was quite dark, the seven dwarfs returned home from the mines. ²They kindled their lights and immediately noticed that their house had been disturbed.

³The first dwarf asked, "Who has been sitting in my chair?"

⁴The second asked, "Who has been eating off my plate?"

⁵The third dwarf wondered, "Who has been nibbling my bread?"

⁶The fourth said, "Someone has been eating my vegetables."

⁷The fifth demanded, "Who has been using my fork?"

⁸"The same person has been cutting with my knife," the sixth said.

⁹"And drinking from my cup," the last dwarf observed.

¹⁰The first dwarf then noticed a slight impression on his bed. ¹¹"Someone has been here," he announced. ¹²Each of the other dwarfs looked on his bed. ¹³The seventh dwarf finally found Snow White, sleeping soundly in his bed.

NO. OF ERRORS

Correct any errors your instructor has found. For additional work in using indirect quotations, choose another selection in STEP 12. Work in the past tense can be found in STEP 9; and in pronouns, in STEP 3 (plurals) and STEP 5 (singulars). Correct any misspelled words below.

---------------------   ---------------------   ---------------------

STEP 12   The short story or fable below contains bits of dialogue. Rewrite the sentences within quotations, rendering them in indirect quotes or reported speech. The changes you will have to make include eliminating quotations, adding "that," changing the tense, and switching the person. Change only the bits of dialogue. Copy everything else and proofread.

The Ant and the Grasshopper

---

¹Weary in every limb, the ant tugged over the snow a piece of corn he had stored up the previous summer. ²"It will taste mighty good for supper," he told himself.

³A cold and hungry grasshopper watched the ant dragging the corn. ⁴Unable to restrain himself, he said, "Can I have a bite of the corn?" ⁵The ant looked at him. ⁶"What did you do all summer long?" he asked. ⁷"I sang from dawn to dusk," replied the grasshopper.

⁸"Because you sang all summer, you can dance all winter," the ant said, and left to enjoy the rewards of his summer labors.

NO. OF ERRORS

Correct any errors your instructor has found. For additional work in using indirect quotations, choose another selection in STEP 12. Work in the past tense can be found in STEP 9; and in pronouns, in STEP 3 (plurals) and STEP 5 (singulars). Correct any misspelled words below.

_____   _____   _____

STEP 12   In the essay below, change all quotations to indirect quotations (reported speech). You will not be reproducing the exact words of the speaker. You are *reporting* what she said. Copy everything else and proofread carefully. Remember that you will be removing quotation marks and adding *that*, as well as making other changes. Underline book titles for italics.

Slaves to Fashion

---

[1]Anne Hollander, the author of *Seeing Through Clothes,* says, "If you want to ignore fashion you will find it impossible." [2]"Partly because we need protection from the elements, but more because we are visual creatures," she asserts, "cloth has been a part of the substance of life as long as bread has, and the naked savage is an illusion." [3]She adds, "Surveys of many cultures lead us to conclude that the truly natural state of the adult human is dressed or decorated." [4]"Because of this everyone must get dressed and give a thought to what we wear," she tells us, "if only to feel comfortable in public and not like a fool."

[5]In fact, the need not to feel like a fool is a generally deep motive in the choice of clothes. [6]"But," she adds, "it also seems like a weakness." [7]And she continues, "The act of choosing can easily make fools of everyone." [8]"One way to escape being bothered by the disturbing importance of clothes in life is to label the whole subject 'fashion' and keep it at a convenient mental and moral distance." [9]She maintains, "If you believe yourself impervious to fashion, it will creep up on you unawares and begin to produce strange effects, like the sudden thought that you need shorter hair." [10]She reminds us, "Men who keep a conservative suit in the closet too long may find it somehow develops too wide or too narrow a lapel to produce the look of confidence; when exposed to lights, such a suit unhappily suggests a tacky hick or a gawky youth."

[11]In conclusion, Hollander states, "Clothes simply cannot be a private matter, and they are never visually neutral." [12]And her final advice is, "Clothes always say something significant about you, and having to think about this can be painful work."

NO. OF ERRORS

Correct any errors your instructor has found. For additional work in using indirect quotations, choose another selection from STEP 12. Work in the past tense can be found in STEP 9; and in pronouns, in STEP 3 (plurals) and STEP 5 (singulars). Correct any misspelled words below.

_____   _____   _____

STEP 12   In the essay below change all quotations to indirect quotations (reported speech). You will not be reproducing the exact words of the speakers. You are *reporting* what they said. Copy what they said. Remember that you will be removing quotation marks and adding *that*, as well as making other changes. *Underline play titles for italics.*

What Oscar Wilde Said

---

[1]During his lifetime the celebrated Anglo-Irish playwright, poet, and novelist Oscar Wilde was better known for things that he said than for his published works. [2]Some of his witty remarks will be long remembered, such as his comment about rich people who went fox-hunting: he said, "They are the unspeakable in pursuit of the inedible." [3]Other examples of his well-chosen, off-the-cuff remarks would fill a small book.

[4]When he was in college, he was required to read aloud from a Greek text of the New Testament and translate into English immediately. [5]Because Wilde was an excellent student, he did this with ease, causing his examination committee to think he was showing off. [6]They said, "Thank you, Mr. Wilde, that will be all." [7]But Wilde continued, causing the chief examiner to plea, "Mr. Wilde, other students are waiting," [8]Then Wilde looked up in surprise, "Oh, do let me go on. [9]I want to see how it comes out."

[10]The usual butts of Wilde's humor were stuffy, self-important persons, especially writers. [11]Once the dull poet Sir Lewis Morris asked, "Oscar, do you know why I have not been appointed poet laureate?" [12]Morris blustered, "It is a complete conspiracy of silence against me," meaning that people had conspired not to talk about him as a way of downgrading his reputation. [13]"What ought I to do?" Sir Lewis asked. [14]"Join it," Wilde replied with readiness.

[15]Understandably, Wilde's plays were most admired for their dialogue, some of which the author was reputed to have said in life. [16]For example, it is really Lord Darlington in *Lady Windermere's Fan* who says, "I can resist everything except temptation." [17]And it is a young lady, Cecily, in *The Importance of Being Earnest,* who says, "I never travel without my diary. [18]One should always have something sensational to read in the train."

[19]Even at life's end, Wilde's wit did not fail him. [20]Drinking some expensive champagne on his deathbed he quipped, "I am dying beyond my means."

NO. OF ERRORS

Correct any errors your instructor has found, and list misspelled words below.

_____   _____   _____

Step 12

Writing Assignments:
Indirect Quotation
Reported Speech

The STEP you have just completed consisted largely of removing quotation marks that would normally surround the exact words of a speaker or writer. You had to remove the quotation marks because you were changing the person and the tense as well as the order of the words in the sentences. Situations still remain, however, where the quotation marks are retained. Keep quotation marks around titles of poems, short stories, articles, chapters in books, essays, and songs. You should also retain quotation marks around distinctive words or phrases the author has used that you have included in your reported version. This will be discussed in STEP 13.

1. Change into reported speech a selection from a famous speech, such as Lincoln's Gettysburg Address, Churchill's call for sacrifice during World War II, Kennedy's Inaugural Speech, Nixon's "Checkers" speech, or any other speech that interests you.
2. Try to transcribe an argument that you had with someone. Then change the exact words into reported speech.
3. Tape or transcribe something your instructor in a course said. Then change it into indirect quotes. (Compare your version to the actual talk.)
4. Listen to a conversation on a TV program, and report on it by making the snippet into indirect quotations.
5. Have someone give you directions on how to get to his or her house. Pass on the directions to someone else.
6. Think of orders that you have recently received—to buy something, do something, or go somewhere. Rewrite those commands as indirect quotations.
7. Watch a question/answer sequence on some quiz show, and change both parts into reported speech.
8. Think of the last time you asked (or were asked) for a date, and rewrite the dialogue in reported speech.
9. Look up a famous exchange in some fairy tale, legend, or story; and rewrite it as reported speech.
10. Write out instructions to someone. Then explain what you had written.

> In situations where there is more than one speaker, remember to indicate clearly who is speaking either by naming the person or identifying the individual in some other way.

Step 13

Direct Quotation

In this STEP you will continue to change the actual words of speakers into reported speech. However, you will discover that at times you will have to retain some of the things the speakers say exactly as they said them. You might want to preserve a whole sentence or just individual words or phrases. You might want to do this either to indicate the authenticity and accuracy of your research or to impart a certain vividness to your account.

The way to preserve a person's exact words is by enclosing them within quotation marks.

Chuck said, "Go ahead. Use my winter rat."

1. The quotation begins with a capital letter because it is a complete sentence.
2. The quotation is set off from other parts of the sentence with quotation marks.
3. The quotation is separated from *Chuck said* with a comma.
4. The punctuation at the end of the quotation goes *within* the quotation marks if it is a comma or a period.

You might decide upon rereading the above sentence that there is no real need to preserve or quote Chuck's entire sentence. Most of it would be communicated effectively and accurately without using his exact words. However, the phrase he uses to describe his car is vivid and unique. You would like to quote it.

Chuck told me that I can go ahead and use his "winter rat."

or, even more briefly,

Chuck said that I could use his "winter rat."

Notice that the reported words still contain some exact words and that those words are set off by quotation marks from the rest of the sentence. STEP 13 is thus a review for the reported speech you had practiced in STEP 12, as well as a STEP in which you can work on including quotations in reports. Notice that when the quotation is not a complete sentence, you do not capitalize the first letter of the quotation.

Do not forget to add "he said" or "she said," whenever it is necessary to indicate the presence of a speaker.

STEP 13   You are listening to the radio and hear the broadcast presented below. You must write a report of it for the next class. In other words, you must transform the direct quotations (the exact words of the speaker) into indirect quotations or reported speech. To do this, add the words *The podiatrist said* or some equivalent phrase to most of the sentences and change the time (to the past) and the person (to third from first). Everything else should remain the same as in the original. As a special feature, place quotation marks around the phrases in boldface type. These are phrases that are unique to the speaker, whose precise use should be preserved with the quotation marks. Proofread carefully.

The Podiatrist's Corner

¹"I can tell a person's self-image by the type of shoes she or he wears. ²A woman's shoes are particularly informative about the way she views herself. ³If she wears boots or high heels, she sees herself as a **sexy, alluring person.** ⁴If she chooses **sensible shoes,** she perceives herself as being **drab** *and* **dull.** ⁵A woman in loafers or sneakers wants to project a neutral image. ⁶Her appearance is unisex.

⁷"I classify men in a similar fashion. ⁸Their footwear indicates whether they consider themselves to be **macho, neuter, or sensuous males.**

⁹"**Speaking as a podiatrist,** however, I must admit that though high heels are sexy and fashionable, they are also **unhealthy and uncomfortable,** ¹⁰High-heeled shoes are made shorter and narrower than usual and thus keep the wearer off balance. ¹¹**The lack of balance and the discomfort lead to hammertoes, bunions, and other toenail problems.**

¹²"**Sensible,** I suppose, is **preferable to sexy,** at least from the point of view of your feet."

NO. OF ERRORS

Correct any errors your instructor has found. For additional work in the punctuation of quotations, choose another STEP 13 selection. You might consult STEP 1 for examples of punctuation around quotations. Correct spelling errors below.

_____   _____   _____

STEP 13   Rewrite the interview below in reported speech (indirect quotations), making the changes you had to make in STEP 12. In addition, however, retain the exact words of the speaker in the phrases in boldface type, as well as in sentences 7 through 15. As you rewrite the essay, alternate sentences 7, 12, 8, 13, 9, 14, 10, and 15, punctuating them and making clear which line is spoken by the wolf and which by Little Red Riding Hood.

Little Red Riding Hood on a Talk Show

---

¹Interviewer: "Tell us, in your own words, what happened at your Grandmother's house?"

²Little Red Riding Hood: "I noticed **something was funny** the minute I walked in and saw the drawn shades. ³Off in the corner of the big four-poster, as far away from me as possible, I could finally make out a shape in a shawl and a nightcap. ⁴**A blind man could see that was no sweet old lady lying there.** ⁵Besides, that wolf wears this **powerful after-shave** you can't ignore. ⁶Time for some hard questions, I thought to myself.

⁷" 'What big eyes you have, Grandma. ⁸And what big ears you have. ⁹And what big arms you have. ¹⁰And what big teeth you have.'

¹¹"That wolf had it all rehearsed, or he must have heard it all before. ¹²He says, 'The eyes are the better to see you with. ¹³The ears are the better to hear you with. ¹⁴The arms are the better to hold you with. ¹⁵The teeth are the better to eat you with.'

¹⁶"Then he jumped me."

¹⁷Interviewer: "Is there a happy ending?"

¹⁸Little Red Riding Hood: "We are not friends or anything, but he's not as terrible as he's been made out to be. ¹⁸He is basically **a misguided little boy.** ¹⁹He is responding very well to therapy. ²⁰Don't believe everything you hear about his punishment or death."

NO. OF ERRORS

Correct any errors your instructor has found in your essay. For additional work in the punctuation of quotations, choose another STEP 13 essay. You might also consult STEP 1 for examples of punctuation around quotations. Correct spelling errors below.

_____   _____   _____

.

Step 13

Direct Quotation

Helpful Hints
and Special Situations

When you indicate the presence of a speaker, you can place the words *John said* or *Jane said* either at the beginning or at the end of the quotation.

He said, "Hand the gun over." *or* "Hand the gun over," he said.

You may even interrupt a quotation with the phrase, but you must be careful with your punctuation.

"The working conditions are fine," she said. "I'm very pleased."

As there are two complete sentences spoken, the second sentence begins with a capital letter. (I, of course, would be capitalized in any case.)

"The working conditions," she said, "are fine."

The interrupted sentence is simply continued, without capitalization, but there is an additional set of quotation marks after *she said*. Notice that the commas and periods after the quotations come *within* the quotation marks.

In general, other punctuation marks also come within the quotation marks, including question marks and exclamation points. One situation that is different is when you are not quoting a question. Then the quotation marks come first.

Is this Fred's "winter rat"?

The question mark in this case refers to the entire sentence; the quotation marks preserve only the words "winter rat." If, however, the entire question is quoted, the question mark would go *within* the quotation marks.

"Who goes there?" the guard demanded.

Notice that *the* does not begin with a capital letter. The clause *the guard demanded* is part of the entire sentence that includes the quotation.

A quote within a quote is indicated by *single* quotation marks.

Tony said, "I read that Jackson told the manager to 'shove it' right in front of the other players."

If you would like to interrupt a quotation in order to insert your own comments or explanations, use brackets.

"He [Frazier] is a bum," Ali yelled. (You are clarifying who the "he" is.)

Sometimes the original sentence contains a grammatical error or some bit of incorrect information. Because you are quoting, you must preserve the *exact words* of the author, just the way they are, without alteration. As the author of the essay, you would like to indicate that the error is found in the original; it is not of your own making. You can indicate this by inserting the word *sic*, within brackets: [sic]. The word means "thus" in Latin. You are saying, "That is the way it was in the original."

Peter wrote, "The fishing is grate [sic] in Onondaga Lake."

Quotation marks do not always indicate someone's exact words. They are also used in other situations.

Titles of articles:	"Back to Yavneh," by Cynthia Ozick "The Podiatrist's Corner"
Titles of short stories:	"The Ambitious Guest," by Nathaniel Hawthorne "Araby," by James Joyce "Barn Burning"
Titles of poems and songs:	"To Autumn" "Lucy in the Sky with Diamonds"
TV and radio programs:	"The Rockford Files" "The Cousin Brucie Show"

Book titles, movie titles, the names of plays and newspapers, and foreign words and phrases are italicized in print and underlined in written or typed essays.

Second Skin—a novel by John Hawkes   The Deer Hunter—best picture, 1979 .

The Zoo Story—a play by Edward Albee   The New Times—A Syracuse newspaper

Sic is Latin for "thus."   Ibid. is an abbreviation of the Latin ibidem.

STEP13   Rewrite the interview below, changing the exact words of the speakers into indirect quotations (reported speech). In the case of the phrases and sentence in boldface type, however, keep the exact words, preserving them in quotation marks. Do make clear throughout that Mr. Allen is speaking. Your first sentence should read: *The interviewer asked Mr. Allen whose throwing arm had "impressed" him most.* (The sentence is in reported speech, but one word has been preserved in quotation marks.)

Golden Arms

¹Interviewer: "Mr. Allen, whose throwing arm has **impressed** you most?"

²"The **best** arms in baseball today belong to Reggie Smith and Bobby Bonds. ³I do remember other arms and other throws over the years that I consider **pretty great.**

⁴"I can still see Willie Mays **race** into right center, make a catch with his back to the plate, **whirl like a dancer,** and throw a Dodger runner out at the plate. ⁵**The Dodger manager still doesn't believe that throw.**

⁶"Another throw I remember is the one by Enos Slaughter against the Yankees, back in the 1942 World Series. ⁷He fielded a base hit along the right field line and got the ball to third so quickly that all the runner could do is **slide right into the tag.** ⁸The Cardinals won four straight after that throw.

⁹"Still, I think that as far as **strength plus accuracy** is concerned, no arm today tops the arms of the three DiMaggio brothers."

NO. OF ERRORS

Correct any errors your instructor has found. For additional work in the punctuation of quotations, choose another STEP 13 essay. You might consult STEP 1 for examples of punctuation around quotations. Correct spelling errors below.

_____   _____   _____

STEP 13   In the essay below, change all quoted material into indirect quotations or reported speech. You would do this because the interview is over and you are reporting what was said. (This is the same as STEP 12.) However, you would like to retain some of the sentences in their original form. Render the sentences in boldface type as they are, adding *He said* or *Dr. Jones said,* as well as proper punctuation. Your first sentence is already in reported speech.

Music and Muscles

¹The interviewer asked Dr. Jones how he was affected by music. ²**All music, whether rock or classical, affects the muscles.** ³Rock and roll generally weakens me, whereas classical music invigorates me. ⁴I know that I feel tired after listening to rock music. ⁵This is because there is a stopped beat at the end of each bar in rock music. ⁶**When people hear that pause, they unconsciously pause, too.** ⁷That is what happens to me. ⁸When the music starts up again, so do I; this stop-start routine is exhausting.

⁹"Classical music, on the other hand, seems to give me energy. ¹⁰**It is not accidental that so many composers and conductors of classical music live longer than other people do.** ¹¹Can I put something on the record player for you?"

NO. OF ERRORS

Correct any errors your instructor has found. For additional work in the punctuation of quotations, choose another STEP 13 essay. You might consult STEP 1 for examples of punctuation around quotations. Correct spelling errors below.

_____   _____   _____

STEP 13   Rewrite the statement by Joe Frazier below in indirect or reported speech. In the case of the phrases and sentences in boldface type, however, retain the original words of the speaker, preserving them within quotation marks. Do make clear throughout that Joe Frazier is speaking. Your first sentence should read: *Frazier said that Ali understood there was a "peace treaty" between them.* (The sentence is in reported speech, with two of the words preserved within quotation marks.)

Frazier and Friend

---

¹Joe Frazier seemed uncomfortable speaking about Muhammad Ali, his opponent in three bruising and memorable fights.
²"Ali understands there is a **peace treaty** between us. ³I don't want to bring back old feelings of animosity, and I don't think Ali does either. ⁴Not that anyone can know for sure what Ali's feelings are.

⁵"I think people should be honest with themselves. ⁶He has to admit that I was **the baddest dude** he ever fought with. ⁷I **knocked** that little fact into him in our last fight. ⁸Right after the first punch **that man** had to know he wasn't on **a picnic.**

⁹"Ali calls it the **'Thrilla in Manila.'** ¹⁰**It was the most brutal fight I was ever in.** ¹¹My face speaks for itself, but Ali's face is not telling jokes either. ¹²I was ready to go out there for the fifteenth round, but Eddie Futch, my manager, told me to sit down. ¹³Ali can't **take anything** away from me. ¹⁴The only thing is, he won't say so. ¹⁵He talks about everything else though. ¹⁶When I'm around him, I make sure I've got some **eyewitness** there. ¹⁷Maybe that guy could hear Ali say something that makes sense.

¹⁸"Ali doesn't know this, but I'll **get him yet.** ¹⁹I'm going to get him to a party and make him **the ex-champ.** ²⁰**He can outtalk me, but I can outdance and outsing him any old time.**"

NO. OF ERRORS

Correct any errors your instructor has found. For additional work in the punctuation of quotations, choose another STEP 13 selection. If you have difficulties with indirect quotations, try STEP 12 again. Correct any spelling errors below.

_____   _____   _____

STEP 13   Rewrite the essay below, changing Ms. Cross's quotations to indirect quotations (reported speech), making the changes you had to make in STEP 12. In addition, however, retain the exact words for other quotations, such as those from advertisements, from Confucius, or chapter titles. After all, you are reporting what Ms. Cross has said, but you should retain the quotations and quotation marks she uses. Underline book titles and other words for italics.

Word Abuses

¹In a new book on the sorry state of the English language, *Word Abuse,* author Donna Woolfolk Cross devotes a chapter to the ways in which advertisers misrepresent the truth. ²She shows us how to read and understand dozens of the ads we hear everyday. ³She titles the chapter, "They Couldn't Say It If Weren't True," and begins it with a quotation from Confucius: "It is a great art to know how to sell wind."

⁴"One of the oldest, most effective of all the advertising man's bag of tricks," she tells us, "is the dangling comparative." ⁵She defines the "dangling comparative" as, "any statement that suggests a product is superior and does not say what it is superior *to*." ⁶A perfect example of the dangling comparative is the Aim toothpaste commercial, "Aim tastes better." ⁷"Better than what?" Cross asks us, "better than dayold bacon fat? ⁸Better than garden fertilizer?" ⁹She cautions us, "The ad writer wants us to think Aim tastes better than other toothpastes on the market, especially Crest, but that is not what the ad says." ¹⁰But she reminds us, "The ad says only, 'Aim tastes better'—and that's all." ¹¹She gives us another example in this tire ad, "Firestone radial tires stop 25% faster." ¹²"Faster than what?" she asks again, "a doughnut?"

¹³Another verbal device cited by Cross is the "weasel word," which sucks meaning out of a sentence the way a weasel can suck an egg without breaking the shell. ¹⁴More literally she tells us, "A weasel word is used to *suggest* or *imply* something that the ad writer cannot come right out and say." ¹⁵A classic example she gives is the long-running Anacin ad: "Three out of four doctors recommend the major ingredient in Anacin for the relief of headache pain." ¹⁶"What is the major ingredient?" she asks us, "some revolutionary medical breakthrough?" ¹⁷"Not at all," she assures us, "the major ingredient in Anacin is plain, unadulterated, inexpensive aspirin, available in economy bottles that cost half as much as Anacin." ¹⁸"Therefore," she concludes, "of course three out of four doctors recommend it. ¹⁹This does not mean that three out of four doctors recommend Anacin. ²⁰It would be equally fair to say that poisoned orange juice has a major ingredient that three out of four doctors recommend—orange juice!"

STEP 13   Rewrite the essay below, changing all of Ms. Elwood's quotations to indirect quotations (reported speech), making the changes you had to make in STEP 12. In addition, however, retain the exact words for other quotations included within Ms. Elwood's quotations. Further, you should retain quotations for the titles of published songs. Underline foreign words for italics.

Chopsticks

¹If there is one song that everyone can play on the piano, it is probably "Chopsticks." ²It is hard to believe that it was composed because most of us assume it was just handed down—like a jump-rope song. ³But music writer Ann Elwood has written, "The creator of 'Chopsticks' was Euphemia Allen, a 16-year-old British girl." ⁴Ms. Elwood goes on to tell us, " 'Chopsticks' was published in London and Glasgow in 1877 under the title, 'The Celebrated Chopsticks Waltz, Arranged as a Duet and Solo for Piano.' " ⁵"Euphemia," Elwood assures us, "published the song under the pen name 'Arthur de Lulli,' and never, so far as we know, published anything else."

⁶Ms. Elwood, who had seen the first edition of "Chopsticks," says page 3 contains these instructions: " 'The first part must be played with both hands turned sideways.' " ⁷"This means," Elwood explains, "that with the little finger lowest, the movement of the hands imitates the chopping from which the waltz gets its name." ⁸"At the same time," Elwood continues, "some people think the name of the waltz comes from the Chinese eating utensil." ⁹She reasons, "This is because the piece is sometimes played with just the forefingers and this looks like someone spearing a morsel of food with chopsticks."

¹⁰But this may not be the whole story. ¹¹"In the same year that Euphemia's 'Chopsticks' was published," as Elwood relates, "Alexander Borodin, the Russian composer, overheard his daughter playing a few bars that sounded like Euphemia's masterpiece." ¹²Elwood reports, "Borodin wrote the song down and named it 'The Koteletten Polka.' " ¹³Koteletten is German for the whiskers called muttonchops in English. ¹⁴Without challenging Euphemia's claim to authenticity, Elwood says, "It is possible that both Euphemia and Borodin's daughter heard an anonymously written version of 'Chopsticks.' "

¹⁵In conclusion, Elwood adds, "Borodin and three other Russian composers, Cui, Liadov, and Rimsky-Korsakov, all published variations on 'Chopsticks' in the next two years." ¹⁶And within three years even the great Franz Liszt had written piano variations on "Chopsticks."

	Correct any errors your instructor has found, and list any spelling errors below.
NO. OF ERRORS	

_____   _____   _____

Step 13

Writing Assignments: Direct Quotation

Remember the importance of punctuation here. Quotation marks go around the exact words of the speaker. Your comments or identification of speakers would go outside quotation marks. Practice (and test) your punctuation skills as you invent or transcribe the conversations suggested below.

1. Sportscasters do this all the time. They see a coach talking to his player, a manager to an umpire, or a pitcher to a catcher; and they invent the dialogue between them. Write your own dialogue for one of those situations, punctuating carefully.
2. Write down a joke that you know that contains dialogue, making sure you present the exact words of the speakers in the joke.
3. Ask a friend to recount an argument he or she has had with someone and try to reconstruct the exact words of the participants in the argument.
4. Try to recall some interview that you have had, and present the exact words the interviewer and interviewee used.
5. Ask three different people for directions to the same place, and write up their exact words.
6. Be the inquiring reporter. Make up a question and get the opinions of five people on the subject. Present these answers in the exact form in which they were given.
7. Listen to a phone call someone you know is making. (Don't eavesdrop; get permission!) Then present the exact words of the speaker, at the same time inventing or imagining what the person on the other end is saying.
8. Cut some photographs out of a newspaper or magazine, and make up a conversation for the situation depicted in the photograph.
9. Watch a famous person being interviewed or making a speech, and write what you think the individual would *really* like to say.
10. Think of a famous moment in history: Napoleon finds out he has lost at Waterloo, Tilden is informed he lost the electoral vote though he had won the popular vote, Ali hears he has lost a decision to Ken Norton, a soldier hears that a peace treaty has been signed, the owner of a property hears that gold has been discovered, slaves hear that they have been freed, or marooned astronauts are returned safely to earth. Make up the conversation between the person delivering the news and the person or people receiving it.

> Even if a speaker speaks ungrammatically, you would
> reproduce that person's words exactly as he or she said them.
> Do not change the actual words when you are quoting them.

Part 2

Style with a Purpose

Step 14

Changing the Active Voice to the Passive Voice

In this STEP you must take the objects of sentences in the active voice and make them the subjects of sentences in the passive voice. In the active voice the subject does the action of the sentence; in the passive voice the subject has the action done to it. For example:

Active	Passive
The tiger bit the man.	The man was bitten by the tiger.

To change the sentence from the active voice to the passive voice, you must first pick out the subject, predicate, and direct object of the active voice sentence so that they may be reconstructed in the passive. The direct object of the active voice sentence becomes the subject of the passive. The predicate is still the predicate although in the passive it usually takes the form of a helping verb like *is, are, was,* and *were* and a participle. The subject of the active voice sentence is usually relegated to a prepositional phrase beginning with *by*, although sometimes it may be omitted when it is understood without being said.

	Active			Passive	
The band	played	a gig.	The gig	was played	by the band.
(subject)	(predicate)	(direct object)	(subject)	(predicate)	(prepositional phrase)
The crowd	admired	the musicians.	The musicians	were admired	by the crowd.
(subject)	(predicate)	(direct object)	(subject)	(predicate)	(prepositional phrase)
The promoter	paid	the performers.	The performers	were paid	by the promoter.
(subject)	(predicate)	(object)	(subject)	(predicate)	(prepositional phrase)

Make sure you change only simple sentences or independent clauses. Do not change the verb forms in subordinate clauses, such as those beginning with *although, whenever,* and so on.

STEP 14   The essay below deals with the different people who did not use or did use soap. Rewrite the essay so that the focus is on soap instead of the people. Change all sentences (except 8, 11, 14, 16, and 19) into the *passive voice*. In other words, make soap the subject of the sentence as often as you can. In addition, use the passive voice in four sentences describing events before soap was invented; the subject for these should be: 3, *plant ashes;* 5, *hot, steaming baths;* 6, *sweat and dirt;* and 7, *strigil.* Make only the changes you must and proofread carefully. Your first rewritten sentence should read: *Soap was not used by ancient peoples to wash themselves.*

Soap

¹Ancient peoples did not use soap to wash themselves. ²They used a harsh soap to wash their clothes, but they did not use it on their bodies because it was too strong. ³The Hittites and other Middle Eastern people employed plant ashes dissolved in water to wash their hands. ⁴Although the Greeks and Romans loved cleanliness, they never utilized soap for bathing. ⁵After gymnastic exercises, they took hot, steaming baths. ⁶Later, they removed sweat and dirt by beating their bodies with twigs. ⁷They also used the strigil, a kind of scraper, to take the dirt off.

⁸While civilized people were beating and scraping, so-called barbarians were making progress. ⁹According to the Roman historian Pliny the Elder, the Gauls made real soap from goat's tallow and beech tree ashes. ¹⁰The fair Gauls used this soap as a shampoo to give their hair extra sheen. ¹¹Perhaps because the Gauls were thought uncouth, their invention did not come into widespread use for almost a thousand years.

¹²By the end of the Middle Ages, the Spanish made some of the best soap, especially in the province of Castile. ¹³Other European countries imported soap in great quantities. ¹⁴Thus today, in many languages, the word "Castile" is still associated with fine soap.

¹⁵Not everyone admired soap for everyday use. ¹⁶Some people thought that too much bathing (more than once a month) was unhealthy and that soap was a frill. ¹⁷Strange to say, the English Puritans distrusted soap, and their leader Oliver Cromwell taxed soap heavily.

¹⁸Common people did not use soap until the 1850s, with the coming of indoor plumbing. ¹⁹As its use became more widespread, the English government took the tax off the cleaner. ²⁰But Prime Minister Gladstone condemned soap as "most injurious both to the comfort and health of people."

STEP 14   In the essay below, the various statements about the way
righties treat lefties are written in *the active voice*. The
statements about Ms. Morlock's actions are written in *the passive
voice*. Rewrite the essay so that all statements about the
behavior of righties toward lefties are also in *the passive voice*.
By thus focusing the sentences away from righties, you will be
making the essay a bit easier for righties to read. You will be
taking the reader's attention away from the doer. Copy
everything else and proofread carefully.

Helping Lefties

---

¹About 10 percent of the American population is left-handed. ²The
right-handed majority has long ignored and maligned this sizable mi-
nority. ³Language informs lefties that to be "right" is to be just, correct,
and skillful, whereas to be "left" is to be sinister, radical, and awkward.
⁴Right-handed parents and teachers routinely force left-handed children
to switch. ⁵In many cases, these misguided people sentence the children to a lifetime of stuttering, poor penmanship, and emotional problems. ⁶Righties also interfere with the way lefties can function with their
hands. ⁷They design simple tools and utensils like scissors, teapots,
and drinking mugs for the comfort of righties. ⁸They make lefties feel
clumsy and inefficient with these objects. ⁹Fortunately for lefties, a store
was opened in St. Louis Park, Minnesota, by Ms. Jackie Morlock, that
stocks tools and gadgets for left-handers.

¹⁰Students have been helped in particular by the items stocked in
Ms. Morlock's store. ¹¹A ruler for lefties enables lefty students to read
the numbers. ¹²"Righty rulers" force lefties to read backwards. ¹³Another
popular item sold by Ms. Morlock is a notebook that opens from front to
back. ¹⁴Notebooks for righties make the lefty student's arm rest uncom-
fortably on the spiral binding. ¹⁵Quick-drying ballpoint pens have also
been made available by the store. ¹⁶These are helpful because lefties
rest their hands on their writing and tend to smear their ink.

¹⁷Lefties in search of other tools and gadgets have also been
helped by The Left Center, Ms. Morlock's store. ¹⁸Fishing rods and
power saws, designed for lefties, are sold, as are lefty sports equipment
and kitchen utensils. ¹⁹There are soup ladles and can openers for lefties. ²⁰There is even a watch for lefties. ²¹The right-handed world had
placed the winding stem on the wrong side of watches for lefties. ²²The
watch offered by Ms. Morlock has the stem on the left side, for easy
winding.

²³To comfort downcast lefties, a bright sign is available in the store.
²⁴It reads, "If the right side of the brain controls the left side of the body
. . . then only left-handed people are in their right minds."

Step 14

Changing the Active Voice to the Passive

Helpful Hints and Special Situations

One of the first difficulties some students have comes with the passive voice constructions in different tenses that require the addition of helping verbs; *be, been,* or *being*.

Active
They are opening the vault tomorrow.
He signed the affidavit.
She is holding your check.

Passive
The Vault will *be* opened tomorrow. (by them)
The affidavit has *been* signed.   (by him)
Your check is *being* held.   (by her)

Make sure you change only simple sentences or independent clauses. Do not change the verb forms in subordinate clauses, such as those beginning with *although, whenever,* and so on.

Active
Although he was sick, he finished the assignment.
  (subordinate clause)

Passive
The assignment was finished by him, although he was sick.
(subordinate clause)

When a sentence contains a compound predicate in the active voice, both must be changed into the passive voice.

Active
Smedley painted the boat and put it into drydock.
 (predicate)   (predicate)

Passive
   The boat was painted and put into drydock by Smedley.
     (predicate)   (predicate)

When a sentence in the active voice contains two independent coordinate clauses, put both of them in the passive voice.

Active
The team won the game, and it held a celebration.

Passive
   The game was won, and a celebration was held by the team.

Sentences containing an objective complement may also be changed to the passive voice.

Active
Tony named his dog   Farrah.
(subject) (predicate) (direct object) (objective complement)

Passive
  His dog was named Farrah   by Tony.
  (subject) (predicate) (objective   (prepositional phrase)
        complement)

Some sentences with intransitive verbs, which do not take objects, can also be changed from the active voice to the passive.

Active   Passive
Supper was cooking.   Supper was being cooked.
The music began slowly.   The music was begun slowly.

Finally, some verbs like *cost, have,* or *weigh*—sometimes called mid-verbs or middle verbs—cannot be changed into the passive voice at all.

STEP 14   The short essay below tells of the beginning of World War II, emphasizing the role of the Germans. The emphasis is on them by the way they are made to be the focus for each sentence. Rewrite the essay so that you will be beginning each sentence by naming the victims. Later in the sentence you will mention the role of the Germans. You can do this by changing each sentence from the active to the *passive voice.* Your first sentence should read: *The world was taught a new word by the German forces in September, 1939.* (Do not change sentences 5, 6, 12, and 16.)

Blitzkrieg

---

[1]The German forces taught the world a new word in September, 1939. [2]They invaded Poland and annihilated its armies in six weeks. [3]They gave the name Blitzkrieg (meaning "lightning war") to the swift method of attack. [4]Nazi planes, tanks, motorized columns, and infantry simply destroyed the courageous but outmoded Polish cavalry. [5]The Germans had used the Spanish Civil War as a training ground for their soldiers. [6]The Polish were helpless against such combat-tested troops.

[7]Until April, 1940, the Germans convinced the world that only a "phony war" existed. [8]Then the Blitzkrieg enveloped all Europe. [9]The Germans hit Denmark and Norway; in Norway they punched through a desperate British Navy. [10]In May the Germans overran Luxembourg and entered Holland and Belgium. [11]They negated France with an "end-run" around the famous Maginot Line. [12]France had thought that line of defense to be impregnable. [13]By June, 1940, the Germans controlled continental Europe. [14]They even forced England into evacuations along the coast. [15]On June 22, 1940, they accepted France's surrender.

[16]They seemed unstoppable, but exactly a year later, on June 22, 1941, the Germans showed that they had not learned from the past. [17]They ignored the lesson of Napoleon's fate and attacked Russia.

STEP 14   The essay below focuses on the people who built, admired, and disliked the Watts Towers. Rewrite the essay so that the focus in each sentence will be on the towers rather than on the people. Change all of the sentences (except sentences 1, 12, and 16) into *the passive voice*. In other words, make the towers the subject of each sentence except 1, 12, and 16. Make only the changes you must and proofread carefully. Your first *rewritten* sentence should read: *Three towers were built by Simon Rodia, an Italian immigrant, on the patio of his home in Watts, a neighborhood in south central Los Angleles.*

Towers of Junk

¹The Watts Towers of Los Angeles are a memorable testimony to one man's creativity and endurance. ²Simon Rodia, an Italian immigrant, built three towers on the patio of his home in Watts, a neighborhood in south central Los Angeles. ³Rodia made the towers of steel, homemade prestressed concrete, and numerous varieties of colored and bottle glass, bits of tile, seashells, scrap metal, even corncobs. ⁴He built the towers to be a memorial to his wife, a symbol of his love for his adopted country, or simply because he wanted to do something big. ⁵After laboring for thirty-three years, Rodia simply gave the towers and his modest home to his neighbors.

⁶Many observers admired the towers, which reach a height of 104 feet. ⁷The Museum of Modern Art in New York has proclaimed the towers works of "great beauty." ⁸Critic Boris I. Chisholm said the towers resembled a harmonious, lacy trio of Oriental temples. ⁹Other critics have compared the towers with the Eiffel Tower in Paris and Angkor Wat in Cambodia. ¹⁰One tourist said, "They're like see-through mosaics."

¹¹City building inspector Harold L. Manley did not admire the towers. ¹²If the towers fell over and killed a passerby, someone would hold the city responsible. ¹³He tested the towers' resistance to wind by trying to pull them down with 10,000 pounds of pressure. ¹⁴Manley built a scaffolding around the towers and looped a steel cable around the tallest of them. ¹⁵His experiment buckled the scaffolding of the towers but did not budge them. ¹⁶Fans of the towers held a celebration and gave free beer to everyone.

¹⁷The Los Angeles Cultural Heritage Committee designated the towers a historical cultural monument. ¹⁸Since then more than a million tourists have visited the three towers made of junk.

STEP 14   The story below tells of the fiasco with the two-dollar bill. If you were an employee of the Treasury Department, you might want to rewrite the story so that the mistakes on the part of the agency appeared minimal. You could do this by changing all the sentences that mention a government agency from the active to the *passive voice*. Then go one step further, and leave off the name of the responsible person or agency altogether. Your first sentence should read: *The two-dollar bill was reissued in 1976 with high hopes.*

The Two-Dollar Bill

---

[1]The United States Treasury, in 1976, reissued the two-dollar bill with high hopes. [2]It expected the bill to replace half of the one-dollar bills in circulation. [3]James A. Conlon, director of the Federal Bureau of Printing and Engraving, foresaw the bills circulating freely and saving $7 million in printing costs. [4]Unfortunately, the bureau miscalculated people's interest in the redesigned note. [5]Neither customers nor retailers liked the new currency.

[6]For one, the bureau ignored the impracticality of the two-dollar bill. [7]It forgot that retail stores had no slots in their cash registers for a new denomination. [8]Nor did bureaucrats realize that people would be reluctant to change their habits. [9]After all, the Treasury had kept the bill out of circulation for ten years. [10]People were afraid they would confuse the two-dollar bills with singles. [11]Finally, the bureau made the error of printing so many of the bills that they had no appeal even as oddities.

[12]Another significant reason for the unpopularity of the bill that the bureau overlooked was its association with bad luck. [13]Because the basic bet at race tracks is two dollars, it was at the track that people had handled the bills most frequently. [14]The agency did not anticipate that the reappearance of the bill would remind people of their losses at the track. [15]The bills did not remind the winners of happy days either. [16]Too often the presence of a two-dollar bill in a wallet had been a clue to the wife that the husband had spent the afternoon watching the horses run.

[17]Just how badly the bureau misread the acceptance of the two-dollar bill can be seen by what it is doing about the bill now. [18]During that first year, the bureau printed 400 million two-dollar bills. [19]It has not produced another since.

STEP 14   The following essay deals with the uses different people have made of bells in religious settings. Rewrite the essay so that the focus is on bells instead of the people. Change all sentences (except 8, 17, and 19) into the passive voice. In other words, make *bell* or *bells* the subject of the sentence as often as you can. Make only the changes you must and proofread carefully. Sentence 1 may be rewritten this way: *Bells were not used by early Christians at all because they did not want to draw attention to places of worship while they were being persecuted by the Romans.*

Church Bells

¹Early Christians did not use bells because they did not want to draw attention to places of worship while they were being persecuted by the Romans. ²Not until at least the eighth century A.D. did worshipers employ bells in services. ³Workmen made early bells from small pieces of concave metal, which is why the word "bell" is derived from the Old German for footpan or basin. ⁴At first people did not use bells for any of their musical properties. ⁵Instead, early worshipers used bells to drive off evil spirits. ⁶The early Hindus had used bells for this same purpose. ⁷Even as late as A.D. 1280 a theological work recommended bells to drive away demons from religious processions.

⁸Although few people still believe in the bell's power to ward off demons, the old belief appears to be behind several continuing uses of bells. ⁹Churchmen have long rung bells, called "passing bells," at funerals. ¹⁰Originally, believers rang bells to drive away the spirits who might pounce on the departing soul. ¹¹Likewise, many people struck bells at times of sickness and natural disaster. ¹²In 1852 the Bishop of Malta ordered bells rung to quiet a violent storm.

¹³Churchmen did not ring bells to remind people of worship until later centuries. ¹⁴Initially, priests sounded bells an hour before services, as a reminder to worshipers. ¹⁵In areas of some Catholic countries, churches still ring bells for the Angelus at noon, 6:00 P.M., and at sundown to remind the faithful to recite a special prayer.

¹⁶Only in recent times have churches sounded bells to count off the hours or to provide entertainment. ¹⁷Some uses of bells today would sound sacrilegious to older ears. ¹⁸A chapel in Evanston, Illinois, uses its bells to play "There's a Tavern in the Town." ¹⁹The joke is that Evanston is the home of the anti-alcohol Women's Christian Temperance Union.

STEP 14   The following essay deals with the contributions of different people to the development of what we now call paper. Rewrite the essay so that the focus is on paper and its ancestors, papyrus and parchment, instead of on the people. Change all sentences (except 1 and 10) into the *passive voice*. In other words, make paper the subject of the sentence as often as you can; make papyrus the subject in sentences 2, 3, and 4, and make parchment the subject in sentences 5, 6, 7, and 8. Make only the changes you must and proofread carefully. Sentence 2 may be rewritten this way: *Papyrus was made by the Egyptians from a tall reed that grew in the marshes of the Nile.*

Paper

[1]Although the word "paper" comes from ancient Egypt's papyrus, real paper as we know it today did not exist in Europe until the Middle Ages. [2]The Egyptians made papyrus from a tall reed that grew in the marshes of the Nile. [3]Egyptians manufactured papyrus from about the year 3000 B.C., and during ancient times traders sold it in all parts of the Mediterranean world, including Greece and Rome. [4]Scribes disliked using papyrus, though, because it was brittle and turned yellow easily.

[5]About the second century B.C., Greeks in Asia Minor began to make parchment out of animal skins, planning it to be a rival to papyrus. [6]Scribes loved parchment because it was tougher, lasted longer, and could take twice the amount of writing, as both sides could be used. [7]Only the very rich could afford parchment, however, as it was highly expensive. [8]Nevertheless, scholars and monks used parchment to preserve learning from the ancient world.

[9]Unknown to Western civilization, the Chinese invented real paper in A.D. 105. [10]We even know the name of the inventor, T'sai Lun, chief eunuch of the Emperor Ho Ti. [11]T'sai Lun made paper from varieties of bark, fibers, and waste, a formula that can still be used today. [12]For eight centuries only the Chinese used paper as they kept its manufacture a secret. [13]When some Chinese workmen were captured by Arab traders, they made some paper in order to win their release.

[14]The Arabs brought paper to the West, even though there was continual warfare between Islam and Christianity in those days. [15]By 1340, Italians made the first paper in Europe in the town of Fabriano. [16]Within another hundred years, Gutenberg used paper in the first printing press.

[17]Over the centuries different national groups made paper by improved methods. [18]In 1800 the Englishman Matthias Hoops first made paper from straw, wood, leaves, and other vegetable material. [19]Improving on his formula, Americans and Swedes made paper by separating fibers from wood pulp through a chemical process. [20]Although the United States once was rich in trees to make pulp for paper, we import most of our paper from other countries, principally Canada.

Step 14

Writing Assignments: Using the Active Voice

You should use the active voice whenever possible. It is livelier and more direct than the passive. Still, the passive can be useful. In some situations using it is unavoidable; in other situations it is even helpful. As the exercises in STEP 14 pointed out, the passive voice can focus attention on the recipient of an action rather than on the doer of the action, and it can actually eliminate the doer of the action altogether. One of those situations might be precisely your aim. If one is, by all means, use the passive. Some writers also use the passive in order to vary their sentences. The passive can be used effectively by skillful writers. It is a skill that is worthwhile developing.

1. List any sentences your instructor has marked in your other essays as appropriate for being written in the passive voice. Write those sentences in the passive.
2. Tell the story of some prank you were part of as a youngster. Write about your role in it, using *the passive voice.*
3. Give a brief description of American involvement in some international event that resulted in a disaster. Minimize the American role by writing about it in *the passive.*
4. Discuss the responsibility for the rising gas prices from the point of view of the gas companies or gas producing nations, using *the passive voice* to describe their involvement.
5. Find a newspaper account of some criminal's activity. Rewrite the account in *the passive.* An actual confession would sound particularly altered when written in the passive.
6. Describe a famous work of art, rendering the artist's role in creating the work in *the passive voice.*
7. Describe the building of some vast project—the Pyramids, Panama Canal, TVA, the Apollo Project, the Tower of Babel—writing about the participants in *the passive voice.* Your emphasis will be on the project, not the builders.
8. Describe the effects of the music *created by some group.*
9. Focus on the effects *created by* a magnificent meal, writing about the people involved in preparing, serving, and eating the meal in the passive.
10. Describe how animals *are treated by* their owners.

Step 15

Changing the Passive Voice to the Active Voice

At the simplest level, this STEP is the reverse of the previous one. In the passive voice the subject has the action done to it. You must change the sentences so the subject does the action.

Passive	Active
The boy was bitten by the dog.	The dog bit the boy.

To change the sentence, you must determine not only the subject and predicate but also the doer of the action. In the sentence above left, the prepositional phrase *by the dog* gives us the doer and thus becomes the subject of the active voice sentence.

When the doer of the action of the sentence is clearly implied, *he, she,* or *it* may be left out of a passive voice sentence. For example:

Passive
The championship was won.
The pedestrian was hit.
Money is kept in a bank.
Snow was piled high beside the road.

In each of these instances, we must assume from the context what the active subject must be, or we must make one up; we often need a "one" or "somebody" to start a sentence.

Active
The team won the championship.
The car hit the pedestrian.
One keeps money in a bank.
Somebody piled snow high beside the road.

STEP 15   The following essay deals with the development of frozen food. Rewrite the essay so that the focus is on people instead of on frozen food itself; after all, two people are really responsible for our having frozen food. Change all sentences (except 5, 8, and 13) into the *active voice*. In other words, make the subject of each sentence the doer of the action. Do not change the subjects or verbs in subordinate clauses. Make only the changes you must, and proofread carefully. Sentence 1 may be rewritten this way: *Over the years hundreds of scientists and workbench tinkerers experimented on frozen food.*

Frozen Food

¹Over the years frozen food was experimented upon by hundreds of scientists and workbench tinkerers. ²One of the first frozen food experiments was conducted in 1626 by Sir Francis Bacon, who gave his life to science in the process. ³But modern frozen foods were developed separately by an Australian, James Harrison, and an American, Clarence Birdseye.

⁴In the 1850s locally produced meat, especially mutton and beef, could not be shipped very far by Australians. ⁵Australia's best market was England, where meat prices were highest, but Australian meat spoiled before it was many miles from port. ⁶A special ice-making machine to freeze meat was patented in 1857 by James Harrison, a newspaper editor. ⁷Earlier model ice makers were adapted by him to keep temperatures stable. ⁸Harrison could not raise the money to develop the freezer, and so he continued editing his newspaper, was elected to Parliament, and worked on his invention in his spare time. ⁹After fifteen years the capital was raised by him, and a ship was outfitted for London. ¹⁰But the equipment was mismanaged by the crew, who did not understand refrigeration. ¹¹Harrison's reputation was ruined by the episode. ¹²The idea, however, was seized upon by other Australians, although their frozen food lacked the good taste and texture when thawed that Harrison's had.

¹³Clarence Birdseye was much luckier. ¹⁴Natural freezing of vegetables was observed by him when he was working on a government survey of Labrador in 1912 and 1915. ¹⁵Fresh vegetables left in a pail of water were frozen by extreme arctic temperatures. ¹⁶Quick-freezing machinery was developed in 1924 by Birdseye back home in Massachusetts. ¹⁷The General Seafoods Corporation was established by Birdseye, and commercial production began the next year. ¹⁸Fruits and vegetables, as well as the abundant sea food of Boston Bay, were all frozen by Birdseye. ¹⁹By 1929, General Seafoods was sold to the Postum Company for $22 million. ²⁰The Birdseye name is still used today by the General Foods Corporation, a great conglomerate that bought Postum.

STEP 15   Rewrite the essay below, changing all of the sentences that have the word "razor" in them into the *active voice*. Some of the sentences already have razor as their subject; do not disturb them. Leave also undisturbed other sentences, whether they are in the active or the passive voice. Changing the specified sentences into the active will help focus away from the item and to the people handling it. Copy everything else and proofread carefully. Your first sentence should read: *Environmentalists do not applaud the invention of the safety razor.*

The One-a-Day Throwaway

[1]The invention of the safety razor is not applauded by environmentalists. [2]The razor has fostered attitudes that are criticized by those who are concerned about diminishing resources.

[3]Using a sharp metal for shaving is not a new idea, of course. [4]"Razors" have been used by men to scrape whiskers off their faces ever since artisans learned how to make metal blades. [5]But the disposable metal blade is a modern invention. [6]King C. Gillette of Brookline, Massachusetts, who made his living selling bottle caps, was determined to invent something. [7]Perhaps because he was already dealing with an item that had a short life expectancy, he cast about for something to invent—anything—that would be used briefly and then be discarded. [8]He got an idea while shaving one morning. [9]His razor was so dull that he knew he would have to get it sharpened by a professional. [10]All razors in those days needed to be honed by an expert. [11]Why not make very thin blades, Gillette asked himself at that moment, and discard them after just a few uses? [12]His disposable razor was marketed by him in 1903. [13]Within fifteen years, disposable razors were being made and marketed by 300 companies around the world.

[14]From one point of view, Gillette's insight was a technological breakthrough. [15]From the point of view of those who seek to preserve scarce resources, however, the razor's invention by Gillette was sheer disaster. [16]The idea of disposable merchandise was made acceptable by the disposable razor. [17]The throwaway razor has led to disposable glass and paper containers, one-wear dresses, single-use diapers, nonwashable paper dishes, and a host of other no-deposit, no-return throwaways. [18]The convenience of these disposables is at the cost of limited resources. [19]The manufacturing concept that was fostered by the disposable razor is, "Build nothing to last except obsolescence." [20]Unfortunately, resources have not been built to last either.

Step 15

Changing the Passive Voice to the Active Voice

Helpful Hints and Special Situations

Because this STEP requires you to put sentences into the active voice, which is used more often in everyday speech than is the passive, many of these sentences should be easier to rewrite than were those in STEP 14. Sentences in the active voice are likely to be a bit shorter, if only because the preposition *by* and the forms of the helping verbs *be*, *been*, and *being* will be missing.

Passive	Active
I was *being* helped *by* the clerk over there.	That clerk helped me.

Perhaps the greatest difficulty in rewriting sentences in the active voice is finding a subject when no doer of the action is named in the passive sentence.

Passive

The Pyramids were built to last forever.

Who built the Pyramids? The sentence names no one. According to what you learn from reading the sentence in context, you must name the subject for the active voice sentence yourself.

Active

Somebody built the Pyramids to last forever.
Workmen built the Pyramids to last forever.
The pharaohs built the Pyramids to last forever.
Pharaoh Khufu built the Pyramids to last forever.

Another problem in switching sentences from the passive voice to the active comes when a relative clause or adjective clause modifies the doer of the action. In the passive voice, such clauses may just be attached to the end of the sentence, but in the active voice, they must find a place earlier in the sentence, closer to the new subject:

Passive

The title was won by Joe Louis, who was known as the "Brown Bomber."
(relative clause)

Active

Joe Louis, who was known as the "Brown Bomber," won the title.
(relative clause)

Because STEP 15 is the reverse of STEP 14, all of the advice about changing the different parts of the sentence still apply. For example, make sure you change only simple sentences or independent clauses. Do not change the verb forms in subordinate clauses, such as those beginning with *although, because,* and so on.

Passive
The assignment was finished by him, although he was sick.
(subordinate clause)

Active
Although he was sick, he finished the assignment.
(subordinate clause)

When a sentence contains a compound predicate in the passive voice, both must be changed in the active.

Passive
The boat was painted and put into drydock by Smedley.
(predicate)   (predicate)

Active
Smedley painted the boat and put it in drydock.
(predicate)   (predicate)

When a sentence in the passive voice contains two independent co-ordinate clauses, put both of them in the active voice.

Passive
The game was won, and a celebration was held by the team.

Active
The team won the game, and it held a celebration.

Sentences containing an objective complement may also be changed into the active voice.

Passive
His dog was named   Farrah   by Tony.
(subject) (predicate) (objective complement) (prepositional phrase)

Active
Tony   named   his dog   Farrah.
(subject) (predicate) (direct object) (objective complement)

STEP 15   In the following passage every sentence is in the passive voice. This means that the subject of the sentence is not the doer of the action in the sentence. Change each sentence into the active voice. Find the subject of each sentence, and then determine who or what did the action of the sentence; often the person or thing that does the action of the predicate will be named in a prepositional phrase. In the first sentence the predicate is "have been used," and the people who did the using were men and women. Therefore, the first sentence can be put in the active voice this way: *Both men and women have been using buttons on clothing since about the thirteenth century.*

Buttons

---

[1]Buttons have been used on clothing by both men and women since about the thirteenth century. [2]Yet from the very beginning, differences have been noticed by everyone. [3]Although buttons on sleeves and pockets might be the same for both sexes, those on the front of clothes, from pajamas to overcoats, are buttoned left to right by men and right to left by women. [4]Why this should be so is a question entertained by many. [5]Although we cannot know for certain the origin of the differences, many reasons have been suggested by scholars.

[6]The left-to-right pattern for men may be explained by medieval man's need to carry a weapon with him. [7]He might be challenged at any time by thieves or rivals. [8]His sword had to be available to him. [9]Because most men held their swords in their right hands, cloaks were designed by tailors with the left flap or lapel on top. [10]Later the left-to-right pattern was maintained by tailors when men began to wear jackets instead of cloaks because men dressed themselves. [11]The left-to-right pattern was found to be more convenient by the right-handed majority of men.

[12]Although women are right-handed in equal proportion with men, the way they buttoned their blouses may be determined by other matters. [13]When buttons were first introduced they could be afforded only by wealthy women, and wealthy women were dressed by servants. [14]Thus, buttons may have been placed right to left by seamstresses for the convenience of servants, most of whom were right-handed.

[15]Another reason given by scholars for the right-to-left pattern is the nursing mother. [16]With the high birth rate in earlier societies, children might be nursed by a mother almost continuously from the time she was eighteen until she was forty-two. [17]Nursing children could be better tended by their right-handed mothers if they were cradled in their mothers' left arms. [18]Freedom of movement was thus given to the right hand. [19]Similarly, the openings of blouses and other garments would be designed by seamstresses to protect the babies' heads.

STEP 15   The transcript below is based on an actual court case in Virginia. As it was originally presented, the transcript focused on the patient or the activity rather than on the hospital staff that performed the activities. Rewrite the entries, changing the *passive voice* to the *active*. In each case, you will be focusing on the doctor or nurse who was responsible for the action. Your first entry should read: *Nurse Chapman admitted John Ferris to Virginia General Hospital.*

The Ferris Case

1:20 P.M. [1]John Ferris was admitted to Virginia General Hospital by Nurse Chapman.

1:30 P.M. [2]Mr. Ferris was scheduled for surgery by Dr. Doherty, the examining physician.

2:30 P.M. [3]A burr hole was drilled to the brain by Dr. Baldwin, to relieve pressure.

3:30 P.M. [4]The operation was completed.

3:50 P.M. [5]The patient was fed intravenously by Nurse Wright.

4:30 P.M. [6]No evidence of cortical activity was found by examining physician.

4:50 P.M. [7]The respirator was disconnected by an unknown individual.

5:00 P.M. [8]Mr. Ferris was pronounced dead by the same doctor who signed the death certificate.

5:10 P.M. [9]The respirator was reconnected by Nurse Chapman.

5:40 P.M. [10]An incision was made by Dr. Jones.

5:50 P.M. [11]The heart was removed and stored for transplant.

5:55 P.M. [12]Another incision was made by Dr. Jones.

6:00 P.M. [13]The kidneys were removed and also stored for possible transplant.

6:30 P.M. [14]Mr. Ferris' relatives were notified of his death by a member of the staff.

[15]Mr. Ferris' brother subsequently sued the hospital, claiming that the organs were removed by Dr. Jones without permission.

STEP 15   The following essay relates some details about the famous building in India, the Taj Mahal. Rewrite the essay so that the focus is on people instead of the building; after all, without people there would be no Taj Mahal. Change all sentences (except 3, 13, and 16) into the *active* voice. In other words, make the subject of each sentence the doer of the action. Do not change the subjects or verbs of subordinate clauses. Make only the changes you must, and proofread carefully. Sentence 1 may be rewritten this way: *Critics everywhere consider the Taj Mahal in north central India to be the most beautiful building in the world.*

The Taj Mahal

---

¹The Taj Mahal in north central India is considered to be the most beautiful building in the world by critics everywhere. ²Although larger than many palaces or temples, the Taj Mahal was not built to be a royal residence or a place of worship. ³Instead, the magnificent building is a tomb to one woman, a monument of love. ⁴The woman memorialized by the Taj Mahal is Mumtaz Mahal or Taj Mahal (in English, "Crown of the Palace"), favorite wife of Emperor Shah Jehan. ⁵Fourteen children were borne by Mumtaz Mahal in eighteen years, after which she died in 1631. ⁶All power and wealth were mustered by the grief-stricken husband to commemorate her.

⁷Architects, sculptors, and jewelers were summoned from all over Asia by Emperor Jehan. ⁸Silver was ordered from Persia, and pearls by the thousand were ordered from Arabia. ⁹Then 20,000 workmen were commanded to labor for nearly twenty years. ¹⁰With the Taj Mahal done in white marble, a duplicate in black marble was planned by Shah Jehan as a mausoleum for himself. ¹¹Before that could be begun, Shah Jehan was dethroned by a rebellious son.

¹²The human eye is deceived by the ornate simplicity of the Taj Mahal. ¹³If we see the building only in pictures, we lack the perspective to appreciate its size. ¹⁴The 70-foot walls are topped by a bulb-shaped dome that reaches a height of 243 feet, equal to that of a twenty-story building. ¹⁵The corners of the marble slab upon which the main building stands are set off by freestanding towers or minarets, each standing 138 feet high. ¹⁶At the same time, the building is not less than impressive on the inside. ¹⁷The solid marble walls are covered with inscriptions, floral designs, and arabesques, all filled with precious stones.

¹⁸In 1830 the Taj Mahal was sold to a British merchant who planned to dismantle the "barbaric structure." ¹⁹All the marble and jewels would be brought back to England to embellish English estates. ²⁰Wrecking equipment was brought to the gardens of the Taj Mahal, but the plan was abandoned by the merchant as too expensive.

STEP 15   In the short essay below there is one person responsible for all the tricks. Rewrite the essay so that in each sentence the identity of this "trickster" is obvious. You can accomplish this by changing the sentences from the passive to the *active voice*. Notice that with many of the sentences you have to add the words *she, he,* or *store manager,* so thoroughly has the person disappeared into the passive voice. Refer to the beginning of this STEP if you are not quite sure what you have to do. Proofread carefully. Your first sentence should read: *The store's manager often manipulates your buying decisions.*

Buying or Being Bought

¹Your buying decisions are often manipulated by the store's manager.

²As part of one scheme, produce and light bulbs are moved near the door. ³These high-profit items are thus made visible. ⁴Other high-yield items such as shaving and camera accessories are placed on aisle displays near cash registers. ⁵Buyers are forced to notice these items and thus often induced to purchase them.

⁶A similar "trick of the trade" is achieved when shelf space that is easiest to reach is reserved for high markup items by the store manager. ⁷Bargains are placed below eye level. ⁸Best buys are there, but they are usually hidden on shelves that are least accessible.

⁹Another frequently used device is "multiplication." ¹⁰You may need only two green peppers but find four of them, presented as a package. ¹¹Chances are you will buy the package of four though by law loose peppers have been made available, too. ¹²Multiple pricing has been devised the same way. ¹³You need only one can of tomatoes but find yourself influenced by the store manager again. ¹⁴Three cans for 99 cents have been placed on sale. ¹⁵You have been caught again.

¹⁶You can become a better shopper if you remember that the store has been arranged to get you to spend your money rather than save it.

STEP 15   The essay below uses the passive voice whenever it discusses the Confederate ship. Rewrite those sentences, changing them to the *active voice*. The change will help focus attention on the "doer" in each sentence. Remember not to change verbs in subordinate clauses. Copy everything else and proofread. Your first sentence should read: *The Federal Navy abandoned the old wooden vessel Merrimac when its usefulness was gone.*

The Virginia, AKA the Merrimac

¹When its usefulness was gone, the old wooden vessel Merrimac was abandoned by the Federal Navy. ²It was then raised by the Confederate Navy. ³Its wooden hull was plated with metal by navy engineers. ⁴Thus outfitted with armor, it was sent out by the Confederates to raid the blockading Union ships at Hampton Roads.

⁵The plan was successful at first. ⁶Several of the Union vessels were sunk by the plated ship. ⁷But the destructiveness of the Merrimac, renamed the Virginia, was limited by its lack of effective armaments or powerful engines. ⁸The Union ships were destroyed only if they were rammed by the Virginia.

⁹To limit the destructiveness of this floating battering ram, the Union Navy sent out the Monitor. ¹⁰The Union ship, also an ironclad, could not be harmed by the Virginia. ¹¹The Confederate ship was thus kept away from other Union vessels by the Monitor, preserving the blockade.

¹²The Confederate Navy, incidentally, introduced another aspect of naval warfare during the Civil War. ¹³Its submersible David, the first "submarine," exploded a torpedo against the hull of the Union Housatonic, sinking it. ¹⁴This was the first attack from under the water in naval history.

Step 15

Writing Assignments: Using the Active Voice

Use the active voice unless you have a particular reason for using the passive. The active voice makes writing more simple, more direct, more "active." The focus, remember, is on the one *doing the action,* not on the one *being acted on.*

1.   Throughout this second half of the book, you should list any sentences your instructor has located in your other essays that seemed inappropriate as written. Rewrite any sentences you had written in the passive, but that your instructor (or you) think would work better in the active voice.
2.   Choose one of the assignments you had completed for STEP 14, and rewrite it in the active voice. (For example, rewrite *"How are animals treated by their owners?"* in the active voice; *"How do owners treat their pets?")*
3.   How do people in power treat people who are more vulnerable? Consider parent and child, teacher and student, men and women, boss and employee, officer and private, and so on.
4.   Discuss a famous work of art, emphasizing the artist's action rather than the appearance of the work.
5.   Describe the role of the United States in some situation that resulted in glory and success. Write about the government's role in the active voice.
6.   Discuss some grand project that needed the cooperation of different people, groups or agencies. Emphasize the role of the participants by using the active voice.
7.   Discuss how you managed to receive an outstanding grade in a course.
8.   Tell a story of how you or other individuals managed to do something against great odds—climbing a mountain, getting into a school, completing a job—using the active voice in your story.

Step 16

Negating and Contradicting

In this STEP you are asked to change sentences making positive statements into sentences making negative statements. Often this will require you only to insert the adverb *not* and reshape the predicate.

> Jennifer *rides* her bike across campus.
> Arnold *does not ride* his bike across campus.

Notice that we could say *rides not* and be understood, but we would sound ridiculous to most native speakers of English. If we use the same form of the verb in this positive statement, "Jennifer *did ride* her bicycle. . . ," we sound a bit overemphatic, as though we were answering a demanding question.

The changes would follow the same pattern in the past tense as well.

> Jennifer *rode* her bicycle across campus.
> Arnold *did not ride* his bicycle across campus.

Along with changes in the verb form, we often have to make other changes in the phrasing of sentences. Here are some other examples:

> Jennifer *has some* mud splashes on her jeans.
> Arnold *does not have any* mud splashes on his jeans.

> Jennifer carries *both* a tire pump *and* and patching kit with her.
> Arnold does *not* carry *either* a tire pump *or* a patching kit with him.

> *Everybody* has seen Jennifer on her bicycle.
> *Nobody* has seen Arnold on his bicycle.

> Jennifer is *both* physically fit *and* healthy from riding her bike.
> Arnold is *neither* physically fit *nor* healthy from *not* riding his bicycle.

Also be careful to keep the statements in other parts of the sentence in agreement with the change from positive to negative:

> Because of her interest, Jennifer will compete in the bicycle race.

> Because of his *lack of* interest, Arnold will *not* compete in the bicycle race.
> *Or*
> Because he is *not* interested, Arnold will *not* compete in the bicycle race.

STEP 16   The essay below contains the opinions of an astronomer, J. Allen Hynek, who supports research into Unidentified Flying Objects (UFOs). Rewrite the essay so it reflects the views of Sir Bernard Lovell, who refutes the claims of those who believe in UFOs. Substitute the name *Sir Bernard Lovell* or *Lovell* wherever you find Prof. *J. Allen Hynek* or *Hynek.* Also negate all statements supporting a belief in UFOs. The first sentence should read: *Sir Bernard Lovell of England's Jodrell Bank Observatory does not believe the question of Unidentified Flying Objects should be pursued.* Do not change sentence 14.

UFOs

---

[1]J. Allen Hynek, retired professor of astronomy from Northwestern University, believes the question of Unidentified Flying Objects should be pursued. [2]He has investigated the more than 60,000 reported sightings of UFOs from the United States and other countries. [3]Because of his interest, he has been happy to associate himself with the thousands of people who insist that UFOs are real. [4]He is a supporter of the Center for UFO Studies in Dayton and of "Ufology" in general.

[5]Prof. Hynek believes that travelers would come to this planet from distant space because he thinks they could come at a speed faster than that of light. [6]He would apply the scientific formula that says that the faster one goes, the slower the passage of time from the launching point. [7]He argues that although it takes light nine years to come from Sirius, one of the brightest stars, a traveler coming at the speed of light or more might not be as conscious of time's passage.

[8]Looking at the question another way, Prof. Hynek speculates that beings in UFOs may be time travelers of one of two types. [9]He thinks they may be members of past civilizations who are coming back to see how we are getting along. [10]Such a theory would explain, he thinks, why UFOs are sighted most often by only one or two observers at a time. [11]Such travelers would have a need only to observe and no need to get cozy, he asserts.

[12]Hynek thinks another theory of time travel offers much to the imagination. [13]He wonders if there may be an extremely advanced civilization somewhere in space that has incorporated the paranormal—things like extrasensory perception (ESP)—into its technology. [14]As any scientist would acknowledge, there are many stars older than our sun, and so the chance exists that there may be many planets older than the earth. [15]This means, Hynek thinks, that there is a good chance such supertechnologies exist out there, too.

STEP 16   The essay below contains the opinion of an astrologer. Rewrite the essay so that it represents the views of an astronomer who would disagree with the views stated in the essay. To do this, simply substitute *Carl Sagan, an astronomer,* for *Linda Goodman, an astrologer;* and negate or contradict each of the statements that asserts the accuracy of reading horoscopes. (Remember to change *she* to *he.*) Proofread carefully.

Sun Signs

¹Linda Goodman, an astrologer and author of many books about the stars, thinks that people need to know what their natal chart is. ²She considers it important that people find out the exact position of the heavenly bodies in the sky at the time of their birth. ³The information can provide dependable predictions about the future. ⁴A precise natal chart, according to Linda Goodman, can be 80 to 90 percent accurate. ⁵She claims that applying sun sign knowledge and casting personal horoscopes are foolproof.

⁶According to the astrologer, the position of these heavenly bodies at the time of birth affects your destiny. ⁷The sun, the most powerful of the stellar bodies in the sky, exerts a particular influence on your fate. ⁸The moon and eight planets contribute also to your personality. ⁹If you were born on June 9, for example, your basic qualities will be determined by the Gemini Sun. ¹⁰You will share qualities with other Geminians born on another day under the sign. ¹¹There will be differences due to the positions of the moon and the other planets at the time of your birth. ¹²Mars, ruling speech, could be in Taurus, so your speech would be slower, closer to a Taurean's pattern. ¹³But you will share with other Geminians most of your characteristics.

¹⁴Linda Goodman argues that everyone can benefit from the knowledge the study of sun signs provides. ¹⁵Knowing horoscopes, she feels, will enable you to have new perceptions about yourself and others. ¹⁶She is convinced that this new understanding will make you a more tolerant and sympathetic person. ¹⁷She also suggests that it might be fun to figure out the natal charts of famous people, real or fictional.

As you proofread, underline the changes you have made.

Step 16

Negating and Contradicting

Helpful Hints
and Special Situations

Although the easiest way to negate a positive statement is to attach the adverb *not* to the predicate, this sometimes produces a lame or unlikely sentence. Often a better way of negating the sentence is to find an entirely new word:

> Jennifer *supports* the college's physical fitness program.
> Arnold *does not support* the college's physical fitness program.
> *Or, improved:*
> Arnold *ignores* the college's physical fitness program.

The verb must be changed in the negative when the positive statement is about time, especially something that continues in time:

> Jennifer *continues* to work out in the gymnasium.
> Arnold *never works out* in the gymnasium.

> Roscoe is *still* driving a Cadillac.
> Marvin *stopped* driving a Cadillac when the finance company paid him a visit.

The positiveness of some sentences is stressed by adverbs. In these instances, a simple *not* is insufficient to make them negative. Instead, the writer must find the negative counterpart or *antonym* of the adverb. Here are some examples:

> It *always* snows in Syracuse.
> It *never* snows in Honolulu.

> It *frequently* snows in Philadelphia.
> It *rarely* snows in Houston.

Sometimes a positive statement may be negated by changing the collective noun serving as the subject or by changing certain adjectives modifying a noun subject.

> *Many* students will play college football.
> *Few* will get bids from professional teams.
> (Notice that *not many* sounds like more than *few*.)

Everyone has heard of Mickey Mouse.
No one has heard of Chakravarti Ragigopolichari.
   (Again, notice that *not everyone* sounds like more than *no one*.)

Much effort has been put forth to help youth unemployment in the city.
Little help came forth from the mayor's office to help youth unemployment.

Some are dancers.
None is a real ballerina.
   (Notice that *none*—not one or less than one—should take the singular.)

Lastly, the English language provides dozens of subtle ways of negating positive statements or, at least, reducing the positive aspects of them. Sometimes this may be done by changing just a letter or two. Consider the differences between *a few* and *few* or *ever* and *every*.

Cher invited *a few* friends over after the concert.
   (This might mean half the theater.)

The deceased man had *few* friends.
   (Maybe only his mother and his dog.)

We go to the opera *ever so* often.
   (Sounds like every two weeks.)

We go to the drag races *every so* often.
   (Sounds like 1959, 1969, and 1979.)

More work of this type will be available in STEPS 17 and 18.

STEP 16   The essay below describes the career of the beloved American movie actor John Wayne (1907–1979). Rewrite the essay, substituting the name *Richard Loo* wherever the name *John Wayne* appears. Richard Loo (1903–   ) is an American-born actor of Hawaiian-Chinese descent. Because of Hollywood's typecasting of Orientals, Richard Loo played sinister villains in hundreds of movies. In many World War II movies, where he played Japanese pilots or officers, his well-trained voice would often intone, "You are surprised I speak your language." Still alive in 1980, he did not make many movies after 1966. Although Richard Loo and John Wayne were about the same age and acted in many films, all the statements about Wayne in this essay are not true of Richard Loo. Copy everything else and proofread. The first sentence should read: *Richard Loo was not the number one box office attraction in the history of American Films.*

Choice Movie Roles

¹John Wayne was the number one box office attraction in the history of American films. ²He was usually a lovable, strong good-guy. ³He often won the beautiful girl in the movie. ⁴Redheads like Maureen O'Hara found him irresistible. ⁵Moviemakers like to portray John Wayne as a symbol of decency and fair play. ⁶People all over the world know the name of John Wayne.

John Wayne first established his reputation in Westerns. ⁸Producers were impressed with the way he sat in the saddle. ⁹John Wayne rode fast and did his own stunts. ¹⁰He was sometimes a soldier in the cavalry. ¹¹Indians in the earlier movies were afraid of him.

¹²During World War II, John Wayne played Marines fighting in the South Pacific. ¹³He was always on the winning side. ¹⁴But sometimes his uniform got ripped and dirty. ¹⁵He often lost his temper in battle. ¹⁶He was still ready to fight.

¹⁷In old age John Wayne made more movies. ¹⁸Blondes fell into his arms when he was old enough to be their grandfather. ¹⁹He was on the side of justice no matter what costume he wore. ²⁰By the 1970s he had won over moviegoers and even the critics who had disliked him. ²¹Popular opinion encouraged Congress to issue a gold medal in his honor.

As you proofread, underline the changes you have made.

STEP 16   The essay below discusses the emergence of robot workers by presenting a description of the way human workers behave. Rewrite the essay so that you will be discussing the way robot workers behave. Substitute *robot* for *human*, beginning with the second paragraph, and change all of the sentences to the negative. Instead of describing what human workers do, you will be describing what robot workers do not do. Proofread carefully.

Robots on the Assembly Line

[1]Industries, particularly automakers, are investing heavily in robots—Ford has been using them since 1958; and GM, since 1970. [2]The later models cost $10,000 each and are employed, according to a Ford spokesman, in "areas of worker discontent."

[3]In extolling the superiority of robots, Don Vincent, manager of the Robot Institute, explained that <u>human</u> workers take coffee breaks and demand vacations. [4]They get sick or injured on the job, and they file union grievances. If their work is dirty or boring, they demand changes and improvements. [5]They have personalities, and that creates problems for their employers.

[6]<u>Human</u> workers become disaffected. [7]Their work suffers. [8]They leave out a couple of welds, and the car that rolls off the assembly line is filled with rattles. [9]They can be inconsistent in their work and put out an inferior product.

[10]Also, he continued, because they are <u>human</u>, their bodies limit them. [11]They get tired. [12]Hot parts can burn them; deadly fumes can choke them. [13]Under such adverse conditions their performance suffers. [14]Mr. Vincent is convinced that robots are here to stay and that there would be no union objection to their presence.

As you proofread, underline the changes you have made.

STEP 16   The essay below presents the opinion of two physiologists who think that a fever helps the body fight disease. Rewrite the essay so that the opposing view is presented. Begin the second paragraph with: *But most physicians disagree.* Then substitute the phrase *most physicians* for the two physiologists in each sentence where they state their opinion about fever in the human being, and negate or contradict the opinion in the sentence. Remember to negate only those sentences where opinions are presented. Copy everything else and proofread.

Hot and Cold About Fever

---

¹Remember the old-fashioned remedy of "sweating out" a bout of flu? ²Two physiologists from the University of Michigan argue that letting a fever run its course is a good idea.

³Doctors Kluger and Rothenberg feel that it would be a mistake to prescribe fever-reducing drugs for moderate temperatures. ⁴Such medication, they argue, will interfere with the body's own defenses. ⁵The physiologists feel that such natural defenses are more effective than drugs in dealing with disease and should be allowed to do their job without interference. ⁶The increased body temperature is successful in combating viral diseases. ⁷Reducing the temperature creates an environment in which viral diseases can flourish.

⁸Kluger and Rothenberg accept the evidence that André Lwoff, a Noble Laureate in medicine, had presented. ⁹Lwoff had discovered that the growth of viruses in laboratory experiments was reduced greatly when the temperature of the cells rose to fever levels of 102°F. ¹⁰The Michigan physiologists extend these findings to human beings. ¹¹They predict that polio viruses, for example, would react to fever in the same fashion.

¹²In their own experiments, Kluger and Rothenberg found that bacilli in the blood of infected rabbits could not multiply when the temperature of the rabbits rose. ¹³They feel that fever would bring about the same results in human beings. ¹⁴They are firm in their belief that fever is a positive force in the body's fight against infection. ¹⁵Though there is no disagreement that high fevers (above 105.8°F) should be treated, the researchers from the University of Michigan also feel that fever in its moderate state is the body's most potent means of thwarting viral diseases.

As you proofread, underline the changes you have made.

STEP 16   The essay below describes traditional Welsh folk beliefs as related by Mr. Gruffydd Jones, aged 76, of Llangynwyd, Wales. Rewrite the essay to reflect the opinions of his granddaughter Julie Jones, aged 18, of Tucson, Arizona, who knows very little of Welsh folklore and rejects what she has heard. Substitute *Miss Julie Jones* or *she* for every *Mr. Gruffydd Jones* or *he* that appears. Copy everything else and proofread carefully. Sentence 1 may be rewritten two ways: *Miss Julie Jones of Tucson, Arizona, does not know a great deal about ancient Welsh folk belief*, or *Miss Julie Jones knows very little about ancient Welsh folk belief*. Do not change sentences 6 and 16, and make the appropriate change in family relationships in sentence 9.

Welsh Folk Beliefs

---

¹Mr. <u>Gruffydd Jones</u> of Llangynwyd, Wales, knows a great deal about ancient Welsh folk beliefs. ²<u>He</u> wants to see the wisdom of his people preserved. ³<u>He</u> respects the beliefs of Wales as they are so many centuries old. ⁴Many of the beliefs, he feels, may be useful in explaining human experience and in giving enjoyment to everyday life.

⁵A folk belief that interests <u>Mr. Jones</u> is called second sight. ⁶Second sight describes the experience of seeing things before they happen. ⁷<u>He</u> can remember seeing the light of a train cutting through the darkness where the tracks were not put down until years later. ⁸<u>He</u> accepts the story of a neighbor who says he saw astronauts on the moon before the Americans landed in 1969. ⁹<u>He</u> is sure <u>his</u> mother was telling him the truth when she saw flying machines before the Wright brothers' flight in 1903.

¹⁰<u>Mr. Jones</u> thinks there are people with special powers, called *dyn hysbys* in Welsh. ¹¹The souls of the Druids, too imperfect for heaven and too good for hell, he says, inhabit the bodies of *dyn hysbys*. ¹²Such people, he will tell you, can always find money that has been lost. ¹³<u>Mr. Jones</u> believes the *dyn hysbys* always had the power to help a Welshman get out of an English jail. ¹⁴Anybody, good or bad, could be helped by the *dyn hysbys*, he adds.

¹⁵The Welsh custom that <u>Mr. Jones</u> thinks should be preserved is the *mari lwyd* procession during the Christmas season. ¹⁶In the *mari lwyd* procession, men follow a leader, who carries a horse's head, and go from house to house, sometimes engaging in a poetic contest with residents and often receiving a coin or a drink in return. ¹⁷<u>Mr. Jones</u> remembers how much people in his village always enjoyed the procession, even though the children were frightened by the horse's head. ¹⁸He believes residents always saved their best liquor to share with the men in the procession.

As you proofread, underline the changes you have made.

STEP 16   The two paragraphs below describe the way college ball is played. Continue to compare college ball to pro ball by continuing the essay and negating each of the statements in the second paragraph. Substitute *pro* for *college,* and make each sentence (except sentences 13 and 14) negative. Copy the first two paragraphs, and then continue with: *By contrast, pro players are not young and immature.* Proofread carefully.

Differences on the Gridiron

---

[1]According to a National Football League coach, there are considerable differences between college and pro ball. [2]College ball, he claims, does what it can whereas the pros do what they must to win.

[3]<u>College</u> players are young and immature. [4]Their skills need polishing. [5]For this reason <u>college</u> coaches prefer to run and are wary of the pass play. [6]They feel that the pass play is too risky. [7]Too many things can go wrong during its execution. [8]<u>College</u> teams are thus content to move on the ground toward the goal line. [9]The crowds at <u>college</u> games accept the slow, "grind it out" strategy without complaint. [10]Because mistakes happen frequently, there is a lot of improvisation, and this makes <u>college</u> games appear more exciting. [11]Crowds tend to think that <u>college</u> athletes are "gung-ho" and daring. [12]They are simply still developing their abilities and trying new things. [13]They have no other choice. [14]If they had one play that was sure to work, they would use it every time and not worry about being daring or exciting.

[15]By contrast, pro players are not young and immature.

As you proofread, underline the changes you have made.

Step 16

Writing Assignments: Negating and Contradicting

Your reader might sometimes be unaware of the fact that opposing views are truly in opposition. The simplest and most straightforward way of indicating disagreement is by negating. You can use your opponent's words and negate them by either adding a negative word or attaching a negative prefix.

1. Choose two antagonists from your field of study, present the view of one, and then have the other directly contradict the words of the first.
    a. Freud on dream interpretation vs. Jung.
    b. Marx on the economic system vs. Adam Smith.
    c. Mendel on heredity vs. Lamarck.
    d. Locke vs. Hobbes on human nature.
    3. Copernicus vs. Ptolemy on the solar system.
    f. Skinner vs. Freud on treatment of neurosis.
    g. Thomas Paine vs. Divine Right of Kings.
2. Choose opposing views from among contemporary ideas, present one, and then negate it from the other point of view.
    a. Gloria Steinem or Phyllis Schlafly.
    b. Adele Davis, natural food advocate, and a junk food enthusiast.
    c. A classical musician and a member of a rock group.
    d. A disco dancer and a ballerina.
    e. A nuclear power advocate and an opponent.
    f. A vegetarian and a meat eater.
    g. An advocate of mass transit and a builder of highways.
3. Find a review of a book, movie, play, or concert that is favorable. Contradict it in detail, turning the author's words against himself or herself.
4. Choose an editorial from your daily newspaper, and disagree with it, once again negating the words of the article.
5. Choose one of the letters to the editor, and negate or contradict it.

Step 17

Simple Synonyms

In this STEP you are asked to provide synonyms—words that mean approximately the same—for words selected in context. Here is an example:

> Version in text: It was dark when the *ship* set sail.
> Revision: It was dark when the *vessel* set sail.

Initially, this seems easy enough. Many students will be able to find a synonym after thinking about it for only a minute, just as in playing a word game. But no synonyms are exact, and many other choices will not work. A paddle-wheeler, an aircraft carrier, a submarine, and a tug are all ships, but we could hardly substitute any of them in this sentence. Similarly, a schooner, a frigate, a man-of-war, and a brigantine each has sails, but each is much more specific than "ship." A schooner is quite small, and the other three were warships before the introduction of steamships. "Vessel" is close to "ship," but it lacks the same flavor. We cannot describe neatness as "vessel-shape," nor can we say a sailor about to leave port is going to "vessel-out."

Many writers like Mark Twain's advice on synonyms: "The difference between the right word and the almost right word is the difference between lightning and the lightning bug." In a sense there are no real synonyms, no words that carry the exact flavor, meaning, and connotation of another. We can see how this works if we examine a list of synonyms in a thesaurus or dictionary of synonyms, the best-known of which is based on one compiled by Peter Mark Roget (pronounced "ro-ZHAY") more than a hundred years ago. Here are some synonyms for "dark" as a modifier in one contemporary thesaurus (not Roget's):

> —unlighted, dim, shadowy, somber, cloudy, foggy, sunless, indistinct, dull, faint, vague, dusky, murky, gloomy, misty, obscure, Stygian, crepuscular, tenebrous, obfuscous.

None of these will serve very well to replace "dark" in the sentence, "It was dark when the ship set sail." All the words have a suggestion of darkness in them, all right, but they carry a different flavor. If we say it was cloudy, sunless, or foggy when the ship set sail, we do not necessarily imply it was after sunset as the original sentence seems to say. If we say, "It was *murky* when the ship set sail," we seem to imply a moral and emotional climate as well as an atmospheric one.

The writer who selects a synonym from a thesaurus without having used the word before is tinkering with a booby trap. A sentence that reads, "It was Stygian when the ship set sail," is describing water like that in the River Styx before the gate of hell because "Stygian" is the adjective form of "Styx." Experienced writers use a thesaurus only as a way of finding a word already known, the lists serving to stimulate memory and imagination. Even at that, a careful writer would still check the newly selected word in a dictionary. Actually, one of the words on the list for "dark" comes close to the meaning of that word in our sample sentence. "Crepuscular" refers to twilight or the time of sunset, but it would sound overly formal in all but some specialized contexts.

Perhaps the best synonym for "dark" is a word not listed in the thesarus at all, "sundown." In the sentence "dark" could have been seen as a noun instead of a modifier; dark is a time as well as a description of the sky.

It was *sundown* when the ship set sail.

STEP 17   In the essay below, forms of two words—*create* and *call*—are used repeatedly. Rewrite the essay, selecting synonyms for the two words. Your objective is to eliminate the repetition, thereby injecting some variety in the choice of words in the essay. Make sure that the *form* of the substituted words is correct. Copy everything else and proofread.

Snap, Crackle, Pop, and the Sundae

---

¹Religion has made some unexpected contributions to the eating habits of Americans. ²The familiar sundae was created by some enterprising drugstore owner as a way of circumventing the Sabbath laws that made the sale of soda water on Sunday illegal. ³The ban forced the storeowner to <u>create</u> a fizzless soda. ⁴He combined fruits, nuts, syrup, and ice cream, leaving out the forbidden carbonated water. ⁵Consumers soon began calling this special dish, "Sunday soda," eventually shortening it to "Sunday" or "sundae." ⁶Religion has also figured prominently in <u>the creation of</u> breakfast foods.

⁷Seventh-Day Adventist Ellen Gould White established the Health Reform Institute at Battle Creek, Michigan, after she had a vision in which she was told that no one should eat meat, use tobacco, or drink whisky, tea, or coffee. ⁸It was at this divinely inspired Institute that Charles W. Post created a cereal beverage as a coffee substitute, <u>calling</u> it "Postum." ⁹It was also Post who <u>created</u> a dry breakfast food that he <u>called</u> "Elijah's Manna," naming it after the heavenly food that fed the Children of Israel in the desert. ¹⁰When the name did not appeal to the public, it was decided to <u>call</u> the cereal "Grape Nuts," and it is by that name that it is <u>called</u> today.

¹¹Patients at the institute lived on a vegetarian diet, with nut croquettes substituting for meat. ¹²It was for the benefit of a patient who had broken her false teeth that a visiting surgeon <u>called</u> J. Harvey Kellogg <u>created</u> crisp flakes made from ground corn. ¹³The patient could soak the flakes in milk and eat without trouble. ¹⁴Today, the name Kellogg and Corn Flakes are synonymous.

¹⁵Originally <u>created</u> for spiritual as well as physical health, breakfast foods made of cereals became immensely popular. ¹⁶At one time, Battle Creek, Michigan, birthplace of the American Manna, listed more than thirty manufacturers of dry cereals.

As you proofread, underline the changes you have made.

STEP 17   Rewrite the entire essay below, substituting synonyms for the underlined words and phrases. You should seek variety but retain precision. Proofread the entire essay carefully.

Occupational Hazards

¹What do beer drinkers, chicken neck wringers, and garage mechanics have in common? ²They have all had diseases of the finger named after them. ³The rings of pop-top beer cans, chicken necks, and high-pressure nozzles have been responsible for swelling, discoloration, dislocation, and perforation of fingers. ⁴The American Medical Association named these <u>diseases</u> after the occupations that caused them. ⁵The association officially lists Beer Drinkers' Finger, Chicken Neck Wringers' Finger, and Grease Gun Finger. ⁶There is even <u>a disease</u> called Scandinavian Blubber finger, common among Norwegian seal hunters. ⁷There is hardly any human activity, in fact, that has not had <u>a disease</u> named after it.

⁸A person taking up sports even casually risks a number of injuries. ⁹Children <u>risk</u> contracting Little Leaguers' Elbow and Frisbee Finger, as well as the more serious Banana Seat Hematuria, which is a contusion of the prostate gland from riding bicycle seats that are too narrow. ¹⁰Adult surfers <u>risk</u> Surfers' Knobs on their feet and legs and Ding String Injury about their ankles. ¹¹Swimmers are continuously <u>risking</u> Bathers' Itch and Bikini Dermatitis, and joggers <u>risk</u> Joggers' Heel and Joggers' Nipples. ¹²Even mountain climbers who survive the dangers of the trip up may be afflicted with Downhill Toe Jam on their way back.

¹³Nor will sitting still in the living room <u>keep hazards from your door.</u> ¹⁴Television Legs, an impairment of the lower back and legs, is acquired mostly by youngsters who spend long hours <u>glued</u> to the TV set. ¹⁵Television Neck <u>strikes</u> viewers of all ages. ¹⁶Perhaps the most deadly physical disease derived from watching television is Video Voodoo. ¹⁷Viewers tend to <u>come down</u> with symptoms they see portrayed on medical programs.

As you proofread, underline any changes you have made.

Step 17

Simple Synonyms

Helpful Hints and Special Situations

As stated earlier, no single word is an exact synonym for any other word. When we choose one word over another that means something similar, we also express something of ourselves. A measure of a creative writer's talent is being able to select the right word, the lightning instead of the lightning bug, as Twain said. We can see how this works when we try to substitute synonyms in the lines of a writer who has taken great pains to polish what is said. Consider, for example, Langston Hughes's famous poem, "Dream Deferred":*

> What happens to a dream deferred?
>   does it dry up
> Like a raisin in the sun?

Now, many things are dried in the sun other than raisins—how about another California product?

>   does it dry up
> Like a prune in the sun?

We can easily change almost every word. A fancier way of saying "happens" is "transpires." A dream is a vision. We can change "deferred" to "postponed," and "dry up" to the more scientific-sounding "dehydrate." And the sun is the star of our solar system. Watch what happens now:

> What transpires to a vision postponed?
>   does it dehydrate
> Like a prune exposed to the star of our solar system?

This may be clear, but it is not what most people would call poetry.

The choice of a synonym is not always poetic expression. Word choice can be used to soften a statement, making it sound less frightening or ugly. If we are describing a fat person in the most pleasant way, we might say the person is portly, husky, robust, or buxom; if the person were a woman we might say, "She is wearing half-sizes." Synonyms that try to say ideas in a nicer way are called *euphemisms*. Sometimes euphemisms are merely a pleasant way of dealing with an ugly or a touchy subject, but other times they are a means of preventing us from thinking clearly. When

---

*"Dream Deferred," copyright © 1951 by Langston Hughes. Reprinted from *The Panther and the Lash* by Langston Hughes, by permission of Alfred A. Knopf, Inc.

a writer substitutes "preowned" for "used" in describing a car, an attempt may being made to make us overlook or forget that we are really talking about a used car. Here are some other euphemisms whose intent may be to mislead:

Misleading Euphemisms	Plain, Honest Words
Internal Revenue Service	tax collector
inoperative statement	lie
released	fired
genuine imitation leather	fake leather
memorial park	cemetery
beautiful music	Muzak, dentist's office music

Another kind of synonym selection works for a different effect—to make the writer look more important. People in any of several professions, especially government bureaucrats, lawyers, and social scientists, seem incapable of saying anything simply. Given a choice, they will always take a more pretentious or self-important synonym. In plain English we can watch a child counting her fingers and say, "She finished counting." By selecting bureaucratic synonyms we get, "The infant in question finalized computation." Instead of answering a simple yes to a question, an inflated and self-regarding synonym is "affirmative."

To a degree this is harmless, if tiresome, unless the reader is actually misled. How many people would recognize a familiar proverb if it were rewritten this way:

Although a substantial plurality of the participants consulted have found that it is within the realm of possibility to escort or conduct any large, hoofed mammal (*viz., Equus caballus*) to a location providing a measurable quantity of a potable mixture of hydrogen and oxygen (not to be consumed in a gaseous or solid state), it is demonstrably affirmative that one cannot coerce the mammal (*Equus caballus*) to imbibe the mixture if it has not expressed a previous desire to do so.

Hint: *Equus caballus* is the scientific term for horse. "Potable" means drinkable, and water is a mixture of hydrogen and oxygen.

Lastly, although we have suggested that a thesaurus is of only limited use in finding the right synonym anyone who writes often will want to keep one handy. The name "Roget" is itself often a synonym for thesaurus, just as "Webster" means dictionary for many people. There are, however, many other fine works on the market compiled by other people. Here is a list of recommendations:

Bernstein, Theodore. *Bernstein's Reverse Dictionary*. New York: New York Times Books, 1975. Especially useful for antonyms.
Laird, Charlton. *Webster's New World Thesaurus*. New York: Collins-World, 1979. Known as *Laird's Promptory* in earlier editions.
G. & C. Merriam Company. *The Merriam Webster Dictionary of Synonyms and Antonyms*. Springfield: G. & C. Merriam Co., 1968.
Rodale, Jerome I. *Word Finder*. Emmaus, Pennsylvania: Rodale Press, 1970.

Roget, Peter Mark. *Thesaurus*, 4th ed. New York: Harper & Row, 1978.

————. *New Roget's Thesaurus in Dictionary Form*. Ed. N. Lewis, New York: Berkley Paperbacks, 1969.

————. *Roget's International Thesaurus*. 3d. ed. New York: Thomas Y. Crowell, 1962.

————. *Roget's Thesaurus of English Words and Phrases*. Ed. R. A. Dutch. New York: St. Martins' Press, 1965.

————. *Roget's Thesaurus of Words and Phrases*. New York: Grosset & Dunlap, 1970.

————. *Roget's University Thesaurus*. Ed. C. O. Mawson. New York: Apollo Paperbacks, 1972.

STEP 17   Rewrite the entire essay below, substituting synonyms for the underlined words and phrases. Do not change the meaning of any of the sentences. Proofread the entire essay carefully. Titles of plays and movies may be italicized by underlining.

The Wicked Witch of Maxwell House

¹American children first came to know Margaret Hamilton more than a generation ago when she played both the wicked witch and the hateful Mrs. Gulch in *The Wizard of Oz.* ²In all she has been in more than seventy movies. ³She has also performed in radio and television dramas as well as in her favorite medium, live theater. ⁴But in the 1970s she began to delight millions as Cora, the New England storekeeper who stocks only one brand of coffee—Maxwell House.

⁵Actually, Miss Hamilton was not born in New England but rather in plain old Cleveland. ⁶When she was in high school and college, she prepared to be a kindergarten teacher. ⁷Her first job was in Cleveland's Hough ghetto neighborhood, where she later opened her own private kindergarten. ⁸After a while she thought she might never get the chance to be a professional actress.

⁹Producers said she could never be a leading lady because of her big nose. ¹⁰In one high school play she had to play a man because of that nose. ¹¹But in college she once played a romantic heroine Jo in the beloved melodrama *Little Women.* ¹²But when she tried to make it as a character actress, the nose became an asset, first on the stage and later in movies.

¹³Although she is pleased with the continuing esteem of *The Wizard of Oz,* she thinks her performance shows no great skill in acting. ¹⁴She feels she did a better job in movies that have been forgotten. ¹⁵She says, "I have done some hard-bitten roles, but most of the time I have been cantankerous cooks or nasty-tempered aunts with a corset of steel and a heart of gold." ¹⁶On the stage she has played everything from classics like Sheridan's *The Rivals* to modern highbrow drama like *The American Dream.* ¹⁷Once she stole the show as the inactive high society courtesan in the Stephen Sondheim musical *A Little Night Music.*

¹⁸More recently Miss Hamilton has sold an immense amount of coffee as Cora the storekeeper, probably the most popular of all her roles.

As you proofread, underline the changes you have made; also underline titles of movies and plays for italics.

STEP 17   The writer in the essay below uses the word "move" in its many forms repeatedly. Rewrite the essay, substituting other words or expressions that mean the same things as the underlined words. Your purpose is to add variety to the essay. Proofread carefully.

Seasickness

¹Within the middle ear is the organ of Corti, which helps the body maintain its balance but is involuntarily also responsible for the dizziness and nausea of seasickness.

²The organ contains stiff hairs or cilia, which are surrounded by liquid. ³When the body moves, the liquid <u>moves</u>, <u>moving</u> the cilia. ⁴The hairs then send a message to the brain, which, in turn, informs the body of the direction it is <u>moving</u> and directs it to maintain its equilibrium. ⁵Under normal conditions, the body's <u>movements</u> are not extreme. ⁶The motions of the cilia are similarly limited, and the body can adjust to its messages easily.

⁷Adjustments become more difficult, however, aboard ship. ⁸As the deck <u>moves</u> beneath the feet, the liquid or lymph around the organ of Corti and beneath the cilia is shaken back and forth. ⁹The violent <u>movement</u> is transmitted to the hairs, which begin to wave wildly. ¹⁰One moment the message to the brain is to shift in one direction; the next moment the order is to shift in another. ¹¹The <u>movement</u> of the ship changes so quickly that the nervous system cannot adjust the balance in one direction before it has to maintain equilibrium in another. ¹²The result is total confusion in the organ of balance and in the part of the nervous system to which it is connected. ¹³Seasickness—headaches, dizziness, gagging—is an expression of this confusion.

¹⁴As there is no way to stop the lymph and cilia from <u>moving</u>, the the pill against seasickness works by paralyzing the part of the brain through which the message from the organ of Corti <u>moves</u>. ¹⁵Some people can cope by remaining in the center of the ship, where the <u>motion</u> is less extreme, both inside and outside the ears.

As you proofread, underline the changes you have made.

STEP 17   Rewrite the entire essay below, substituting synonyms for the underlined words and phrases. Do not change the meaning of any of the sentences. Proofread the entire essay carefully.

Tennis, Everyone?

¹Although tennis as we know it has been played for only about a hundred years, <u>predecessors</u> of the game go back a long way. ²Games in which <u>some kind of</u> ball was hit back and forth were played in ancient Egypt, Persia, and Greece. ³Historians believe the true ancestor of the <u>game</u> was brought from the Middle East by the Crusaders in the twelfth century. ⁴Tennis has gone through so many changes since then that few <u>early</u> players would recognize today's game.

⁵French monks played tennis inside their monasteries until 1245, when an archbishop <u>forbade</u> all clergy to play. ⁶Meanwhile, French <u>monarchs</u> had taken up the sport, and from then it spread to the royalty of other nations. ⁷The early form of tennis <u>was something like</u> handball. ⁸Both monks and kings <u>batted</u> the ball with their bare hands. ⁹The French still <u>designate</u> tennis "the game of the hand." ¹⁰After years of <u>injuries</u> and blisters, a protective glove was developed. ¹¹And by 1500 the first tennis rackets <u>superseded</u> the gloves.

¹²From the earliest times until just recently, tennis was a game for the elite. ¹³Royal palaces in Austria, England, and even Scotland <u>incorporated</u> tennis courts within their walls. ¹⁴King Henry IV of France <u>built</u> 250 courts in Paris alone. ¹⁵Not surprisingly, when the French Revolution came, one of the first <u>developments</u> against the royalty was in the tennis court at the Palace of Versailles.

¹⁶Outdoor tennis or "lawn tennis" is played over a <u>larger</u> area and with different rules. ¹⁷Major Walter C. Wingfield <u>developed</u> outdoor tennis at Wimbledon, England, in the 1860s when he noticed people getting <u>bored</u> watching croquet. ¹⁸A few years later an <u>upper-class</u> American lady, Mary Ewing Outerbridge, saw tennis played by English soldiers while she was vacationing in Bermuda. ¹⁹She brought home nets, rackets, and balls and <u>set up</u> the first modern American tennis court on Staten Island, New York, in 1877.

²⁰Today tennis is no longer just a game for the <u>rich</u>. ²¹One of the world's finest players <u>learned</u> on the public courts in Richmond, Virginia—Arthur Ashe.

As you proofread, underline the changes you have made.

STEP 17   Rewrite the entire essay below, substituting synonyms for the underlined words and phrases. Do not change the meaning of any of the sentences. Proofread the entire essay carefully.

Francesco A. Lentini:
The Three-Legged Man

[1]Not long ago a real three-legged man, Francesco or Frank Lentini, traveled with Ringling Brothers Circus. [2]Doctors who investigated him saw that a third leg was growing out of his right hip. [3]Lentini's third leg was actually a part of an undeveloped or incomplete twin. [4]The early diagnosis was that Lentini's appendage would not be cut off surgically without grave danger of death or paralysis. [5]Although other people with three or even four legs have been recorded, Lentini was the only one known to live a normal or nearly normal life or to have lived to the old age of seventy-seven.

[6]When Lentini was born in Rosolini, Sicily, the midwife who delivered him was said to have hidden him under the bed and run screaming from the room. [7]Feeling he was doomed to live as a human oddity, young Lentini suffered terribly from acute embarrassment and sank into deep depression. [8]Anxious to help their son, Lentini's parents took him to an institution for handicapped children. [9]There he saw blind, crippled, and terribly malformed children who were far worse off than he was. [10]"From that day to this," Lentini said later, "I have never complained; life is beautiful and I enjoy living it."

[11]When he was eight, Lentini's family came to the United States. [12]For years his father held off circus managers who wanted to sign the boy for a tour until young Frank could finish his education. [13]He traveled nineteen seasons with Ringling Brothers and later traveled with the W. L. Main Circus, Buffalo Bill's Wild West Show, and others. [14]He was traveling with the Walter Wanous Side Show when he died in 1966. [15]Part of his act was in employing his third leg as a stool as he sat with his two better legs crossed. [16]He could also kick a ball with the third leg.

[17]Although he had full control over his extra leg, he did not walk on it because it was three inches shorter than the others. [18]He could, however, leap, ride a bicycle or horse, drive his own car, ice-skate, and even roller skate. [19]He also swam, insisting that he could use his third limb as a rudder.

[20]When he bought shoes, he had to order two pairs. [21]From the second pair he used the right and gave the left to a one-legged friend. [21]"You see," he said late in life," my extra leg helps me to do good deeds."

As you proofread, underline the changes you have made.

STEP 17   Rewrite the entire essay below, substituting synonyms for the underlined words and phrases. Do not change the meaning of any of the sentences. Proofread the entire essay carefully.

The World Trade Center

¹Although the Sears Tower in Chicago and the CN Tower in Toronto are taller, the World Trade Center in New York is the world's <u>largest</u> building. ²The twin 1,350-feet, 110-story towers contain <u>such capacious</u> office space that each one has its own zip code. ³About 50,000 people work in the building, and another 80,000 visit it every <u>working</u> day. ⁴This means the building accommodates more people than <u>reside</u> in Albany, the state capital. ⁵The World Trade Center <u>holds</u> more than 40 percent of the population of the State of Alaska. ⁶Even at that, the towers <u>occupy</u> no more than two acres on the ground.

⁷Naturally, the designers of such a complex were faced with numerous problems, each of which they solved with imagination and daring. ⁸More than 1.2 million cubic yards of earth and rock had to be <u>dug up</u> from the site. ⁹The job of transporting such a massive load to a distant landfill site seemed <u>overwhelming</u>. ¹⁰Builders <u>cleared up</u> the problem by deciding to dump the dirt and rock on the shoreline, thus <u>actualizing</u> 23.5 acres of new land. ¹¹This new <u>territory</u> was then deeded to the city.

¹²To provide <u>sufficient</u> elevator service for so large a building looked as though it would require more than half the floor space of each tower just for elevator shafts. ¹³The <u>answer</u> to this problem was the "sky lobby." ¹⁴The towers <u>include</u> lobbies on the forty-fourth and the seventy-eighth floors as well as on the first. ¹⁵Passengers <u>bound</u> for the upper two-thirds of the building board large express elevators that scoot them to a sky lobby, where they board a second, local elevator that takes them to their floor. ¹⁶The system assures that no <u>passenger</u> will have to stop more than six floors before reaching a destination. ¹⁷More <u>significantly</u>, because the local elevators run only between one lobby and another, three elevators actually use the same shaft. ¹⁸In this way the 104 elevators in each tower <u>take up</u> only 13 percent of the floor area, as compared with 23 percent in most office buildings.

¹⁹Not the least of the problems was <u>figuring out</u> a way to wash 43,600 windows. ²⁰The solution to this was an automatic washing machine that slides up and down <u>the surface</u> of the building on a stainless steel track.

²¹The <u>bad part</u> about the World Trade Center is that it is going to cost much more to operate in the future. ²²It currently uses more energy than the <u>entire</u> city of Troy, New York, and the cost of that energy is going through the roof—even of the World Trade Center.

As you proofread, underline the changes you have made.

Step 17

Writing Assignments: Simple Synonyms

You should remember that words never mean exactly the same thing. Words can resemble each other, but they will ultimately separate. Their connotations will differ. The search for synonyms through a thesaurus or a dictionary is thus often no more than a search for just the "right" word rather than a search for another word that "means the same." You should remember this as you work on the exercises below. The exercises are important and helpful in that they will enable you to practice the search as well as the placement of the right word. When you find a word to replace the one you already have, you must make it "fit" the sentence grammatically.

1. Rewrite the selection in STEP 14 entitled "Towers of Junk." Substitute a synonym for at least one verb in each of the sentences.
2. Find alternative labels for "shopper" and "store manager" in the selection "Buying or Being Bought" in STEP 15.
3. Collect a list of phrases that newspapers use to identify political figures and find alternatives for them. (the junior senator from Oklahoma, the freshman congressman, the woman mayor)
4. Rewrite the selection "How Did They Begin?" in STEP 1, substituting synonyms for the work the various people are described as having done. (Desi Arnaz cleaned birdcages. Henry David Thoreau worked as a pencil maker.)
5. Write a brief description of a person you love or admire greatly. Find an alternative for each adjective that you use. Explain why one is more appropriate than the other.
6. Choose one of the selections in STEP 2 of this book. The instructions for the STEP ask students to substitute a number of words for the words already in the text. Consider the appropriateness of the substitutions. Discuss how close or how far from the original the "synonyms" are.

Step 18

Difficult Synonyms

When you are asked to substitute more difficult synonyms in this STEP, you may often have to come up with words that cannot be found in a thesaurus:

> Version in text: The platoon met *pockets* of resistance.
> Revision: The platoon met *isolated groups* of resistance.

The selection of synonym will depend entirely upon context. Anyone checking a thesaurus of "pocket" would find something like "purse, pouch, receptacle," and so on. Clearly, none of these will serve in the sentence above. Neither will they serve in the following sentences:

> Version in text: Arson was isolated in several *pockets* of the city.
> Revision: Arson was isolated in several *corners* of the city.

> Version in text: The commissioner always *pockets* a percentage of the fee.
> Revision: The commissioner always *steals* a percentage of the fee.

In a general sense, "pocket" refers to that part of our trousers or jeans where we carry our change, keys, broken pencils, tickets, and so on. We would not usually find a synonym for "pocket" in "isolated group," "corner," or "steal," unless "pocket" is used figuratively—as a metaphor. We often use figures of speech—especially metaphors—to enliven and make more vivid what we want to express. The metaphors we use so often that we barely think of them are called "dead metaphors" because they are now a part of the language in their metaphorical meaning. For example, if we call some one we think intelligent "bright" or "brilliant" we are apt to forget that those two words literally refer to light. Similarly, we use different parts of the body in metaphors that may not literally require the body to be used at all. For example, in helping two people resolve an emotional conflict, a counselor should try to help define just what is bothering the couple:

> The counselor *put his finger* on the problem.
> (Metaphor: he did not use his finger or his hands at all.)
> The counselor *pinpointed* the problem.
> (Metaphor: he did not use a pin.)
> The counselor *pointed out* the problem.
> (Still a metaphor: he did not use a pointer either.)
> The counselor *discovered* the problem.
> (Literal: we discover what we did not know before, whether it is a lost island, an unknown element, an idea, an emotion, and so on.)
> The counselor *named* the problem
> (Literal: to put a name on something is to discover it.)

The name for a word that means the opposite is *antonym*. "Bad," for example, is an antonym for "good." For the most part, antonyms are trickier to come by than synonyms are. "Dry" might be a good antonym for "wet," but what is a good antonym for "humid"? "Light," "fresh," or "airy" might do in the case of weather that is not humid, but what about a humid cellar or a humid complexion? Returning to weather, if we describe a day that is not humid as a "dry day," some listeners will assume only that it is not raining. Similarly, a day described as "sunny," "bright," or "clear" may or may not be one low in humidity.

For these reasons, a thesaurus will be of only limited use in finding antonyms. The best thesaurus will list only a few antonyms, perhaps only about one per two hundred synonyms. In general, however, antonyms are best determined from context.

STEP 18   In the essay below, note those words that suggest that it is foolish to be wary of Friday the thirteenth. Replace these underlined words with others that mean the same thing but are less harsh. Change only the words you must. Copy everything else and proofread.

Friday the Thirteenth

¹The <u>idiotic</u> belief in the dangers of Friday the thirteenth has its source in two <u>irrational</u> notions. ²Unpleasant events have been associated separately with Friday and with the number thirteen.

³The <u>ignorant</u> fear of the number goes back to pre-Christian days. ⁴According to the <u>unreliable</u> testimony of Norse mythology, a banquet with twelve gods in Valhalla was interrupted by Loki, the god of evil and strife. ⁵His presence, the thirteenth at the feast, led to the death of Balder, the most beloved of all gods. ⁶This <u>unreasonable</u> ill-will toward thirteen was also shared by some Greek philosophers. ⁷Fascinated by mathematical relationships, these thinkers preferred the easily divisible even numbers to the unpaired odd numbers. ⁸The number thirteen is unfortunate enough to be not only an odd number but also a prime number, divisible only by itself and one. ⁹<u>Incredible as it seems</u>, that was sufficient reason for the Greeks to develop an aversion toward thirteen. ¹⁰The Christian association of thirteen with calamity is based on the belief that there were thirteen participants at the Last Supper. ¹¹Judas, the thirteenth to appear, betrayed Christ, according to the Gospels, and was responsible for the crucifixion.

¹²The "bad press" that Friday has received can also be blamed on beliefs <u>accepted without question</u>. ¹³According to Hebrew legends, devils and demons were created on Friday, the sixth day of creation. ¹⁴Despite this, some primitive people thought Friday a lucky day, until the early Christians pointed out that the crucifixion occurred on Friday.

¹⁵Because <u>the superstitious are slaves</u> to these ideas, many hotels have no thirteenth floor, the house address between twelve and fourteen is often rendered as 12½, and airlines omit numbering the thirteenth seat on airplanes. ¹⁶When the thirteenth falls on Friday, some <u>absurdly credulous</u> people stay in bed, fully convinced that the forces of evil are at their most powerful and must be avoided.

As you proofread, underline the changes you have made.

STEP 18   Rewrite the entire essay below, substituting synonyms for the underlined words and phrases. Do not change the meaning of any of the sentences. Proofread the entire essay carefully.

Barry Manilow

---

¹Pop composer and singer Barry Manilow is <u>celebrated</u> by people who barely know his name. ²Nevertheless, he did have several albums <u>in the charts</u> during the seventies, five simultaneously. ³And even though some people hate his music as bubblegum, he has been the single most listened-to-musician of the past ten years. ⁴Not only have his albums sold, but his music has also been <u>hawking</u> Big Macs and Pepsi, too.

⁵Barry Manilow was born Barry Pincus in Brooklyn's tough Williamsburg neighborhood, but he took his mother's name when his father <u>walked out on</u> the family. ⁶He was, by his own <u>admission</u>, the kind of boy other kids beat up. ⁷His mother <u>gave</u> him music lessons on piano and accordion with tunes like "Tico, Tico" and "Lady of Spain." ⁸His stepfather, <u>a trucker</u> named Willie Murphy, introduced him to jazz. ⁹Still, Manilow was not <u>confident</u> enough in his talent to major in music in college, and so he started in business, which bored him. ¹⁰After some career indecision, he started working for CBS, <u>progressing</u> from mail boy to editor of commercials. ¹¹Meanwhile, his musical career <u>blossomed</u> when he learned more about the intricacies of arranging instruments in a band.

¹²His interest in music and his experience with advertising eventually <u>married</u> when Manilow began to write music for television commercials. ¹³Within a short time he had written commercial music for some of the giants of American industry and commerce. ¹⁴He <u>started rolling</u> with Maxwell House Coffee, Dodge Charger, and Kentucky Fried Chicken: "Get a bucket of chicken/Have a barrel of fun." ¹⁵He knew his career in writing commercials had <u>taken off</u> when he got commissions from Band-Aid, Stridex, and Pepsi Cola: "Join the Pepsi people/Feelin' free, feelin' free." ¹⁶The commercial song that the public <u>took to its heart</u> was the one for McDonald's: "You deserve a break today." ¹⁷But according to critic Jack Kroll, Manilow's greatest composition is the misty, <u>haunting</u>, lyrical cry of the insurance agent: "Just like a good neighbor, State Farm is there."

¹⁸What about the songs on his own albums? ¹⁹Hits like "Mandy" and "Weekend in New England" <u>bid</u> to be with us for a long while. ²⁰His "Daybreak" has been so popular that it has been translated more than twenty times, including into sign language for the deaf.

As you proofread, underline the changes you have made.

Step 18

Difficult Synonyms

Helpful Hints and Special Situations

Part of what makes this STEP more difficult than STEP 17 is that you must often think about the form of the word changed as well as the word itself:

The building was prepared for *a possible* breakdown.
The building was prepared for *a hypothetical* breakdown.
The building was prepared for *an imagined* breakdown.
The building was prepared for *a delusive* breakdown.

Each of these modifiers has a different ending, and as only one of them begins with a vowel, only one takes the article *an*.

Often a change of synonym means a change of more than one word:

The driver *took advantage* of the lead he had over the other racers.
The driver *capitalized on* the lead he had over the other drivers.

The warden *released* the prisoner.
The warden *let* the prisoner *go*.

The matters we are dealing with here are rarely problems for native speakers of English, but they pose continuing difficulties for people learning English as a second language. Why should we end the predicate "take advantage" with *of* and "capitalize" with *on* if both mean approximately the same thing? There is no logical reason for making the distinction. We just follow the customs and habits of the English language developed over the past thousand years. When these customs and habits become a fixed part of our language, we call them *idioms*. Some handbooks on writing give lists of idioms, and good dictionaries and thesauruses will tell much about them, but the best way to learn idioms is by continual immersion in the English language, speaking, reading, and writing.

One problem that even native speakers of English have with the customs and habits of the English language is the mixed metaphor. A metaphor is "mixed" when we forget that it is a figure of speech and ultimately refers to something unseen. For example, the expression "keep your eye on the ball" comes from a batting coach's advice or possibly a golf coach, but we also know that it means, "Pay attention." To "keep your nose to the grindstone" is a metaphor that means "work hard," but ultimately refers to treating one's body as if it were a farm tool such as a scythe. And to "keep your shoulder to the wheel" means to make great effort as one would in pushing a large wagon out of a ditch in earlier times. If we put all these expressions together, we get one of the best-known joking mixed metaphors: "Keep your eye on the ball, your nose to the grindstone, and your shoulder to the wheel." Outwardly, it means to pay attention, work hard, and make great effort, but the metaphors are so absurdly mixed that the sentence just sounds ridiculous. Other mixed metaphors are not so obvious:

> Literal version: Fred went to the Adirondacks *to begin learning* skiing.
> Mixed metaphor: Fred went to the Adirondacks *to try his hand at* skiing.
>
> (Does he ski on his hands?)

As we considered in STEP 17, words that denote approximately the same idea may come in a wide range of connotations. For example, a person who does not weigh much may be called "slender," "svelte," "trim," "thin," "hollow-eyed," "gaunt," or "skinny." The difference between "slender" and "skinny" may be more in the person making the judgment than in the person described; just how do we want to make the underweight person appear? The difference in connotation of words is frequently no simple matter; it may determine the way we understand social or political questions. For example, we may call the dominant economic system of the United State "capitalism." Enemies of the system call it "economic imperialism." Others may call it "free market economy" or the "profit and loss system." The differences in connotation here are so great that two speakers may not appear to be dealing with the same subject at all:

> The energy crisis should be solved by *the free market economy*.
> The energy crisis should be solved by *somebody who can make a buck on it*.

When the difference in connotation substantially changes our understanding of the idea denoted, we call that difference *semantic*.

STEP 18   In the report below, the Potters are complimented repeatedly for their ingenuity. The adjectives that describe the house are careful not to mock them. Rewrite the report by substituting for the underlined words other modifiers that do mock the couple. Make them appear to be crackpots rather than creative builders. Change only the adjectives. Copy everything else and proofread.

House of Hay

¹An <u>enterprising</u> Minnesota couple has created an <u>unconventional</u> but cozy home. ²Richard and Donna Potter have assembled 200 bales of hay into a house that seems surprisingly comfortable. ³The smell is a bit odd, but the Potters do not mind. ⁴"The whole thing cost me four hundred dollars to build," said the <u>clever</u> husband. ⁵"I can afford plenty of pine deodorant to cover up the hayloft smell."

⁶The two <u>ingenious</u> people utilized many different models in designing their <u>unusual</u> looking home. ⁷They got the idea for using hay from reading about Nebraskan settlers in the 1860s who had to resort to baled hay when they found no wood or stone in the area. ⁸The idea for the pole structure that shapes their home came from pictures the Potters had seen of Manitowoc Indian earth lodges. ⁹Twentieth-century technology supplied the layers of plastic beneath the sod and hay that keep the place dry. ¹⁰Light filters down from skylights, and heat is provided by a wooden stove, which is surrounded by six posts in the center of the house. ¹¹The total effect is somewhat <u>offbeat,</u> but the Potters prefer comfort to style inside their living quarters.

¹²The outside of the house is as <u>striking</u> as the inside. ¹³It has a peak where spruce poles radiate like the spokes of a wild umbrella. ¹⁴The house is hexagonal in shape and <u>interesting</u>-looking from all sides because of the stained-glass windows. ¹⁵The <u>inventiveness</u> of the Potters extends to the greenhouse, which takes advantage of the southern exposure.

¹⁶The couple is <u>justifiably</u> pleased with the <u>creative</u> living arrangement. ¹⁷The Potters seem to have managed to simplify their lives in an <u>unusual</u> but <u>ingenious</u> way.

As you proofread, underline the changes you have made.

STEP 18   "Avoid" and "Do not touch" convey a similar message, but the negative often carries a more powerful message. In the essay below, change the underlined directions or warnings in each sentence to a negative form of the word. Use *no* or *not* whenever you can but also try a negative prefix (*un, in*), or suffix (*less*). Make sure that you do not change the information in the essay. Proofread carefully.

Food and Drugs

¹Next time your doctor prescribes medication for you, make sure to ask him which foods and drinks you must <u>avoid</u> combining with the drug. ²Many foods and drinks can make ordinarily safe medicine either dangerous or ineffective.

³Milk, no matter how "natural," is a <u>bad</u> choice for washing down a tetracycline pill, one of the most common antibiotics. ⁴Separately each is fine. ⁵In combination, they are <u>harmful.</u> ⁶Another drug, MAO, frequently prescribed for depression, is <u>risky</u> if combined with aged cheese, chianti wine, yogurt, bananas, and chicken livers. ⁷Mixing drugs with foods that "clash" makes them <u>lose their effectiveness</u> or renders them downright dangerous.

⁸Other liquids to <u>keep away from</u> when taking medicine are carbonated drinks, beer, and fruit or vegetable juices. ⁹These drinks stimulate excess acid in the stomach, dissolving the drugs and bringing about their absorption too early. ¹⁰The drugs do more good if they dissolve in the intestines instead of the stomach. ¹¹They are more easily absorbed into the bloodstream from the intestines.

¹²In general, <u>beware of</u> taking alcohol with either prescription or over-the-counter drugs. ¹³It makes for a <u>hazardous</u> companion to antibiotics, antihistamines, and tranquilizers.

As you proofread, underline the changes you have made.

STEP 18   Rewrite the entire essay below, substituting synonyms for the underlined words and phrases. Do not change the meaning of any of the sentences. Proofread the entire essay carefully.

A Useful Optical Illusion

¹Motion pictures or movies do not really move at all. ²Our eyes <u>tell us</u> the pictures move because of a principle of optics called "the persistence of vision." ³The phrase "persistence of vision" was <u>coined</u> in a scientific paper in 1828 by Peter Mark Roget, compiler of the famous thesaurus. ⁴In the forty-seven years he labored on his book, he had time to <u>increase</u> his knowledge in other areas as well. ⁵Roget's report was an <u>observation</u> of <u>a small toy</u> that still exists. ⁶The device consisted of a stiff paper disk with strings attached to opposite sides so that the disk would <u>rotate</u> quickly when the strings were pulled tight. ⁷On one side of the disk was a picture of a horse and on the other a jockey. ⁸When the disk was spun, the jockey appeared to be on the horse's back because the viewer's brain still <u>remembered seeing</u> one side of the card by the time the other has come into view.

⁹Although Roget was working <u>at the same time</u> as several other investigators, not much was done to apply the persistence of vision <u>for several decades.</u> ¹⁰In the 1870s the governor of California, Leland Stanford, wanted to win a $25,000 bet. ¹¹He was sure the feet of a galloping horse all <u>left the ground</u> at the same time. ¹²To prove his point, he hired an English photographer named Eadweard [sic] Muybridge to <u>find a way.</u> ¹³Muybridge took twelve pictures at short intervals of a running horse along a track. ¹⁴When the pictures were put together and flipped through rapidly, the running horse <u>appeared to move</u> before the viewer's eyes. ¹⁵Under the principle of the persistence of vision, the brain retained one image of the photographed horse when the next one appeared. ¹⁶Although many more inventions, including a mechanized camera and celluloid reels, would have to be invented before what we call movies or the cinema could exist, Muybridge's experiments did in a real sense <u>father</u> the motion picture.

¹⁷Anyone who has ever handled a reel of movie film understands the persistence of vision very well. ¹⁸The reel comprises thousands of little frames, each complete in itself. ¹⁹By holding the reel up to the light, we see still photographs—sometimes of people now dead: John Wayne, Marilyn Monroe, W. C. Fields, or Charlie Chaplin. ²⁰But if we run those frames through a <u>machine</u> at the rate of twenty-four per second, we have the illusion of the dead coming to life before us.

As you proofread, underline the changes you have made.

STEP 18   Consider the underlined words or expressions in the essay below that speak of the use of tobacco negatively. Substitute synonyms that make the practice seem even more unpleasant. Change only the words you must. Copy everything else and proofread carefully.

Smoking

¹Tobacco and smoking have earned their <u>unsavory</u> reputations. ²The history of the <u>foul</u> activity contains many examples of unpleasant events that should have forewarned of the present <u>disrepute</u> of smoking.

³Tobacco was brought back to Europe by the Spanish in 1558, along with syphilis, another native American <u>product.</u> ⁴The use of tobacco spread rapidly. ⁵Jean Nicot, French ambassador to Portugal, did so much to popularize the <u>plant</u> that his name, in "nicotine," remains forever paired with "tar," the other <u>deadly</u> component of the leaf. ⁶The English adventurer Sir Walter Raleigh made perhaps the most dramatic endorsement of smoking when he chose to smoke a pipe as a last pleasure before his execution in 1618. ⁷Another notorious champion of the <u>habit</u> was the great lover Casanova. ⁸In his memoirs he speaks of puffing on Brazilian tobacco "wrapped in a little paper tube." ⁹Within a century, smoking had <u>enthralled</u> the entire Continent.

¹⁰North America fared little better. ¹¹The English at Jamestown had turned to tobacco as a cash item when they could find neither gold nor silver. ¹²John Rolfe, Pocahontas's husband, discovered the commercial possibilities of the leaf in 1612. ¹³In 1619 a Dutch ship delivered twenty African field hands to the tobacco growers at Jamestown. ¹⁴Well before it had a chance to bring about emphysema, smoking <u>triggered</u> human slavery in America.

¹⁵For three centuries the foolish prescribed tobacco to the credulous for all ailments. ¹⁶Users smoked it, chewed it, and snuffed it, <u>convinced of</u> its healing powers. ¹⁷Smoking was done mostly by wrapping loose tobacco in a leaf. ¹⁸The development of cigarettes was aided not only by Casanova but also by war. ¹⁹Discarded containers of gunpowder, "Dutch tubes," are thought by some to have been the first wrappers used around tobacco. ²⁰By the late 1800s demand had grown so great that industry accepted responsibility for cigarette production. ²¹In the United States it was the American Tobacco Company that <u>made addiction easier,</u> in the process developing into one of the <u>nastier</u> monopolies until "trust-busted" in 1911. ²²The <u>vice</u> has, of course, enriched a generation of lung surgeons as well as made the fortunes of the James B. Duke family. ²³It has given this country slavery, lung cancer, and Duke University.

As you proofread, underline the changes you have made.

STEP 18   Rewrite the entire essay below, substituting synonyms for the underlined words and phrases. Do not change the meaning of any of the sentences. Proofread the entire essay carefully.

The Great Wall of China

¹Of all the structures on earth built by human beings, only one is visible to someone on the moon: the Great Wall of China. ²<u>Wending</u> its way over more than one-twentieth of the earth's surface, the wall is an unparalled feat of engineering and human determination. ³In size, materials, and human labor, it is the <u>most herculean</u> construction project ever undertaken. ⁴If the wall were <u>picked up</u> and moved to the United States, it would stretch from New York City to Topeka, Kansas, not counting the branch walls that run off at angles. ⁵Enough stone was used in the entire project to build an eight-foot <u>belt</u> around the globe at the equator.

⁶Such an <u>enterprise</u> could not spring up overnight. ⁷The first eastern portion of the wall was built by an emperor <u>reigning</u> 200 years before Christ who employed an army of three million working for eighteen years. ⁸Later emperors continued the work for the next 1,700 years, but the <u>major</u> portion was done during the Ming Dynasty (1368–1643). ⁹In the eastern regions, the wall is built of stone <u>faced</u> with brick, reaching an average height of twenty-five feet. ¹⁰Here the wall is generally twenty to thirty feet wide at the base, <u>tapering</u> to fifteen feet at the top, wide enough to allow six horsemen to ride abreast.

¹¹In the west, however, the wall is not as <u>well made.</u> ¹²Here the wall is simply dirt covered with stone or merely <u>earth</u> piled into mounds. ¹³Today much of this section of the wall has <u>fallen into ruin</u> and, at points, is almost covered by drifting sands.

¹⁴Why such a Gargantuan project was <u>undertaken</u> is not known for certain. ¹⁵Historians once thought the wall was built for defense against <u>barbaric</u> Mongolian invaders, but if that was its purpose, it failed repeatedly. ¹⁶Many determined invaders were successful in <u>breaching</u> the wall. ¹⁷Because of its size, the wall was expensive to maintain. ¹⁸More than 24,000 gates and towers <u>dot</u> the wall over its <u>serpentine</u> course. ¹⁹For all the soldiers it took to <u>man</u> the wall, there were only a few in any given mile.

²⁰More recent historians have suggested that the wall was really only a make-work project. ²¹For example, many ancient Chinese cities had <u>decorative</u> walls that did not serve defensive <u>ends.</u> ²²Perhaps the Great Wall was really a <u>guard</u> against unemployment for 1,700 years.

As you proofread, underline the changes you have made.

Step 18

Writing Assignments: Difficult Synonyms

Once again, "synonym" is a bit inaccurate in that the new words you seek very clearly intend to do something else than the words already in the text. Still, the forms have to be grammatically correct and the words "similar" to the ones already in the text. The exercises below ask you to continue the type of work you were doing in STEP 18, as well as to work in opposites, or "antonyms."

1. Consider the essay "Helping Lefties" in STEP 14. Rewrite the essay, softening the harsh terms used in it against right-handed people.
2. Find a "rave review" of some book, movie, concert, play, or restaurant; and make the adjectives be more restrained. Soften the enthusiasm.
3. Find a nasty review of one of the above (nasty reviews are easier to find), and try to negate the pejorative statements by changing adjectives.
4. Ask around and list all the names that you and your friends use to address various members of the family. Does the variety correspond to a variety in attitudes?
5. Listen to some advertisements, and make a list of the words they use that suggest positive attributes. How do these words make their appeal? What happens if you substitute words similar in meaning?
6. Find a description of some invention or discovery that is considered beneficial. Rewrite part of it from the point of view of someone who has been harmed by it. (the railroad—farmers, dams—environmentalists, aviation—homeowners near airports, nuclear power—pacifists, space exploration—people in humanities)
7. Find a description of some unpleasant or unfortunate situation. Try to extract from it a "silver lining." One defender of the Vietnam War has argued that more people have been saved through medical advances developed during the war than died in it.
8. Make a list of the nouns used in articles to indicate a female human being. Compare the list to a selection of nouns used to indicate males. Any differences? Is "woman" used as an adjective? In what situations?

Step 19

Appropriate Language

Usage describes the many aspects of spoken or written English determined by habit or custom. One of those aspects is appropriateness; one kind of English is appropriate where we work or at a party, and another kind is appropriate in writing. In this STEP you must find the usage appropriate in college *writing* and avoid those usages found only in *speech*. For example, we might hear some one say, "The editor is plastered," and we would understand that the editor was drunk. "Plastered" is *colloquial* or *informal* English, often appropriate in speech, whereas "drunk" is *standard usage*, a kind of usage more appropriate in college writing. *Standard usage* does not mean stuffy or pompous English. Instead, it is the usage that is appropriate anywhere, in speech or in writing. Although *informal* or *colloquial* English is appropriate only in speech, there are other kinds of usage appropriate only in writing: *formal, legal literary,* and *scholarly;* in one of these we might describe the editor as intoxicated or inebriated.

This chart will partially explain the relationship:

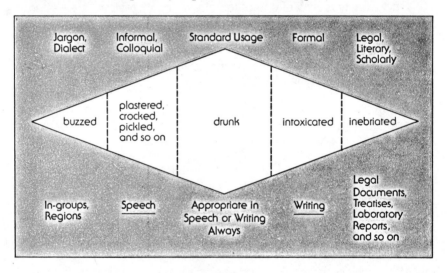

Though "drunk" is appropriate most often, "buzzed" and "inebriated" are appropriate less often, in part because fewer people recognize what they mean. Neither "buzzed" nor "inebriated" is bad English, however. "Buzzed" would be spoken by very few people and would rarely be written. "Inebriated" sounds put-on in speech and would be appropriate in writing only among readers used to such words.

As our chart tries to show, the lines between standard usage and colloquial or formal usage may be crossed from time to time. Many writers today try to imitate the flavor of spoken English in their writing, but there are still many kinds of writing where the author does not have that choice. A student writing a term paper on alcoholism cannot describe a person as "plastered" and still expect to be taken seriously. The words we have under-lined and asked you to change are all of the kind that would not be appro-priate in standard written English.

This STEP does not deal with *nonstandard usage* or what used to be called "bad English," such as "the editor ain't sober" or words like "irre-gardless," "nowheres," "anywho," and so on. Although we hear such usage every day, the speaker of such words is simply unused to the habits and customs of the majority of educated people.

STEP 19   In the following passage several words and phrases are underlined because they are inappropriate for usage in college-level writing. Find substitutes for the underlined words and phrases so that the entire passage will be in standard usage.

The Pyramids of Egypt

¹Few people realize how old or what a <u>gigunda</u> building project the Pyramids of Egypt were. ²<u>Building on</u> the Pyramids got started <u>around about</u> five thousand years ago. ³That means there is more than half again as much time between the building of the Pyramids until the time of Christ as there is from the time of Christ <u>until us.</u> ⁴They are more than twice as old as the Parthenon of Greece.

⁵There are a lot of pyramids <u>all over the place</u> in Egypt, but the biggest of them all are the three at Giza, <u>right next</u> to the Sphinx. ⁶The biggest of these three is that of Cheops (or Khufu). ⁷The immensity of this construction <u>blows the mind.</u> ⁸Visualize a large tract of land like a modern athletic field, <u>say,</u> Shea Stadium. ⁹Over this area is a <u>pile of rocks</u> more than forty stories high. ¹⁰As Cheops' <u>thing</u> was meant to be a tomb, it is interesting to realize that one could <u>squeeze</u> in the Vatican and Westminster Cathedral in the same area and still have room left over.

¹¹<u>And</u> it <u>sure</u> took <u>a lot</u> of man hours to build the Pyramids. ¹²The work was done without the use of machinery or animals of any kind—not even the wheel. ¹³To build Cheops' pyramid, the <u>boss on hand</u> needed 100,000 men working full time for a period of twenty to thirty years. ¹⁴Each stone in the pyramid had to be carved out of solid limestone. ¹⁵Each one weighed about two and a half tons and had to be dragged up a ramp that surrounded the pyramid during construction. ¹⁶Because of the number of stones the <u>guys</u> had to repeat this <u>backbreaker</u> two and a half million times.

¹⁷<u>But</u> how much stone was used is <u>the real gasser.</u> ¹⁸If the pyramid of Cheops were <u>knocked down</u> there would be enough stone to build a wall all around France. ¹⁹If all the pyramids of Egypt were <u>busted down,</u> there would be enough stone to build a wall ten feet high and five feet wide running <u>clear across</u> the United States from New York City to Los Angeles.

As you proofread, underline the changes you have made.

STEP 19   Rewrite the essay below, substituting more appropriate language for the underlined words or expressions. Copy everything else and proofread carefully. Remember, you would like to make the language appropriate for a college essay.

Getting Drunk

¹The first alcoholic drink people could <u>get high</u> on was beer. ²An 8,000-year-old clay tablet from Babylonia describes the preparation for a kind of beer. ³By the year 4000 B.C. (nearly 6000 years ago), Babylonians could <u>shop around</u> and <u>get bombed</u> on sixteen different kinds of beer. ⁴In fact, beer (and probably the <u>lush</u>) was known to most of the ancient peoples. ⁵There are records that the Egyptians, the Chinese, the Incas of South America, and the natives of North America were <u>getting a nice buzz</u> from beverages made of fermented corn, barley, or other cereals. ⁶Why this interest in <u>tanking up</u>?

⁷Alcohol, like all narcotics, paralyzes nerve cells, but, before it paralyzes, it stimulates those nerves, <u>getting them all stirred up.</u> ⁸Booze, especially if <u>it's</u> sweet and warm, stimulates the gastric and salivary glands into producing juices. ⁹<u>That's why, first of all,</u> alcohol makes people hungry. ¹⁰For this reason, many people stir their appetite with a cocktail or sweet wine before the meal. ¹¹<u>Then, as you start dumping more and more of the stuff inside you,</u> alcohol begins to affect the brain. ¹²People breathe more quickly and their heart rate <u>goes up.</u> ¹³Their skin flushes, their blood pressure rises, and their speech and movements <u>go out of whack.</u>

¹⁴While alcohol is taken into the body slowly, in weak solutions, it continues to act as <u>an upper instead of a downer.</u> ¹⁵But, eventually, people <u>get good and stewed</u> if they continue drinking. ¹⁶Their ability to think and concentrate becomes affected as their nerve cells are paralyzed. ¹⁷Other nerves in the body called "inhibitory fibers" also become paralyzed. ¹⁸Restraints people have built up over the years through training and education relax. ¹⁹When they have reached a state of drunkenness, they may do things that they would never do if they were sober.

As you proofread, underline the changes you have made.

Step 19

Appropriate Language

Helpful Hints
and Special Situations

The most difficult part of this STEP in trying to know what informal or slang expressions really mean. Most standard dictionaries will be of little help as will dictionaries of slang, such as you might find in the college library. One of the disadvantages of slang and informal expressions, especially the ones that get used all the time, is that they are imprecise. The word "hassle," for example, may mean anything from a duty or responsibility to being arrested for a felony. These examples should show what we mean:

> The dean *hassled* Cheryl about her grades. (Did he mention them in passing? Put her on academic probation? Dismiss her from college?)

> Improved: The dean *advised* Cheryl about her grades. (He told her to take fewer hours and easier courses.)

> It is too much of a *hassle* to go to the ball game. (Long lines at the ticket windows? Inadequate parking? The disappointment of losing teams? Marauding street gangs?)

> Improved: It is too much of *an expense* to go to the ball game.

> Kathy *is hassling* Ed about his breath. (Does too much garlic make his kisses undesirable? Halitosis? Does Ed have smoker's hacking cough? Emphysema?)

> Improved: Kathy *is complaining* to Ed about his breath. (She gave him some breath mints to cover the halitosis.)

An additional difficulty with informal or slang usage is that it dates so quickly. Out-of-date slang has a way of characterizing a speaker or writer as much as hair styling or clothes. "Kook," "kooky," and "mod" were popular words in the sixties, but their use today tends to give them a meaning quite different from what they were intended to mean. If we call something "mod," which is supposed to suggest "modern" and "contemporary," we are more likely to imply something fifteen years old. Similarly, easy college courses were Mickeymouse in 1965, gut courses in 1970, and cake courses today.

Although you have been asked to change examples of slang and informal usage to a kind more appropriate in college writing, that does not mean to imply such expressions are somehow wrong or that they are never appropriate. For one thing, we are—as a culture—much less formal than we used to be. We can see this in our dress as well as our language; before 1940 all college graduation photos featured men in tuxedoes and women in long

204

gowns. In such a context a word like "hassle" might be as out of place as a belch. One good reason to use slang or colloquialisms from time to time is that some are more vivid and direct than their more formal counterparts. That is why "rip-off" is now used more frequently than "robbery" or "thievery" even in such a formal environment as a presidential news conference.

There are, in addition, some situations in which slang and informal English are more honest and fitting than their formal counterparts. If you were writing about pop musicians (themselves a rich source of colloquial English), you would sound a bit stilted if you said they went out to buy clothes instead of threads. If the pop musicians were British, they would go out to buy gear. Likewise, if you were writing about an army private in World War II, you would refer to the lower-ranking officer as a second louie.

Many of us were told in grade school that any informal or slang expression was all right in writing as long as we put it in quotes. Doing this implies we are using an expression some one else said and that we would not stoop to it ourselves. This is not only prissy, but the quotation marks themselves tend to imply we have some doubt about this word we are quoting. Look what happens when we put quotation marks around an ordinary word in standard usage:

Bonita knew she could rely on her "real" friends.

This reads as though the friends are not real friends at all—only that they said they were. Now, this is what happens when we put quotation marks around an informal or slang expression:

The meter maids kept "hassling" Clyde for parking there.

This sounds as though the meter maids may not be pestering Clyde at all; maybe he just *says* they are.

(Quotation marks may be used for other purposes that do not suggest quotation of any kind. We use them frequently in this book to designate words spoken of as words; for example: "Hassle" is a rather vague slang word.)

STEP 19   In the following essay, several words and phrases are underlined because they are inappropriate for usage in college writing, even for an essay about a pop music star such as this one. Find substitutes for the underlined words and phrases so that the entire passage will be in standard usage.

Elton John

¹Little Reginald Dwight was a <u>fatso kid</u> growing up near London in the fifties. ²His father <u>hassled</u> him so much that he was afraid of playing in the family garden for fear of <u>mashing</u> the roses. ³An only child, ugly, with glasses, he was virtually without <u>sidekicks.</u> ⁴Who would ever expect that this <u>little schnook</u> would grow up to be Elton John, the world-famous <u>honcho</u> of glitter rock?

⁵Although his father <u>bad-mouthed</u> pop music, John's mother used to <u>slip</u> him Little Richard and Jerry Lee Lewis records. ⁶American rock 'n' roll blew young John's mind, and he started <u>thumping out</u> the music on the family piano. ⁷He took piano lessons at the <u>big-shot</u> Royal Academy of Music from ages eleven to sixteen. ⁸After that he started playing with <u>piddly</u> suburban bands. ⁹For a couple of years he played with a group called Blues Energy, whose members included Elton Dean and John Baldry, giving him the <u>brainstorm</u> for his new name. ¹⁰" 'Reg Dwight sounded like a cement mixer," he remembered later.

¹¹Answering a newspaper ad for a songwriter when he was twenty, John found his professional career really <u>begin to take off.</u> ¹²Answering the same ad was Bernie Taupin, John's future <u>buddy-buddy</u> collaborator on <u>oodles</u> of songs. ¹³John and Taupin began to write for singers they secretly <u>mocked-out,</u> like Engelbert Humperdinck and Lulu, but soon they were writing the kind of music they wanted to write. ¹⁴Their first salable single was "Lady Samantha," which critics said sounded like a <u>rip-off</u> of Paul McCartney and José Feliciano. ¹⁵Their first album was an <u>el cheapo,</u> produced in a basement for $1,200, but it sounded lavishly orchestrated and highly professional.

¹⁶The <u>big thing</u> holding back John's career was that he did not want to make live appearances; the reason he was shy was that he was too fat and self-conscious. ¹⁷After struggling to get the <u>blubber</u> off, John <u>took a gander</u> at his conservative wardrobe and knew he needed new threads for the stage. ¹⁸In Los Angeles at his first live concert he wore the wildest outfit he could find: the Elton John style was born. ¹⁹The <u>mousy</u> little <u>butterball</u> from London was now the <u>weird</u> hero of theater rock, doing handstands on his keyboard in front of thousands of <u>bellowing</u> fans in Madison Square Garden.

As you proofread, underline the changes you have made.

STEP 19   The essay below contains many words or expressions that are too informal or colloquial. They may be quite clear or effective, but they are also inappropriate in college essays or inconsistent with the diction elsewhere. Rewrite the essay, substituting more appropriate diction for the underlined words or phrases. Copy everything else and proofread carefully.

The World Is a Garden

¹The gooseberry <u>isn't</u> related to a goose, the strawberry has no connections with straw, and walnuts <u>don't flop off walls.</u> ²Actually, <u>a lot</u> of the familiar fruits and vegetables have names that reveal their international origins.

³The names describe either the <u>looks</u> or the origin of the fruits. ⁴The goose in gooseberry is a version of the Saxon word "gorst," meaning "rough," a reference to the berry's thorny shrub. ⁵"Grape" is the <u>same in</u> English as the Italian "grappo" and the French "grappe," meaning "bunch," whereas melon is <u>just plain</u> Greek for "apple." ⁶On the other hand, currant and cherry come from Corinth and Cerasus, two <u>really old</u> cities where the fruits <u>supposedly</u> originated, say <u>various folks in the field.</u> ⁷The greengage plum is a combination of description and discovery. ⁸Lord Gage introduced it into England, and, unlike most fruits, this one is green when ripe.

⁸Vegetables <u>show</u> their homelands and sources <u>the same way.</u> ¹⁰Tomato (not really a vegetable) is the West Indian word for love-apple. ¹¹Chestnuts, according to some sources, <u>came across</u> from the city of Castana. ¹²The "wal" in walnut is from the Saxon "wahl," which <u>translates out into</u> "foreign," which is how the Saxons described it because it <u>could've come</u> from Persia. ¹³<u>In the meantime,</u> spinach <u>started life</u> as "Hispanach," the Arabic word for any plant from Spain. ¹⁴A <u>funny</u> name like "pomegranate" is <u>really exactly right</u> because it means "a fruit with many seeds," in Latin "pomum" for fruit and "granatus" for many seeds.

¹⁵<u>By the way, like I said before,</u> the names are descriptive. ¹⁶The straw in strawberry is a form of "stray," a description of the way in which the runners <u>went off every which way.</u> ¹⁷The "cran" in cranberry was once "crane," a characterization of the stalks looking like the long legs and neck of a crane.

As you proofread, underline the changes you have made.

STEP 19:   The essay below, although well organized and free of mechanical problems, contains underlined words and phrases written at an inappropriate level of diction. Rewrite it, choosing language that is closer to college writing. Do not change the meaning or alter the overall organization. Proofread carefully.

Jogging Junkie

¹I've been running for years. ²My greatest problem has not been stamina or strength but people. ³I can deal with dogs that snap at my heels but not with cars that have tried to run me off the road and people who have thrown things at me from their front lawns. ⁴I'm finally getting the message that nonjoggers really have it in for joggers.

⁵What gets them about us is our sense of freedom. ⁶We're not controlled by the weather the way everyone else is. ⁷I was once on a four-mile run in weather most people would consider pretty crummy. ⁸It was around zero and was snowing a lot. While I was loping along, ignoring the storm, I could see the people in their cars getting pissed off at me. ⁹I was moving and they were standing still. ¹⁰They looked like they were baby-sitting their cars. ¹¹I looked like a free man. ¹²They sure looked resentful of my freedom.

¹³The other thing that ticks them off about us is that we're in better shape than they are. ¹⁴People who don't exercise very often are aware of the fact that they are mistreating their bodies, and they don't want to be reminded of it. ¹⁵They know that jogging is the best way to get into shape. ¹⁶Coaches know that nothing builds stamina and endurance like running. ¹⁷Nonjoggers can ignore athletes, but they can't ignore a plain guy like me who's in shape because he gets off his butt and works at it. ¹⁸So they try to run you down.

¹⁹Finally, sedentary people envy us our peace of mind. ²⁰We have this serene look on our faces when we jog because it was no hassle being out there running. ²¹We didn't have to wait for anyone to get ready. ²²We just picked up and ran. ²³Also, we are at peace because we are not competing with anyone else. ²⁴We run for the fun of it. ²⁵A successful mile for me is one that was pleasant, not one that was fast. ²⁶Oh yeah. ²⁷That peaceful look on my face also tells that I'm calm about my health. ²⁸I don't have that worried look those jerks in their cars have who think any sudden move will bring them a heart attack.

As you proofread, underline the changes you have made.

STEP 19: In the following essay, several words and phrases are underlined because they are inappropriate for usage in college writing. Find substitutes for the underlined words and phrases so that the entire passage will be in standard usage.

April Fool's Day

[1]There are lotsa reasons given for the origin of April Fool's Day or All Fools' Day, but we cannot be sure which, if any, of them is right on. [2]The custom of setting aside a day for dopey practical jokes, like putting salt in sugar bowls, may go back to ancient India or Rome. [3]It all depends on whatcha call an April Fool's joke.

[4]The essence of the April fool's joke is an errand, question, or riddle designed to make the guy responding look like a jerk. [5]Kids and greenhorns are often sent on April Fool's Day errands, partially as a means of showing them just how out of it they are. [6]A typical April Fool's Day errand would be to look for a left-handed monkey wrench. [7]In short, the point of that day in April is to make a nudnick of somebody who is unaware or inattentive.

[8]Some explanations of the origin of the day seem off the wall. [9]For example, a lot of historians think the custom may date from a time when asylums let the loonies out for a day at a time; however, no record of such a policy exists. [10]Some holy joe cultural historians see the origin of the day in as many as two different episodes in the Bible. [11]One was when Noah sent out a dove to find land and it never showed up again. [12]Or the day may be an ironic commemoration of Christ in that lily-livered Pilate and the stuffed-shirt priests sent Christ back and forth on fool's errands. [13]Both of these are unlikely, however, as customs much like April Fool's Day exist in non-Christian countries.

[14]Maybe the best bet to explain the day comes from the change in the calendar over the years. [15]Under the Julian Calendar used in the old days, New Year's Day was March 25. [16]Because the jollies of New Year's Day sometimes coincided with Easter Week, the festivities were delayed until April 1. [17]In 1564 the Catholic countries of Europe took on the Gregorian Calendar, which jumped New Year's Day back to January 1. [18]Almost 200 years later in 1752, the Protestant countries, including England and her colonies in America, followed suit. [19]In all countries hayseeds from the sticks were slow to adapt to the new calendar. [20]They were the continual butts of city slickers' jokes when they came to town to pay their taxes for the new year.

[21]However it got started, April Fool's Day is now our international holiday for tomfoolery.

As you proofread, underline the changes you have made.

STEP 19: In the following passage several words and phrases are underlined because they are inappropriate for usage in college writing, even for an essay about a personal recollection such as this one. Find substitutes for the underlined words and phrases so that the entire passage will be in standard usage.

Being a Stranger in Canada

¹When I first went to Canada, I thought <u>a lot</u> of it looked like an <u>add-on</u> to the United States. ²Roadsides have the same visual blight: McDonald's Golden Arches, Holiday Inns, and Shell Gas Stations. ³But after <u>moseying</u> around, I could see I was in a <u>bona fide</u> foreign country, one where the average U.S. citizen might feel <u>like a creature from outer space.</u>

⁴While I was still in the car, I <u>got a load of</u> speed signs that read, "Limit 100." ⁵But down in the corner they sneak in "kph," meaning "kilometers per hour." ⁶In the metric system 100 kilometers per hour is <u>even Stephen</u> with about 62 miles per hour. ⁷<u>That</u> metric system <u>can throw you</u> until you get used to it. ⁸For example, when I left Buffalo, I knew Toronto was about eighty miles away, but the first marker I <u>took a gander</u> at said, "120"—kilometers, of course. ⁹Then again, some of the metric system sounds really <u>mellow.</u> ¹⁰Although Canadian gasoline costs just a little less than ours, they sell it at twenty cents a liter.

¹¹When Canadians <u>gab</u> about their money, they sound as though <u>they're</u> talking about our money; they have pennies, dimes, quarters, and dollars. ¹²All their coins have the <u>real live</u> queen on them instead of dead presidents as we do. ¹³Their <u>folding money</u> comes in different colors. ¹⁴The only greenback they have is the $1 bill, but the front of it is yellow. ¹⁵They use the $2 bills <u>a lot,</u> which is a <u>weird</u> orange-brown on both sides. ¹⁶The $5 bill is plain blue, but the bigger bills are <u>really wild.</u>

¹⁷I found that most Canadians think <u>it's</u> bad manners for us to use our American money in their stores as though we were putting down their currency as Monopoly money. ¹⁸It was a <u>weird</u> feeling to be in a Canadian crowd, blending in with the <u>locals,</u> until I opened my wallet. ¹⁹With all the money in there the same color, I felt like <u>some kind of freak.</u>

As you proofread, underline the changes you have made.

Step 19

Writing Assignments: Appropriate Language

Formal language also needs its appropriate time. Used in the wrong situation, it can sound pretentious and pompous. Formal language can also be vague, long-winded, and meaningless. In short, neither formal nor informal language is "better." Rather, each is apt for particular situations. You can move more easily through language if you can distinguish among the choices available for various situations. The assignments here ask you to practice transforming informal language to more formal language.

1. Write down the sentences in your other essays in which your instructor found language he or she considered too informal. Rewrite them, using more appropriate language.
2. Compare the language in two newspapers, using the same news items as a basis for comparison.
3. Select an article or story from a magazine that specializes in informal writing, *People,* for example, and rewrite the piece, using more formal language.
4. Choose some letter you have received that was written using an informal style. Rewrite it, using formal language. (Is anything lost?)
5. Exchange essays with a fellow student. Read each other's essay for informal language. Rewrite informal sentences, making them formal.
6. Tape a conversation (or transcribe one). Rewrite it, making it formal.
7. Read the essay "Frazier and Friend" in STEP 13 in this book. Rewrite it substituting formal language for Frazier's informal words.
8. Select a passage in a textbook that seems particularly incomprehensible because of the jargon, and "translate" it.

Step 20

Fresher Diction

In writing, "diction" means the use, choice, and arrangement of words. Some words cause a writer to lose a reader, not because they are misspelled or ungrammatical but because they are tiresome. Words and phrases that once sounded vivid or witty often become simply boring through too much use. Using some of these may be forgivable in conversation when a speaker cannot think of anything better quickly, but a phrase like "sticks out like a sore thumb" or "a sight for sore eyes" at the beginning of a piece of writing is likely to announce that the author has little new to say. Any writer interested in reaching a reader can find better ways of phrasing hackneyed and trite phrases, clichés, and redundancy.

Here are the kinds of words and phrases to avoid:

Hackneyed words/phrases: these include stock words and phrases that are used so often they barely mean anything anymore. They are called "hackneyed" because they are like hacks or taxis, always available for hire. Examples would include: "a blushing bride," "a cold sweat," "old man winter," "a ripe old age," and so on. But most brides don't blush; and even if one does, why not try something original like "the flustered, shamefaced, embarrassed, deep-breathing, or laughing bride."

Triteness: this describes something that was once meant to be funny but is no longer. There apparently was a time when "dead as a doornail" or "raining cats and dogs" struck someone as witty, but that time has long since passed. Although triteness should generally be avoided, some trite phrases can be regenerated with a little work. For example, "lower than a snake" comes alive again when it is "lower than a snake in a wagon track." Or he's not a "diamond in the rough," he's a "zircon in the rough."

Clichés: these are hackneyed or trite expressions whose meaning is made unclear though overuse. "Cute as a bug's ear" is a cliché; are bugs' ears really cute? "Let him stew in his own juices" is a more ambitious cliché, but a person might be more likely to pickle than to stew in his or her own juices. Similarly, grasshoppers' knees are really only .015 inches high, so anyone would be taller than one. Some sore thumbs fold in instead of sticking out. Avoid clichés like bad breath—as well as the plague, smallpox, and bad habits.

Redundancy: redundant expressions say the same thing more than once. Someone who writes, "My car is red *in color*" has wasted the last two words; what else is red but a color? There is no need to write, "The globe is spherical *in shape*," because the word "globe" means spherical. Other examples are more likely to slip by; the sentence "The *reason* I am broke *is because* my check did not arrive" is redundant because *the reason* means *because* and *because* means *the reason*. The sentence could be improved in two ways: "I am broke because my check did not arrive," or "The reason I am broke is that my check did not arrive."

STEP 20:   The essay below contains many examples of trite and redundant diction. Substitute fresher or more vivid language for the underlined expressions, and eliminate redundancies. Copy everything else and proofread carefully.

The Busy Fortune Cookie

¹Over the years the fortune cookie has been <u>as busy as a bee,</u> carrying a variety messages.

²There is a <u>traditional custom</u> in ancient China of slipping wedding and birth announcements into small cakes and sending them around with messengers. ³There is also a game in which players are handed cookies containing bits of paper. ⁴The participants must compose <u>impromptu</u> essays <u>right on the spot</u> on the subjects written on the pieces of paper. ⁵And, according to legend, leaders of an uprising <u>spread the word</u> about the exact time of the revolt by stuffing notes into moon cakes and distributing them to the revolutionaries.

⁶The modern fortune cookie was devised around 1918 by a Chinese immigrant <u>fresh off the boat</u> named David Jung. ⁷World War I had just ended; times were hard and jobs scarce. ⁸Jung thought of wrapping little messages of <u>good cheer</u> into tiny pastries and sending them to his depressed Los Angeles neighbors. ⁹Unsure of his <u>command of the English language,</u> Jung enlisted the services of a Presbyterian minister, who filled the cookies with <u>Biblically inspired bits of wisdom.</u> ¹⁰Later, Mrs. Marie Raine, a greeting card <u>versifier,</u> took over the writing of the messages, which Jung had begun baking into cookies his Hong Kong Noodle Company was supplying to <u>establishments for dining pleasure.</u>

¹¹More recently, Billy Wilder used fortune cookies to promote his movie, "The Fortune Cookie," and Kathleen Parker, a California politician, <u>buttonholed</u> potential voters with them. ¹²Fortune cookies have also been used to <u>hawk</u> jobs, cars, and electricity. ¹³Today cookies with messages <u>spread like wildfire.</u> ¹⁴The messages range from X-rated notes to warnings of misfortune. ¹⁵The persistent shopper can also locate Pot Luck Fortune Cookies, packaged especially for <u>your friendly neighborhood</u> marijuana smoker.

As you proofread, underline the words you have changed.

STEP 20:   In the following essay, many examples of clichés and trite or hackneyed diction have been underlined. Substitute fresher, more vivid words or phrases for the underlined examples. In addition, some examples of redundancy are underlined; in the case of those, you may decide to eliminate the underlined word entirely.

The Director of *Star Wars*

[1]When George Lucas was growing up in Modesto, California, nobody thought he was as smart as a whip. [2]He used to hang around the main drag, McHenry Street, in his souped-up Fiat. [3]He thought he might become an auto racer until an accident doomed him to disappointment. [4]The reason he barely squeaked through high school was because he wasted so much of his time. [5]With his poor grades, his parents did not want to fork over the money to send him away to art school, and so he settled down at Modesto Junior College.

[6]It certainly was a red letter day in young George's life when Hollywood cameraman Haskell Wexler visited the college. [7]The old master Wexler took one look at Lucas's short films, and he could see the boy was a budding genius. [8]He helped Lucas to get into the grand and glorious film department at the University of Southern California. [9]While there, he had the great good fortune to sell his student film project, *THX-1138*, to big-time move distributors.

[10]Although *THX-1138* was arty and somewhat depressing, it met with thunderous applause from the critics. [11]Real success came fast at its heels with *American Graffiti*, a nostalgic look down memory lane about Lucas' high school days in Modesto. [12]Because in reality Lucas had been a rank outsider, a car customizer, and a bookworm, his own life serves as a basis for three characters in the film. [13]This movie really stood out from the crowd. [14]Made for a mere $780,000, the movie brought in $50 million. [15]After this Lucas was the producers' fair-haired boy who could do no wrong.

[16]Although *American Graffiti* had been made for adolescents and teen-agers, Lucas said his next movie would be "for children of all ages." [17]He really put on his thinking cap and pored over what he had loved as a boy, from Marvel Comics to Flash Gordon serials. [18]He really burned the midnight oil for three years, putting his nose to the grindstone eight hours a day on a new filmscript. [19]He scared up more than $9 million for production in Tunisia and England.[20] Upon its release in 1977, *Star Wars* was a success beyond Lucas's wildest dreams. [21]Audiences and critics went for it head over heels. [22]At present it is the numero uno financial success of all times, with box offices receipts and attendance plus spin-offs, books, toys at approximately around a half billion dollars.

As you proofread, underline the changes you have made; also underline the titles of movies for italics.

Step 20

Fresher Diction

Helpful Hints and Special Situations

You will doubtlessly find this STEP more difficult to do than the three before it that also require substitutions. Part of the reason for that is the lack of reference books providing answers. More importantly, you must now think about expressions that most people use without thinking at all. What is the author who uses a trite expression or a cliché really trying to tell us?

In geology class Marcia *stuck out like a sore thumb*.

From this we can tell that Marcia felt uncomfortable in the class and that she felt many eyes upon her. It also seems that Marcia's discomfort is related to her being noticed. When someone attracts unwanted or undue attention, we may call that person conspicuous. We can now revise the sentence with less tiresome diction:

In geology class Marcia *was painfully conspicuous*.

The word "painfully" can easily be overdone as some writers cannot describe someone as shy without adding "painfully shy." In any case, "painfully conspicuous" is better than a "sore thumb" because the clichéd phrase can mean so many different things:

The teams' yellow uniforms *stood out like sore thumbs* in the league.
The teams' yellow uniforms *were the most garish* in the league.

The drive-in *stood out like a sore thumb* on the block (which is also a mixed metaphor).
The drive-in *contrasted badly with the fine houses* on the block.

The green and maroon geisha wallpaper *stood out like a sore thumb*.
The green and maroon geisha wallpaper *was incredibly ugly*.

Some writers may wonder how anyone—such as an English teacher— can say that an expression is trite, hackneyed, or clichéd. Why should anyone have such authority? Well, the judgment is not personal. It comes to anyone with experience, just the way anyone can know that a joke is old or that a style is out of date. No expression was tiresome or clichéd the first time it was used. Some, indeed, were first used by our finest writers; expressions like "all Greek to me," "paint an inch thick," and "green-eyed monster" first appeared in the plays of Shakespeare. But if Shakespeare were alive today, he would not use them again because they have been heard so often the wit has been beaten out of them. Their use today would imply to the reader or listener that the author was not thinking very hard or that he had little new to say; this was never true of Shakespeare.

Many writers ask, What is wrong with phrases like "dead as a doornail" or "scared as a rabbit" if everyone uses them and everyone understands them? Everyone who studies writing seems to agree that the writing that communicates best is the simplest.

The problem with trite or hackneyed diction and clichés is not that they are tiresome or imple. Instead, such words and phrases most often indicate that the writer has given up thinking about what he or she is trying to say. For example, we might meet and have to describe a person who can give us a good deal of background on a subject. If we say, using the cliché, that the person is a "veritable mine of information," we imply that this person seems to be endowed, as if by nature, with what we need to know; we need only go to the person and draw out what we want. "Veritable" is just an excuse to say the person really is like a mine. But the expression pays no attention to why or how the person has the information, whether he or she is always telling the truth, or why the person might want to share the information with us. Trite and hackneyed expressions and clichés becomes less and less true when they are used millions of times by hasty writers who just stick them into the middles of lines without thinking. Do we speak of "intensive purposes" or "intents and purposes"? Do we "tow the line" or "toe the line"? Is a whip smart or does it make a smart? Anyone who cannot answer these questions—and even those who can—should never use such expressions in writing that readers are supposed to believe.

STEP 20:   The essay that follows contains words and expressions that are trite, redundant, or meaningless. Substitute fresher, more vivid language for the underlined phrases. In the case of repetition, you might want to eliminate one of the expressions altogether. Copy everything else and proofread.

American Classics

---

¹There are certain products made in the <u>good old U. S. of A.</u> that have become <u>virtual</u> classics for their trustworthiness and dependability. ²The Zippo lighter is <u>number one</u> <u>at the top of this list;</u> the company is still receiving unsolicited <u>testimonials that extoll the product.</u> ³A Mississippi man wrote that he lost his Zippo while quail hunting and found it two months later, <u>still in perfect working condition.</u> ⁴A fisherman swore he landed a flounder and discovered a Zippo in its belly that still zipped when he flicked it. ⁵Part of the popularity of even the <u>basic, no-frills</u> Zippo was the distinctive little wind chimney that allowed it to light in the <u>stiffest</u> breeze. ⁶The lifetime guarantee, a <u>one-of-a-kind deal</u> <u>unique</u> to Zippo, did not hurt business either.

⁷Another classic item people <u>swear by</u> is the old Singer sewing machine. ⁸<u>No less a famous personage</u> than Mahatma Gandhi spoke up for this <u>great</u> <u>little</u> machine. ⁹The Indian leader had learned how to sew loincloths while in jail and is said to have remarked that the Singer was "one of the few useful things ever invented." ¹⁰One upstate New Yorker had a model from 1920 that she claims lasted <u>through thick and thin</u> for fifty years, never needing a repair.

¹¹Other products of American <u>know-how</u> that have earned <u>soft</u> <u>spots in people's hearts</u> are the Hoover upright vacuums, the Kodak 2A Box Brownie camera, and the Waring blender, bankrolled and popularized by bandleader Fred Waring. ¹²And, of course, the Duofold, a fountain pen from Parker, was <u>ahead of its time.</u> ¹³It survived, for one Ohio man, a toboggan ride down the Swiss Alps, and three years in a Japanese POW camp.

¹⁴Many of these products still survive, though they can be found under different names and are made by different companies. ¹⁵The Duofold, for example, <u>resurfaced</u> in 1972 as Big Red.

As you proofread, underline the changes you have made.

STEP 20:   In the following essay, many examples of clichés and trite or hackneyed diction have been underlined. Substitute fresher or more vivid words or phrases for the underlined examples. In addition, some examples of redundancy are underlined; in the case of those, you may decide to eliminate the underlined word or phrase entirely.

Happy Birthday to You

¹One of the <u>most widely known</u> songs <u>that all people love</u> is "Happy Birthday to You." ²Many people think this <u>little gem</u> is a folk song, but that—<u>amazingly enough</u>—is not the case. ³Actually, two <u>dear little</u> sisters, Mildred J. and Patty S. Hill, wrote the song. ⁴Their original version, titled "Good Morning to You," was published in 1893. ⁵It was not a <u>rousing success.</u> ⁶At first the sisters worried about the song's lack of popularity <u>to no avail.</u> ⁷Then they <u>put on their thinking caps.</u> ⁸Eventually, they <u>got a bolt from the blue.</u> ⁹Birthdays are more a cause for singing than a simple good morning, and so they decided to change the first two words of the song to "Happy Birthday."

¹⁰The rest is history. ¹¹This plain and simple song is part of the <u>universal</u> birthday ritual <u>known round the world.</u> ¹²Modern people <u>from all walks of life</u> know the song today. ¹³Many of the worlds' children know the song more readily than their nations' national anthems. ¹⁴In many parts of the globe a waitress carrying a <u>birthday</u> cake with <u>candles</u> will cause a restaurant's patrons to burst <u>spontaneously</u> into song <u>without encouragement.</u>

¹⁵<u>Last but not least,</u> the sisters renewed their copyright on the song in 1939, which means the copyright is still in effect. ¹⁶This requires <u>professional</u> musicians who perform "Happy Birthday to You" for money to pay royalties to the sisters' estate. ¹⁷The cost of each performance is small, but the worldwide total of the royalties is <u>a tidy sum.</u> ¹⁸Of course, if every single performance of the song paid royalties, the sisters would have ended their days <u>by rolling in dough.</u>

As you proofread, underline the changes you have made.

STEP 20: Sports stories are often filled with their own clichés and redundancies. In the story below, substitute more vivid or more precise language for the underlined expressions. Proofread carefully. Remember, the objective is to make the language fresher and more exact. Clichés eliminate meaning. Restore it.

Costello's 32 Straight

[1]Wilt Chamberlain's 100-point game for Philadelphia against the New York Knicks on March 2, 1962, was the greatest shooting exhibition in NBA history. [2]But that same season, on December 8, 1961, Larry Costello of the Syracuse Nationals went on a <u>shooting binge</u> that is still <u>inscribed in the record books.</u>

[3]The Nationals were facing the Celtics in Boston in front of their always <u>rabid and partisan</u> fans. [4]Costello, one of the last two-hand set shot artists on <u>the hoop circuit,</u> was Syracuse's <u>playmaker and floor general,</u> usually content to <u>dish off</u> to teammates with <u>accurate, pinpoint</u> passing. [5]That night, however, Costello <u>shot the eyes out of the nets,</u> connecting repeatedly with his <u>patented</u> set shots. [6]He took eleven shots in the first half and made them all, keeping the Nats in the game. [7]Not even a <u>brief bout of fisticuffs</u> between Boston's Jim Loscutoff and the Nats' Dave Gambee could slow him down. [8]<u>Cool as a cucumber,</u> Costello <u>stayed hot.</u>

[9]In the third quarter he hit his twelfth and thirteenth consecutive baskets. [10]Because he had also <u>pumped in</u> six straight from the foul line, those baskets gave Costello 32 straight points. [11]His first miss was a <u>desperation heave</u> from midcourt just before the buzzer ending the period.

[12]Costello took only one more shot after that, missing it. Boston's early <u>scoring barrage</u> proved too much, and the Nats found themselves on the <u>short side</u> of the final 123–111 score. [13]But Costello had the satisfaction of a shooting performance that the game's greatest shooters have not been able to match.

As you proofread, underline the changes you have made.

Step 20

Writing Assignments: Fresher Diction

Clichés are bad habits. They are automatic responses to words. "Sky" comes with "blue" without thinking. Thinking might help the writer remember other colors; looking will certainly reveal different shades. Worn expressions, even redundancies, indicate stock responses. Consider what you want to say, and select the word or expression intentionally; don't allow your "automatic pilot" to take over.

1. Write down the sentences that contain trite language in other essays you have written. Rewrite the sentences, choosing fresher diction.
2. Listen or read a politician's speech. Catalog the repetitions and clichés. Substitute more original expressions.
3. Listen to an inning of baseball or to a series of downs. Try to list the very familiar expressions with which sports announcers fill their descriptions. Try to substitute words or expressions closer to what you can actually see. (Is a "line drive" always hit on a line? What is a "slashing type of a runner"? What is "some kind of a game"? A "tailor-made double play"?)
4. Read the official explanation for some disaster—a plane crash, flood, snowstorm—and try to rewrite the repetitious and trite statements.
5. Make a list of expressions people use at special occasions. What language is used when congratulations, condolences, good wishes are offered? What expressions are used to respond to those statements? Can those expressions be revived?
6. Consider the language of various advertisements. Do they utilize clichés? Trite expressions? Redundancy? Rewrite some well-known jingles. Is their impact lost?
7. Make a list of clichés (8 to 10) that utilize comparisons, for example, green as grass. Write another list alongside the first one. At random, crisscross the comparisons. How do the new expressions sound? Rearrange them again, trying for matches.
8. Read the gossip column in your local newspaper or in a magazine. List the clichés and repetitions. Substitute more vivid language.
9. As an alternative to the previous assignment, substitute straightforward language for the roundabout expressions and clichés in the columns. Write what the author really means when he or she writes that two famous stars are "on the outs" or "consoling each other."

Step 21

Choosing Premodifiers

A common defect in a writer's style is using too many words when fewer would do as well. We call this "verbosity." Reducing verbose writing takes effort. The writer must learn how to cut words from each sentence and still communicate the same ideas. The examples in the following STEP are designed to do just that. Consider the following:

> Hal is interested in buying insurance *to cover his car in case of an accident*.

The last nine words in that sentence are a postmodifier of the word "insurance." Because we know that insurance is supposed to provide coverage, we can communicate the meaning of the entire nine words with one three-letter word, "car," if we make it a premodifier:

> Hal is interested in buying *car* insurance.

Here are some more examples:

> The antiques will be sold at an auction *that is open to the public*.
> (postmodifier)
> The antiques will be sold at a *public* auction.
> (premodifier)

In these two examples, one word selected from the postmodifier could serve unchanged as the premodifier. In some other instances in this STEP, the word may have to be changed a little.

> The policeman ticketed the cars *of all the residents of the apartments*.
> The policeman ticketed all the *apartment residents'* cars.

> The coach made the team perform exercise *each and every day*.
> The coach made the team perform *daily* exercise.

STEP 21:   In the essay below, form a single word from the underlined phrases or clauses. Then place the newly formed word before the word in **boldface** type that precedes each of the underlined phrases. Copy everything else and proofread. Your first sentence should read: *Close your eyes and try to walk in a straight line.* (*That is straight* became *straight* and was placed before *line.*)

Walking in Circles

---

¹Close your eyes and try to walk in a **line** that is straight. ²Inevitably you will move toward one side. ³If there would be sufficient space for it, you would stray further and further from the center, eventually completing a circle. ⁴People lost in the fog or in a snowstorm invariably circle back to the **point** where they started, thinking all the while that they are walking in a straight line. ⁵This inability to avoid the circle can be explained by the asymmetry of the **body** of a human being.

⁶The left side and the right side of the human body are not balanced. ⁷The heart on the left side has no **organ** that corresponds to it on the right. ⁸The liver on the right is not balanced by an organ on the left. ⁹The spine is more or less in the center, but it is not **straight** to a perfect degree. ¹⁰The thighs are **different** to a slight extent in size and shape. ¹¹The **feet,** also undependable, are of unequal length, which is why you should always try on your new shoes on both feet.

¹²As a result of this lack of symmetry in the organs and bones, the muscles are **asymmetrical** in structure as well. ¹³The lack of balance **affects** as a consequence the way a person walks. ¹⁴When the eyes are closed or external means of guidance are obscured, the control of the gait or walk depends on the message of the muscles and body structure. ¹⁵Because there is no balance, one side dominates, and that side forces the wanderer to turn in a certain direction. ¹⁶The **person** who is lost ends up walking in a circle.

As you proofread, underline the changes you have made.

STEP 21:   In the essay below, words in **boldface** type are followed by underlined phrases or clauses. Rewrite the essay, choosing from the underlined expressions a word that would come *before* the word in **bold print.** *The standard Hershey bar consisted of two ounces of milk chocolate and sold for ten cents in 1950. (The Hershey bar we consider standard* became *The standard Hershey bar.)*

The Chocolate Chase

[1]The **Hershey bar** <u>we consider standard</u> consisted of two ounces of milk chocolate and sold for ten cents in 1950. [2]Today it weighs 1.2 ounces and sells for twenty-five cents or more. [3]The rising cost of **chocolate** <u>that is found naturally</u> has prompted experimentation with 500 different chocolate substitutes. [4]True "chocoholics" do not, however, accept **flavoring** <u>that is artificial.</u> [5]They would rather not interrupt their 400-year-old romance with chocolate and pay willingly for the "real thing."

[6]In the seventeenth century cocoa was brought back to Europe by the Spanish. [7]The Aztecs had enjoyed the naturally bitter taste of cocoa, but the Spanish preferred it sweetened with sugar. [8]**Chocolate** <u>that was both hot and sweet</u> became the rage of the Spanish court. [9]Perhaps because it was thought to have **powers** <u>as a restorer of tired spirits</u> and to work as an aphrodisiac, the use of cocoa spread to Italy, Austria, and French. [10]**Artisans** <u>from France</u> created elaborate chocolate servers for the court of Louis the XIV, whose wife, Maria Teresa of Spain, presented him with chocolates as a **gift** <u>on the occasion of their engagement.</u>

[11]**Developments** <u>in the nineteenth century</u> helped make chocolate more accessible. [12] A Dutchman, C. J. Van Houten, patented a process that made cocoa easier to mix with water, and **Daniel Peter** <u>from Switzerland</u> created milk chocolate under the name "Nestle." [13] Finally, Milton Hershey, an American businessman who had failed as a printer and candy maker, developed a formula for making **chocolate** <u>that was successful.</u> [14]Derry Church, Pennsylvania, became the town of Hershey, and **chocolate bars** <u>made by Hershey</u> became available to millions.

[15]The best chocolates in the world? [16]According to Adrienne Marcus, author of *The Chocolate Bible,* Sidney Bogg Chocolates of Detroit and Van Leer Chocolates in Jersey City make **products** <u>that are outstanding.</u> [17]On the other hand, she suggests, French chocolates are **inferior** <u>without any question.</u>

As you proofread, underline the words you have changed.

Step 21

Choosing Premodifiers

Helpful Hints
and Special Situations

What difficulties you encounter in this STEP should be minor. As you are to choose a premodifier, you need only pick out the key word from the postmodifier, the whole of which is clearly identified. Often you can make this switch without changing a key word at all:

> Thomas Edison patented many inventions *that were useful.*
> Thomas Edison patented many *useful* inventions.

Some other premodifiers will require slight changes. Of these, the trickiest by far is the switch from plural postmodifiers to singular premodifiers, even when the noun modified does not change number:

> Pancho bought a racket *that cost 200 dollars.*
> Pancho bought a *200-dollar* jacket.

> The pilot announced a delay *of twenty minutes.*
> The pilot announced a *twenty-minute* delay.

> Kathy drove a car *made by the Germans.*
> Kathy drove a *German*-made car.

This change from plural to singular will come easily to native speakers, but it is difficult to understand for people learning English as a second language. There is no logical reason for our making such a change; it is just English idiom—the way we do it by custom.

Other changes are easier to classify. If the word being modified is a noun, the premodifier must take the form of an adjective:

> Geraldine was not interested in the career *of an athlete.*
> Geraldine was not interested in *an athletic* career.

> Senator Claghorn praised the accomplishments *of blacks.*
> Senator Claghorn praised *black* accomplishments.

This also means that when the key word chosen from the postmodifier is a verb, it, too, must take the form of an adjective—as a participle. The present participle, which you are likely to use more often, always ends in *-ing*. The present participle of "start," for example, is "starting." The past participle, which you are likely to use often, usually ends in *-ed*. The past participle of "chill" is "chilled." Many commonly used verbs take irregular past participles; see Appendix 2, pages 284–286.

The horses approached the gate *where they started*.
The horses approached the *starting* gate.

Wayne would only buy wine *that was put in the cooler to chill*.
Wayne would only buy *chilled* wine.

The most versatile premodifier is the adverb, which nearly always takes the ending *-ly*. An adverb may modify a verb, an adjective, or another adverb:

The Brinks guards handled the big diamond *with care*.
The Brinks guards *carefully* handled the big diamond. (modifies the verb "handled")

When the guards opened the safe, they noticed the gem was different *to a slight degree*.
When the guards opened the safe, they noticed the gem was *slightly* different. ("different" is an adjective.)

That night a new guard left the office so quickly *it seemed exceptional*.
That night a new guard left the office *exceptionally* quickly. ("Quickly" is an adverb.)

Lastly, when two or more premodifiers come in a row, they may need a comma to separate them:

Bobbie bought a red blouse *that was washable*.
Bobbie bought a *washable*, red blouse.

On the other hand, some premodifiers are so much a part of the words they modify that there is no need to separate the additional premodifier with a comma:

Donna bought a fur coat *that was large*.
Donna bought a *large* fur coat.

STEP 21:   In the essay below, form a single word from the underlined phrases or clauses. Then place the newly formed word before the word in **boldface** type that precedes each of the underlined phrases. Copy everything else and proofread. Your first sentence should read: *Most people do not realize that many of the characters in Wonder Women comic books are drawn from ancient mythological gods and heroes.* In sentences 2 and 3 you should observe that the adjective form of "King Arthur legends" is "Arthurian" and the adjective form of "Norse mythology" is simply "Norse."

Wonder Woman and Mythology

[1]Most people do not realize that many of the characters in Wonder Woman comic books are drawn from **gods and heroes** that come from different ancient mythologies. [2]By checking over back issues one can see hundreds of examples from the **mythology** of the Greeks and Romans, or Norse mythology, and from the **legends** about King Arthur. [3]Often characters like Merlin, the **magician** of King Arthur, and **Odin,** the chief god of Norse mythology, will appear in the same episode with the Roman Mars and Hercules.

[4]Even Wonder Woman herself, who goes through life under the alias of Diana Prince, is a blend of different myths. [5]The name "Diana" comes from the **goddess of the hunt** in Roman mythology. [6]At the same time she is one of the **Amazons** of Greek legends. [7]The comic book Amazons are ruled over by **Hippolyte,** the queen of the Amazons, who lives on Paradise Island, where men are not allowed. [8]Although the ancient Hippolyte is also queen of the Amazons, she has several **friends** who are male, unlike the modern one. [9]The **Hippolyte** of Wonder Woman comic books worships Aphrodite, goddess of love, but the ancient one is independent of her.

[10]Some other changes are more startling. [11]Neptune, the **god** of the sea in Roman mythology who is male, is transformed into a female Olympic swimming champion named Leona Masters in 1944. [12]During World War II this **Neptune** who is female sinks **ships** of the Allied cause until Wonder Woman stops her. [13]Similarly, in ancient mythology, Pegasus is a **horse** who can fly. [14]But in an **issue** appearing in 1962 the comic book Pegasus undergoes a miraculous transformation so that he becomes a silent **airplane** that is invisible.

[15]One **god** of Roman mythology who is male is always a baddie when he deals with Wonder Woman. [16]This god is Mars. [17]The **Romans** who were military-minded worshipped Mars, the god of war, but in the modern comic book he is the **ruler of the planet Mars** who is iron-

<u>fisted.</u> [18]He believes that women are the natural spoils of war and will not tolerate giving them **freedom** <u>of the slightest kind.</u> [19]In **issues** <u>of more recent vintage</u> Wonder Woman has had the best of him. [20]He has not been seen since 1967 when Wonder Woman defeated his crimson centipede.

As you proofread, underline the changes you have made.

STEP 21:   In the short essay below, change the underlined phrases and clauses into one or two words that come before the word or words in **boldface** type. Essentially, you will be simplifying the language, reducing the number of words and phrases. Copy everything else and proofread. In your first sentence, for example, *with X-ray vision* can be written as *An X-ray satellite.*

The Violent Cosmos

[1]A **satellite** with X-ray vision has sent photographs back to earth that show space to be "wildly active," not at all the **sky** that is filled with serenity human beings have thought it to be.

[2]The stars appear to be fixed and unchanging to the **eye** of a human being. [3]This is because radiation from **stars and galaxies** that are distant is filtered by the earth's atmosphere. [4]The satellite's X-ray vision makes this radiation visible. [5]Photographs showed **quasars** that were twinkling and **X-ray stars** that were blinking, going off and on every few seconds. [6]The sky, seen with X-ray eyes, is a "violent, changing thing," said Dr. George Clark, one of the principal scientists in charge of this project.

[7]Another dramatic **event** of the cosmos the satellite photographed was the cataclysmic explosion of a star. [8]The supernova, as this is called, occurs when a **star** that is massive and fast-burning runs out of nuclear fuel and collapses, ejecting its outer layer into a shell known as a supernova remnant. [9]Astronomers believe that the universe began as hydrogen and helium, which **combined** after a while into higher forms and became the complex elements necessary for life. [10]These elements were then shot into space by supernovas. Billions of years later they coalesced into new stars and planets. [11]Only a dozen of these explosions have been recorded since the birth of Christ, making the present photographs **valuable** in the extreme. [12]They are, after all, shots of the birth process of the universe.

[13]The photographs also revealed **information about "black holes"** that is fascinating. [14]There is no upheaval apparent near black holes, but much **activity** of a violent nature is taking place about them. [15]The density of black holes is so great that gravity keeps even light from escaping.

As you proofread, underline the changes you have made.

STEP 21:   In the short essay below, change the underlined phrases and clauses into one or two words that come *before* the word or words in **boldface** type. The new modifiers may force you to make other alterations. Make only the changes you must. Copy everything else and proofread.

Arthur Ashe: Classy Pro

[1]After he passes his thirtieth birthday, the **character** of an athlete is tested severely. [2]Many athletes find it difficult to restrain their exuberance when their talent is at its peak. [3]Accepting **the diminution of those skills** with grace is impossible for most **sports figures** who are thirty years old. [4]This is particularly true in tennis, a sport filled with **teenage stars** who are as quick as panthers. [5]Compared to them, a **player like Arthur Ashe,** who is older, should look awkward and out of place. [6]But Ashe, well in his thirties, is a tennis pro who has never lost his dignity on or off the courts.

[7]On the playing court, Ashe is as trim and sleek as a greyhound. [8]He has a **face and body** that are youthful, not very different from the way they appeared when he was an undergraduate at UCLA. [9]What is most remarkable about his fluid movements is that he has been "under the knife." [10]He carries **marks** of surgery on his eye and heel. [11]He was out of competition for all of 1977, yet has somehow retained his **swift reflexes,** which characterize him. [12]His gutsy comeback has made him a **favorite** of crowds in recent matches. [13]Watching him beat **Vitas Gerulaitis,** who is much younger, made the spectators believe that they, too, could stop time and come back from adversity.

[14]Off court, Ashe's competitive spirit is under control. [15]He possesses a calm **manner** that is unruffled, eliciting the adjective "classy" from fellow players. [16]His speech is cool and elegant. [17]Above all, there is a sense of dignity about him that cannot come easy to a black man in a **sport** of whites and to an older man up against young bombers with **serves** that are big and **voices** that are loud. [18]Somehow Arthur Ashe has managed to sustain the intensity of his spirit without losing his self-control and sense of proportion.

As you proofread, underline the changes you have made.

Step 21

Writing Assignments: Choosing Premodifiers

The assignments below have been designed to familiarize you with modifiers. STEP 21 asked you to practice forming modifiers that came *before* certain words. You should remember that grammatically the phrases that *followed* those words were also correct. You were asked to make premodifiers out of them in order to reduce the number of words and make your writing smoother.

1. Reduce wordiness in your other essays by transforming phrases that begin with *which, who* or *that* into premodifiers. (Not all of them can be transformed.)
2. Reduce wordiness in other essays you have written by transforming as many prepositional phrases as you can into premodifiers. (These are phrases that indicate location or relation: in the house, over the roof, of the tree, the street *on the left.*)
3. Reduce wordiness in a fellow student's essay by making premodifiers out of postmodifiers.
4. Consider the essay "Snap, Crackle, Pop, and the Sundae" in STEP 17. Try to form *postmodifiers* of any adjectives you can locate.
5. Write a series of sentences that state someone's attributes (physical, emotional, spiritual). Let each sentence have the following pattern: She (he) is a person who is _____ . Then transform each of the sentences, making premodifiers that come before *person,* out the postmodifiers.
6. Consider the essay "Seasickness" in STEP 17. Try to convert some of the adverbs in that essay into postmodifiers.
7. Consider the essay "Smoking" in STEP 18. List the words that modify in one column and the words being modified in another. Make postmodifiers out of premodifiers and premodifiers out of postmodifiers.

Step 22

Creating Premodifiers

The following STEP is also designed to help a writer reduce verbosity. As with the previous STEP, you must make briefer premodifiers from lengthier postmodifier. What makes this STEP different is that no one word from the postmodifier will serve for the whole. You must find a new word that does the work of the whole postmodifier phrase or clause. This is how it can be done:

> They are looking for a home *in which they can settle down.*
> (postmodifier)
> They are looking for a *permanent* home.
> (premodifier)

> The old radio did not work because it had too many tubes *that were not in good working order.*
> The old radio did not work because it had too many *defective* tubes.

> The ship failed to give a warning *that came on time for the* lighthouse keeper.
> The ship failed to give *adequate* warning *to* the lighthouse keeper.

> Foods *having high quantities of starches and sweets* were off Lorraine's list.
> *Fattening* foods were off Lorraine's list.

STEP 22:   As in Step 21, you will find a number of underlined phrases and clauses that come after modified words and phrases in **boldface** type. In each instance try to come up with a different word—not contained in the original—that means what the underlined words mean and put that one word before the boldface word. For example, *for the band* can be restated as *ring*. Your first sentence should thus read: *The ring finger continues to be the third finger of the left hand.* Notice that you are streamlining your sentences by reducing the number of words. Be careful with punctuation. Proofread carefully.

The Ring Finger

---

¹In many countries, the **finger** <u>for the band</u> continues to be the third finger of the left hand. ²The custom persists despite the fact that the **reasons for its use** <u>at the very beginning</u> have become invalid.

³Ancient Greek and Roman anatomists **believed,** <u>not rightly,</u> that a vein or nerve led directly from the heart to the third finger. ⁴Naturally, this was the finger selected for the **ring** <u>that indicates matrimony.</u> ⁵The ring, a symbol of love, would thus be connected to the heart, the source of love. ⁶Though this error was discovered, the ring remained on the third finger owing to another **reason** <u>that had to do with the body.</u> ⁷It was observed that the third finger could not be extended by itself. ⁸In order to be stretched fully, it needed a **finger** <u>that would work together with it.</u> ⁹As this other finger would help keep the ring from slipping off, the ring remained on the third finger of the left hand.

¹⁰The other reason for the selection of the finger on the left hand seems **humiliating** <u>to a great extent</u> today. ¹¹According to tradition, the husband is the master in the household and thus the "right hand" of the family. ¹²The wife, slave to the master, is then the "left hand." ¹³The ring on the left hand was thus intended to mark the **female** <u>who gives in easily and has little power.</u> ¹⁴Today, when such a symbol is considered onerous, the wedding band remains on the left hand, but for a different reason. ¹⁵As most people are right-handed, their left hand is the less active hand. ¹⁶**Women** <u>who are employed</u> can thus keep the ring hand conveniently out of the way.

As you proofread, underline the changes you have made.

STEP 22:   As in STEP 21, you will find here a number of underlined phrases and clauses that come after modified words in **boldface** type. In each instance try to come up with a different word—not contained in the original—that means what the underlined words mean, and put that one word before the boldface word. For example, *for unattached men and women* can be restated as *singles* (strictly speaking, this word should take the plural possessive but the phrase "singles bar" has entered the language without the apostrophe). Your first sentence should thus read: *Research by two psychologists indicates that the action in a singles bar follows easily observable patterns.* Notice that you are streamlining your sentences by reducing the number of words. Be careful with the punctuation. Proofread carefully.

Singles and Science

¹Research by two psychologists indicates that the action in a **bar** for unattached men and women follows **observable patterns** that are simple to determine.

²A man who approaches a woman has **seven seconds,** give or take a second, in which to make a favorable impression and request a date. ³Within those seven seconds a woman makes up her mind, usually rejecting the invitation. ⁴Most men risk making this **request** that is so important only once every fifteen to twenty minutes, say the researchers. ⁵They suggest that bars for singles hardly teem with **activity** that is hot, heavy, and excited. ⁶The frequency of the approaches does increase, however, as the number of women in the bar increases. ⁷Naturally, the more frequent the approaches become, the shorter the conversation per approach gets.

⁸The psychologists also found that men did not approach attractive women any more frequently than **women** whose appearance was less appealing. ⁹Apparently, men are less interested in looks than in **signals** that are given without speaking. ¹⁰They look for eye contact, facial expression, and body posture for clues whether they were approaching **women** who would be likely to accept their proposition.

¹¹The psychologists believe that their research could help singles improve their technique. ¹²Knowing what they can expect and what is expected of them could help singles enhance their social skills and eliminate their **anxieties** while interacting with people.

As you proofread, underline the changes you have made.

Step 22

Creating Premodifiers

Helpful Hints and Special Situations

STEP 21 should have been a preparation for the problems you will face in this STEP. Once again, you must be mindful of the kinds of words your premodifiers must describe. Adjectives and participles modify nouns, and adverbs modify verbs, adjectives, and other adverbs. Once again, a string of premodifiers must be separated by commas:

> Critic Brode said he saw an insipid, tasteless, disorganized, stupid, and incompetent movie.

What makes STEP 22 more difficult, of course, is that you must find a word on your own that does the work of from two to ten others. Finding that right, useful word is the kind of struggle all thinking writers face all the time. A thesaurus may be of limited help in jogging your imagination, but most often you you will simply have to think about the meaning of the words in the lengthy postmodifier. The strongest advantage you have is that there is always more than one choice to be made. Here is a sample sentence:

> The Upper Peninsula of Michigan is an area *where relatively few people live*.

What is meant by "where relatively few people live"? The Upper Peninsula is almost half of a large, Midwestern state bordered by the Great Lakes. If few people live there, that means there are many green open areas, trees, bushes, and—very likely—much wild game. In such a place one would find little traffic on the roads, and one would not likely find an expensive French restaurant. One would expect an abundance of fresh air but not very many housing tracts. We can know all this without counsulting a map or a geography book. And how we understand the words *where relatively few people live* depends on who we are:

> The Upper Peninsula of Michigan is an *uncrowded* area.
> (This sounds positive; "uncrowded" means there are not many people there.)
> The Upper Peninsula of Michigan is an *undeveloped* area.
> (This implies there are few towns, shopping centers, and housing tracts.)
> The Upper Peninsula of Michigan is a *wilderness* area.
> (It does follow that there is much wilderness if there are few people.)
> The Upper Peninsula of Michigan is an *underpopulated* area.

(This is a geographer's term that means there is room for more people to move there.)

The Upper Peninsula of Michigan is a *low-density* area.

(This is a sociologist's term that means people do not live close together.)

The Upper Peninsula of Michigan is a *hunting and fishing* area.

(This is a positive view some people would have of a wilderness area.)

The Upper Peninsula of Michigan is a *desolate* area.

(This is a negative view some people take of there being few people in the area.)

By thinking a few moments more, you should be able to think of as many as ten more ways of looking at an area where few people live. Some would call it "God's country," perhaps because it does not belong to commerce or industry; others might call it "godforsaken" because it does not have posh department stores and expensive restaurants.

Our discussion here should not suggest that any premodifier can do the work of a lengthy postmodifier. Sometimes those extras words are not wasted and may make meaning more specific. If we talk about ideas instead of an expanse of land, we can see the difference:

Feldman in *The New Times* praised the play *for its funny lines*.

Notice that the postmodifier refers only to the lines of the play, not to the performance of the actors, the quality of the sets or lighting, the reactions of the audience, and so on. Further, the reviewer, Feldman, says the lines were funny; this apparently means the play was not a slapstick comedy—where the actors use pies-in-the-face, seltzer bottles, or whoopee cushions. Here are some attempts to reduce the wordage of *for its funny lines:*

Feldman in *The New Times* praised the *witty* play.

(Yes: lines that are funny are frequently called "witty.")

Feldman in *The New Times* praised the amusing play.

(Not as good: "amusing" might exclude slapstick, but it also sounds less than really funny.)

Feldman in *The New Times* praised the *comic* play.

(This does not do it well at all; now we do not know what he thought was funny.)

STEP 22:   As in STEP 21, you will find here a number of underlined phrases and clauses that come after modified words in **boldface** type. In each instance try to come up with a different word—not contained in the original—that means what the underlined words mean, and put that one word before the boldface word. For example, *a night creature* can be restated as *nocturnal.* Your first sentence should thus read: *The nocturnal scorpion uses its long, curved tail for both defense and destruction.* Notice that you are streamlining your sentences by reducing the number of words. Be careful with the punctuation. Proofread carefully.

The Scorpio's Sting

---

¹The **scorpion,** a night creature, uses its long, curved tail for both defense and destruction. ²It can **paralyze** with alacrity its enemy or prey by injecting a poison with that tail. ³Some people fear that the Scorpio personality, like its namesake, also carries a **sting** that kills. ⁴Astrologists feel that though Scorpios do possess some of the qualities of the scorpion, they are not **people** who arouse concern.

⁵Ancient astrologers called the scorpion a serpent and also associated the eagle with the sun sign. ⁶Scorpios seem to have inherited from these creatures an **intensity** that is easily seen. ⁷They have a steady **gaze** that mesmerizes. ⁸People on whom this stare is focused often feel that their innermost secrets are being penetrated. ⁹The passion of **Scorpios,** mentioned in ancient stories, is a source of much curiosity. ¹⁰More apparent is the determination in the Scorpio voice. ¹¹Whether **smooth** as soft cloth, rough, or sharp, the tone is always direct and self-confident. ¹²Even **Scorpios** at rest project what one astrologist calls, "a crackling, electric vitality."

¹³This intensity naturally unnerves enemies of Scorpios, but it is a boon to those Scorpios befriend. ¹⁴With friends, Scorpios are **genuine** without any limitations. ¹⁵They tell the **truth** even when it hurts but also offer their boundless generosity and utter fearlessness when necessary. ¹⁶The eagle in their sign has made them fierce, but that trait merely strengthens their loyalty to friends.

As you proofread, underline the changes you have made.

STEP 22:   As in STEP 21, you will find here a number of underlined phrases and clauses that come after modified words in **boldface** type. In each instance try to come up with a different word—not contained in the original—that means what the underlined words mean and put that one word before the boldface word. For example, **gray hair** that turned while he was still in his twenties can be restated as *prematurely* **gray hair.**

A Wild and Crazy Guy

[1]Steve Martin is a young comedian with **gray hair** that turned while he was still in his twenties, who specializes in the unlikely. [2]So far he has had a **career** that was unexpected. [3]After eight years of working at Disneyland, Martin was a **philosophy student** with top grades and a warm-up comedian for **rock groups** that indulged in controlled substances. [4]He was always a **fellow** who was uncontrolled and insane-appearing.

[5]Growing up in Anaheim, California, Steve Martin was ten when he started to work at **Disneyland,** which was in the same town. [6]Putting on silly costumes, he sold **books** that told you how to get around the place, but he went on to a dozen other jobs. [7]He did magic tricks, sold novelty items, and learned to play the **banjo** in the manner of the old musicians of a long time ago. [8]He was especially attracted to a Disneyland employee, an old vaudevillian named Wally Poag, who made **animals** that were insane by bending balloons.

[9]Although Martin had been a **student** who wasted his time in high school, he almost became a scholar when he entered a local junior college. [10]The **difference** that was significant was made by a girlfriend Martin names only as Stormy, who told him, "Knowledge is the most important things there is." [11]He transferred to Long Beach State College and maintained an **average** that had no B's, C's, D's, or F's for three years. [12]Then he encountered a **philosopher** who was hard to read named Wittgenstein, who made him think all philosophical problems were only a matter of language. [13]Disillusioned, Martin abandoned academia and dedicated himself to **business** involving night clubs, movies, and television.

[14]He got his first break writing for **comics** broadcasting over the boob tube. [15]After some of his writing was nominated for an Emmy award, he played a **character** in the supporting cast of *Sonny and Cher.* [16]He was not a success, however, and left to start a discouraging tour of **night clubs** that were not first class. [17]Worse, he was a **comic** who prepared the audience for chaotic rock groups. [18]Out of this his **style** of the present moment emerged, a mixture of Disneyland, philosophical absurdity, and disorder. [19]A **Martin joke** that represents his style is, "I gave my cat a bath but the fur stuck to my tongue."

As you proofread, underline the changes you have made.

STEP 22:   As in STEP 21, you will find here a number of underlined phrases and clauses that come after modified words in **boldface** type. In each instance try to come up with a different word—not contained in the original—that means what the underlined words mean, and put that one word before the boldface word. For example, **pie** _judged tops in taste_ can be restated as _best_ **pie**.

Blue Ribbons

¹Anyone who has ever been to a county fair has seen a blue ribbon given to a **pie** judged tops in taste in a baking contest. ²To win a blue ribbon means to come in **place** ahead of the others in anything, racing, selling, or even alligator wrestling. ³Red or yellow ribbons may be given to a **place** that is runner-up, but first place is always blue. ⁴The **origin** that is genuine for this custom is difficult to explain.

⁵Although blue is the **color** of the heavens, not all of our associations with it are good ones. ⁶Blue language is **language** that is obscene. ⁷A blue nose is a **person** with very puritanical tastes; although, when capitalized, a Blue Nose is a person from Nova Scotia, puritanical or not. ⁸Blue laws are ones that try to make Sunday a **day** when there is no recreation. ⁹And someone who sings the blues is a **person** feeling dejection of the spirit. ¹⁰So why a blue ribbon?—or even a ribbon for that matter?

¹¹Ribbons were the **way** that had been handed down to signify an order of knighthood. ¹²About 1349, King Edward III of England established an order of **knights of his realm** who had shown the most accomplishment. ¹³He called the group the Order of Saint George and gave the men in it an inscribed blue ribbon to be worn just under the knee of their medieval costumes. ¹⁴As fashions changed, men no longer wore the kind of clothing that would allow the **ribbon** of distinctive color to show, but they continued to represent the ribbon in their coats of arms. ¹⁵Later the **Order of Saint George** for knights of greatest distinction came to be known as the Order of the Garter.

¹⁶But the phrase "blue ribbon" appears never to have applied to anything but knighthood until the time of **Benjamin Disraeli,** who was head of the English government in 1868. ¹⁷A friend challenged Disraeli, saying he could not even identify the Derby, the **horserace** that was the best-known in the country. ¹⁸Disraeli's **reply** that came immediately was, "Indeed I do; it is 'the blue ribbon of the turf.' " ¹⁹Although we cannot be sure our **definition** at the current time for the phrase comes from Disraeli, he is the first person we know of to use it this way.

As you proofread, underline the changes you have made.

Step 22

Writing Assignments: Creating Premodifiers

In the previous STEP you could be sure that the premodifier you formed meant exactly the same thing as the postmodifier from which you had formed it. In this STEP, you have to be aware of the possibility that, in *creating* or choosing a premodifier that is not found in the postmodifier, you are altering slightly the meaning of the modifier. If you remember, this was the caution that was raised in STEP 17 and STEP 18. Each new word brings new connotations. Be aware of this possibility as you do the assignments below.

1. Consider the essay "Wonder Woman and Mythology" in STEP 21. Rewrite the essay, this time *creating* instead of *finding* premodifiers in the underlined postmodifiers.
2. Consider the essay "The Violent Cosmos" in STEP 21. Rewrite the essay, creating premodifiers that mean the same thing as the postmodifiers. (Not all of the postmodifers can be replaced by new modifiers.)
3. Rewrite the essay "The Chocolate Chase" in STEP 21, creating new premodifiers.
4. Rewrite "Arthur Ashe: Classy Pro" in STEP 21, forming new premodifiers.
5. Rewrite "Walking in Circles" in STEP 21, creating new premodifiers.
6. Write a series of sentences that describe the appearance of some object, using the pattern: It was a book that had _____. Then transform the sentences, finding new premodifiers.
7. Reduce wordiness in a fellow student's essay by creating new premodifiers.

STEP 23

Combining with Coordinators

The following sentences were heard in a local pizzeria at 11:00 P.M.:

Kevin wants pizza with anchovies.
Debbie wants just a plain, cheese pizza.

Although there is nothing wrong with these two sentences as they stand, they do not imply any relationship between Kevin and Debbie. Suppose they were sitting at the same table; then the two sentences would go better together:

Kevin wants pizza with anchovies, and Debbie wants just a plain, cheese pizza.

This sentence, too, is fine. Now, suppose Kevin and Debbie have gone out on a date; the reason they are both at the pizzeria is that they wanted a snack after the movie they saw. Unfortunately, they have only enough money for one pizza:

Kevin wants pizza with anchovies, but Debbie wants just a plain, cheese pizza.

Perhaps because we have put Kevin first, we appear to favor him. The two sentences may be made one and remain simply a statement of facts:

Debbie wants a cheese pizza; Kevin wants a pizza with anchovies.

We started with two simple sentences. When we joined them with a comma and a coordinating conjunction or a semicolon, we created two coordinate clauses. Notice that we did not have to change any other words in the sentences to coordinate them. The only matter requiring attention is the way in which we join them. Two independent coordinate clauses need the glue of punctuation to hold them together, either a comma and a conjunction or just a semicolon by itself. It is possible to use a semicolon with a conjunction, too, but in short sentences it looks like punctuation overkill. We would more likely use a semicolon with a conjunction if there were already many commas in the sentence:

Kevin's pizza had oregano, sardines, bay leaf, maraschino cherries, and anchovies; and Debbie's pizza had mushrooms, grape leaves, fried won-ton, and collard greens.

There are only a few coordinating conjunctions, and they are easy to remember: *and, but, or nor,* and *yet.* Often *for* and *so* are also coordinating conjunctions, depending on the construction of the sentence. Each of them acts differently: *and* is the only conjunction that joins in the sense of "adding to"; *but* excludes or contrasts; *or, nor,* and *yet* provide different alternatives.

STEP 23: Some of the facts about energy consumption in the following essay might make more sense if mention of them were brought into relation with comparable information in nearby sentences. Fourteen of these sentences can be reduced to seven, following the suggestions we give. You must decide on the proper punctuation in each instance.

Join sentences 1 and 2 with *yet.*
Join sentences 5 and 6 with *but.*
Join sentences 8 and 9 with *or.*
Join sentences 10 and 11 with *and.*
Join sentences 12 and 13 with *but.*
Join sentences 15 and 16 with *or.*
Join sentences 18 and 19 with no conjunction but with the necessary punctuation.

Sentences 1 and 2 may be joined this way: "Gasoline has been called a 'precious natural resource,' yet few of us realize just how precious it is."

Dwindling, Precious Energy

[1]Gasoline has been called a "precious natural resource." [2]Few of us appreciate just how precious it is. [3]Just a thimbleful of gasoline provides enough energy to drive the average automobile 100 yards on level roadway. [4]Ever try pushing a car that distance? [5]We know it takes a great deal of fuel oil to heat an average home in winter. [6]Do we know we would have to run a half-million miles on a treadmill to generate the same amount of heat? [7]Meanwhile consider that at a practical 20 percent efficiency, a gallon of gasoline will generate one horsepower for eleven hours. [8]That is enough energy to lift a one ton load to the top of a 10,000-foot mountain. [9] It is equivalent to 330 hours, or two months, of what we call "heavy labor" for a human being.

[10]The energy consumed by Americans in 1975 was enough to bring Lake Erie to a boil. [11]With normal growth, each of us would consume twice as much energy by the year 2000, enough to bring nine lake Eries to a boil.

[12]Much energy, however, does not work at all. [13]Instead, it is wasted. [14]Much energy is wasted in heat loss through windows. [15]In the Philadelphia area during winter the heat loss of one square foot of double glass is roughly equivalent to the amount of energy a person expends in running 200 miles. [16]This is the same amount of usable heat gathered in a solar energy collector in the same period.

[17]Perhaps our greatest waste of energy is what we never collect at all. [18]Within a two-week period, the earth receives as much energy from the sun as is stored in all the earth's known reserves of oil, coal, and natural gas. [19]One day of average sunlight on Lake Erie surpasses the total energy used by the United States in a day.

STEP 23   The essay below contains a number of choppy sentences. Connect those sentences with coordinators as specified below. Connecting the sentences with coordinating conjunctions will also help establish relationships between pairs. You must punctuate in each instance. Copy everything else and proofread carefully.

Join sentences 1 and 2 with *but.*
Join sentences 5 and 6 with *and.*
Join sentences 7 and 8 with *but.*
Join sentences 10 and 11 with *but.*
Join sentences 12 and 13 with *but.*
Join sentences 16 and 17 with *or.*
Join sentences 19 and 20 with *but.*
Join sentences 23 and 24 with *but.*
Join sentences 25 and 26 with *and.*

Blowing in the Wind

¹Primitive tribes did not carry flags into the battle. ²They did carry carved poles that displayed the tribal totem on top. ³This totem was usually the figure of an animal. ⁴The Vikings made use of a raven; the Saxons, of a white horse; and the Romans, after 100 B.C., of an eagle. ⁵Held aloft, the staff identified the forces. ⁶It served as a rallying point. ⁷Next, a banner was substituted for the totem. ⁸Its purpose remained the same. ⁹Finally, streamers or tassels were tied to the banner.

¹⁰These colored streamers were not there to decorate the pole. ¹¹They were meant to indicate the presence of the divine amid the battle. ¹²God is invisible. ¹³The wind, as it moves streamers, is visible. ¹⁴That was the magical means by which the outcome of the battle could be determined. ¹⁵During battle it was carefully guarded. ¹⁶Its capture or fall could cause confusion. ¹⁷It could cause defeat. ¹⁸These banners led to the flags we recognize.

¹⁹National flags appeared in Europe in the twentieth century, A.D. ²⁰The Europeans did not invent them. ²¹They got the flag from their Saracen foes who did not invent it either. ²²They got it from the Indians, who probably appropriated it from the Chinese. ²³It is not known for certain that the Chinese invented it. ²⁴A leader of the Chou dynasty, in the twelfth century B.C., is known to have had a white flag carried in front of him. ²⁵More than 2,000 years later, the Crusaders brought the idea of flags back from the Holy Land. ²⁶They naturally chose the cross as the emblem for the flag. ²⁷Denmark, Finland, Greece, Norway, and Sweden still retain the cross in their national flags.

As you proofread, underline the changes you have made.

Step 23

Combining with Coordinators

Helpful Hints and Special Situations

The introduction to this STEP stated that independent coordinate clauses had to be held together by a kind of punctuation glue, either a comma and a conjunction or a semicolon. Leaving out that glue makes for problems that composition teachers classify under different names. For example, if the writer leaves out any kind of punctuation, we get this:

> Kevin wants pizza with anchovies Debbie wants just a plain, cheese pizza.

This may be called a *run-on sentence* or a *fused sentence*. Either term works; the two parts of the sentence run into each other, and thus are running on; and the two clauses are fused because they are just jammed together without any punctuation. The problem with them is not simply that teachers do not like them but rather that they are difficult to read.

Another mistake is to join the clauses with just a comma:

> Kevin wants pizza with anchovies, Debbie wants just a plain, cheese pizza.

Such a sentence is called a *comma splice* because a comma is not enough to splice or join them together. Comma splices are frequently confusing for readers because a simple comma usually ties something smaller to the rest of the sentence.

Another problem with coordination is simply overdoing it. Most writers learned in grade school that it is unwise to use the word "and" too often, which is another way of saying too much coordination is a bad idea. This is what it looks like:

> Kevin picked up Debbie at her house, and he took her to the movies, and they drove to a pizzeria, and he sat down to order.

There is nothing wrong with the punctuation of such a sentence, but reading it is like sitting at a railroad crossing and watching the boxcars in a slow freight train. Coordination keeps your writing style loose, which may or may not be a good idea. You can tighten up your style, making it more emphatic, with some of the methods we give you in the next three STEPS.

You may have noticed in the introduction to this STEP that the list of coordinating conjunctions is very short. There is also another kind of word put between coordinate clauses that is usually called the *conjunctive adverb*. There are many of these, and they serve different purposes:

Addition: also, too, furthermore, likewise, moreover, besides, in fact
Emphasis: indeed, that is to say, to be sure
Drawing distinctions: however, nevertheless, anyway, on the contrary, on the other hand
Illustration: namely, that is, for example, for instance, by way of illustration
Conclusion and result: accordingly, consequently, hence, therefore, thus, as a result
Time and space: first, second, third, then , later, finally, in conclusion, at the top, further on

---

In general, keep the same voice in both clauses. Do not switch to the passive voice if the first clause is in the active:

Kevin loved anchovies,   but Debbie hated them.
                          not
                          , but they were hated by Debbie.

And do not use the subject of the first clause as anything but the subject of the second clause, providing the subject is repeated at all. Avoid sentences like the following:

Kevin proposed to
Sheila,   and Debbie has not spoken to him since.
                     instead, make that
                     , and he has not heard from Debbie since.

Students often have a good sense of sentence rhythm, particularly in the case of run-on sentences or comma splices. The presence of a comma suggests that the writer is aware of the need for a pause or break at that point in the sentence. With that in mind, you should ask yourself during proofreading if a period might be the appropriate punctuation in those places where you have placed a comma. If the resulting sentences make sense, substitute the period for the comma. What is merely a pause (a comma) in speech, is often a stop (a period) in writing. Of course, the new sentence begins with a capital letter.

The children were playing, they were making a great deal of noise.
                         ↑

Even inexperienced writers would put the comma in. Let yourself be guided by the presence of the comma. Try a period in its place. That is the correct punctuation.
                                    ↓
The children were playing. They were making a great deal of noise.
                          ↑

STEP 23   The essay below is choppy, and its sentences lack connections. Rewrite the essay, joining the sentences with coordinating conjunctions as specified below. You must decide on the proper punctuation in each instance. Copy everything else and proofread carefully.

Join sentences 1 and 2 with *but.*
Join sentences 3 and 4 with *and.*
Join sentences 5 and 6 with *and.*
Join sentences 8 and 9 with *or.*
Join sentences 10 and 11 with *but.*
Join sentences 12 and 13 with *and.*
Join sentences 14 and 15 with *yet.*
Join sentences 16 and 17 with *and,* then to 18 with *but.*
Join sentences 20 and 21 with *but.*

Tips for Shoppers

[1]According to the American Council of Life Insurance, most people spend most of their time spending money. [2]They are nervous about their ability to manage their finances. [3]The council offers simple suggestions to these unsure shoppers that may ease their discomfort. [4]It can save their money in the process.

[5]Before buying a used car, shop around. [6]Consult an expert. [7]The council also urges you to resist pressure from salespeople. [8]Avoid making a quick decision. [9]Avoid signing anything you find confusing. [10]To protect yourself, you can always request a written guarantee. [11]Most people are reluctant to ask for one. [12]You should also know the total cost of installment payments. [13]You should not be afraid to add the figures right in front of the salesperson.

[14]Supermarket purchases seem less important than used-car deals. [15]Great opportunities for saving exist here as well. [16]The important instruction to remember while purchasing food is "Compare!" [17]You must compare the prices. [18]You must compare the weights. [19]Above all, you must compare the quality. [20]Remember that a name brand may indicate quality. [21]The supermarket's own brand may be just as satisfactory.

As you proofread, underline the changes you have made.

STEP 23   The sentences in the essay below lack a sense of relationship among them. Rewrite the essay, establishing connections with the use of coordinating conjunctions as specified below. You must decide on proper punctuation in each instance. Copy everything else and proofread carefully.

Join sentences 1 and 2 with *but.*
Join sentences 3 and 4 with *but.*
Join sentences 6 and 7 with *and.*
Join sentences 9 and 10 with *and.*
Join sentences 12 and 13 with *yet.*
Join sentences 16 and 17 with *or.*
Join sentences 19 and 20 with *but.*

Out Damned Spot

[1]No cleaning job is too big for a handy person. [2]What about little jobs that seem simple yet prove difficult? [3]Spots on clothes, cars, and outdoor furniture can often defy the efforts of the most persistent cleaner. [4]There are ways of dealing even with these deceptive spots.

[5]For removing spots in fabrics, you need a solvent and some cloth. [6]Get a bottle of mineral spirits. [7]Get two pieces of clean, cotton cloth. [8]Do not start rubbing immediately. [9]Moisten one cloth with the mineral spirits. [10]Put the other cloth under the spot or stain. [11]Next, gently blot the spot with the damp cloth. [12]Rubbing can harm the material. [13]Few people can resist using their strength.

[14]When eliminating oxidation spots on automobiles and outdoor furniture, you do not need to be as concerned with harming the metal. [15]You need soap and water. [16]Buy a rubbing compound. [17]You may prepare your own rubbing compound by combining toothpaste and baking soda. [18]Once again you will need two pieces of cloth. [19]Dampen one cloth for rubbing. [20]Keep the cloth dry for buffing. [21]The procedure then is to wash the oxidized area. [22]After drying the area, rub on the compound with the damp cloth. [23]Buff for luster with the dry cloth.

As you proofread, underline the changes you have made.

STEP 23   Some of the details about the lemming in the following essay might seem more emphatic if they were brought into relation with comparable information in nearby sentences. Eighteen of the sentences in the following essay can be joined together to make nine following the suggestions we give:

Join sentences 1 and 2 with *yet*.
Join sentences 3 and 4 with *and*.
Join sentences 5 and 6 with *and*.
Join sentences 7 and 8 with *but*.
Join sentences 9 and 10 with *but*.
Join sentences 11 and 12 with *but*.
Join sentences 14 and 15 with *but*.
Join sentences 16 and 17 with *and*.
Join sentences 18 and 19 with *but*.
Join sentences 20 and 21 with no conjunction but with the necessary punctuation.

Lemmings

[1]The instinct for self-preservation is perhaps the most basic drive in all living things. [2]Lemmings, small, mouselike creatures who live in the icy, northern reaches of Scandinavia, frequently commit mass suicide. [3]No one seems to know why thousands of them hurl themselves off cliffs into the sea. [4]Thus their name has come to mean mindless self-destruction.

[5]Lemmings are about six inches long. [6]They have small eyes and ears, short legs, and very stumpy tails. [7]Their fur is grayish black. [8]Some northern varieties change their pelts to white in winter. [9]They usually eat green vegetation like reindeer moss. [10]When that is scarce, they will eat almost anything. [11]When food is plentiful, one female can produce from thirty to fifty young in a year. [12]When their numbers increase, the food supply always decreases. [13]Then lemmings migrate by the millions, eating everything as they go.

[14]Normally, lemmings fear and avoid water. [15]During their mass march they brave streams and lakes, heedless of predators, leaving a swath of destruction behind them. [16]After running for weeks, the lemmings finally reach the sea. [17]Then, row upon row, they cast themselves headlong into the water. [18]For a short time the frantic rodents remain afloat. [19]Soon the creatures tire, sinking one by one to their doom.

[20]During one lemming suicide, the bodies of the animals completely covered the surface of the water. [21]A Norwegian steamer captain reported that he had to steer his way through a shoal of lemming corpses for more than an hour.

As you proofread, underline the changes you have made.

Step 23

Writing Assignments: Combining with Coordinators

Remember to use correct punctuation as you utilize coordinators in combining sentences. Coordination helps produce a smoother style. More important, it helps your reader's understanding because it shows connections between sentences.

1. Rewrite sentences in your other essays in which your instructor felt coordination would be helpful.
2. Evaluate another student's essay, determining first if coordination is necessary, then rewriting it with coordinators.
3. Write a paragraph in which you describe your feelings about the morning. Write another short paragraph in which you describe those same reactions at night. If there is a difference in the feelings, alternate a sentence from the first paragraph with one from the second, combining them with *but*. If your feelings are the same morning and night, alternate sentences from the first paragraph with sentences from the second, combining with *and* or *or*.
4. Consider the essay "Differences on the Gridiron" in STEP 16. Combine as many of the sentences as you can (two at a time), using coordinators.
5. Consider the essay "UFOs" in STEP 16. If you have done STEP 16 using that essay, place it side by side with your version. Combine the two essays, alternating sentences from your essay and the original, and use the coordinator *but*.
6. Make a list of various records set by a sports figure you admire. Make complete sentences out of each item on the list. Try to combine the sentences, using coordinators.
7. Consider one of the essays you had worked on from STEP 19. Try to combine sentences, using coordinators.
8. Write a brief description of a number of couples that you know. Name each member of the couple separately but link sentences that describe them with coordinators. (*John is quiet. His daily companion is a loud Labrador→John is quiet, but his daily companion is a loud Labrador.*)

Step 24

Combining with Relative Pronouns

Here are some sentences about a man in the news:

Alfred E. Newman has been elected senator.
He got his start in journalism.

His magazine has just taken over the *Congressional Record*.
His magazine is sold in every supermarket.

This is the kind of writing many composition teachers call "choppy." Not only are the sentences all short and simple (nothing wrong in that by itself), but they overlap; the first two have the same subject as do the second two. In both sets of sentences, the second gives relative information to help identify the subject of the first. The choppiness of the sentences could be eased and the style made more emphatic if we could reduce the four sentences by two by using the relative pronouns *who* and *which:*

Alfred E. Newman, who got his start in journalism, has been elected senator.

His magazine, which is sold in every supermarket, has just taken over the *Congressional Record*.

We call the two clauses beginning with *who* and *which* relative clauses because they give additional—relative—information about the subject of what is now the main clause. You may have heard such clauses called "adjective clauses" because they do indeed modify nouns.

You will notice that these relative clauses have been set off with commas at either end. This simple convention is the most difficult kind of punctuation for many students to remember. One way to reinforce it in your mind is to apply the general rule about commas, that is, set off any elements you could lift out of the sentence without changing the meaning of the main clause. If we leave out Newman's having been in journalism or his magazine's having been sold in supermarkets, we do not change his political career or that of his magazine. Grammarians call such relative clauses *nonrestrictive* because they do not limit or restrict the meaning of the main clause. When nonrestrictive relative clauses describe things, they often begin with *which*.

We would use only one comma, of course, if the nonrestrictive relative clause came at the beginning or the end of the sentence, leaving room for only one comma:

The senator-elect is Alfred E. Newman, who got his start in journalism.

The other kind of relative clause is not set off by *any* commas and is called *restrictive*. Here is a memorable example:

People who live in glass houses should not throw stones.

If we lift this relative clause out of the sentence, we would be left with only "People should not throw stones." Of course they should not, but the sentence with the relative clause means much more. That "much more" is what makes "who live in glass houses" a *restrictive* relative clause. When restrictive relative clauses describe things, they often begin with the relative pronoun *that:*

The magazine that Newman founded is the only one to support his candidacy.

The relative pronouns are: *who, whom, whose, that,* and *which.*

STEP 24   Some of the wordiness in the following essay can be reduced by turning six sentences into relative clauses and joining them with nearby, more important sentences. In each instance, the relative information is about persons, so you may use the relative pronoun *who* each time. You will have to decide, however, whether the new relative clause is restrictive or nonrestrictive. Sentences one and two become: *Historians who have traced the evolution of tableware generally agree that the fork was developed much later than the knife or the spoon."*

Join sentence 1 to 2: *who* have traced the evolution . . .
Join sentence 7 to 6: *who* was chancellor of England . . .
Join sentence 9 to 10: *who* was an English traveler . . .
Join sentence 13 to 12: *who* was the son . . .
Join sentence 18 to 17: *who* showed his impatience . . .
Join sentence 20 to 19: *who* had first seen them . . .

Learning to Use Forks

¹Historians have traced the evolution of tableware. ²They generally agree that the fork was developed much later than the knife or the spoon. ³Perhaps the oldest forks were used by South Sea Islanders. ⁴Although they were cannibals, their religion did not permit them to eat human flesh with their fingers.

⁵Whereas forks are mentioned in the Bible and early chronicles, they were first widely used among the upper classes of Italy in the eleventh century. ⁶Thomas Becket tried to introduce them to English royal society, but he did not succeed. ⁷He was chancellor of England under Henry II (1162–1170). ⁸Most Englishmen preferred to use their fingers instead of the newfangled invention.

⁹Thomas Coryate was an English traveler. ¹⁰He returned from a walking tour in Italy in 1611 and tried again to get his countrymen to use forks. ¹¹The English now considered forks to be jewelry and their use to be finicky and effeminate. ¹²Nevertheless, the first English monarch to use a fork was James I. ¹³He was the son of Mary, Queen of Scots. ¹⁴But the common people did not adopt forks for another three centuries.

¹⁵In the years while the fork was battling for acceptance, some priests condemned its use as most unsuitable and most irreligious. ¹⁶An angry preacher told his congregation that to eat meat with a fork was to declare impiously that God's creatures were not worthy of being touched with human hands. ¹⁷Clergyman Jonathan Swift added this in 1738, "Fingers were made before forks, and hands before knives." ¹⁸He showed his impatience with trendy innovation in *Gulliver's Travels*. ¹⁹Later, when John Adams tried to set his table with forks in 1785, he was criticized as undemocratic. ²⁰He had first seen them in France.

As you proofread, underline the changes you have made.

STEP 24   In the essay below, combine the following sentences by adding *who, which,* or *that:* 1 and 2, 8 and 9, 11 and 12, 14 and 15, 19 and 20. Copy everything else and proofread carefully.

Fair Weather or Foul

---

[1]Weather forecasters use sophisticated equipment. [2]It is designed to recognize a simple change in atmospheric conditions. [3]Dropping air pressure is a sign for approaching rain or storm. [4]Rising air pressure signals fair weather ahead. [5]Nonprofessionals who are observant can determine air pressure without having to turn to technology.

[6]Nature calls attention to falling air pressure in many ways. [7]Fowl, as hunters know, tend to fly lower because the lower air pressure affects their ears. [8]Birds perch more before a storm because of dropping pressure. [9]It reduces air density, making flying more difficult. [10]Dogs and other animals begin to sniff the air as inclement weather approaches. [11]The dropping air pressure releases odors. [12]These odors were being held captive by high air pressure. [13]The animals sniff because the released smells are stronger.

[14]Higher pressure (and fair weather) is indicated by dew. [15]Dew accumulates on grass at night and in early morning. [16]Dew forms only when the air is dry and the skies clear. [17]Smoke that rises from chimneys and funnels of ships also tells of improving weather. [18]Lower air pressure drives smoke downward; higher pressure allows it to escape upward.

[19]Another trustworthy weather guide could be the family's elderly member. [20]He has corns on his toes. [21]If the corns begin to ache, prepare for foul weather. [22]As air pressure falls, body tissues swell painfully.

As you proofread, underline the changes you have made.

Step 24

Combining with Relative Pronouns

Helpful Hints and Special Situations

We frequently delete relative pronouns and the verbs *is, are, was,* and *were* in informal contexts, and we may leave them out of some formal contexts without loss. Here is an example from one of the exercises in this STEP:

> Nevertheless, the first English monarch to use a fork was James I, who was the son of Mary, Queen of Scots.

This goes just as well as:

> Nevertheless, the first English monarch to use a fork was James I, the son of Mary Queen of Scots.

The relative pronoun most likely to be left out is *whom.* For reasons hard to explain, *whom* has come to sound affected and stuffy in informal English, and it is also becoming less common in formal English as well.

> The Highlanders whom Bonnie Prince Charlie led were defeated at Culloden Moor in 1746.

Nothing is lost when the *whom* is deleted:

> The Highlanders Bonnie Prince Charlie led were defeated at Culloden Moor in 1746.

Whom could not be replaced by *who* in a formal context, such as history term paper, because Bonnie Prince Charlie is the subject of the verb *led.* But *whom* could be replaced by *that,* the most versatile of relative pronouns, as it may replace nouns referring to either people or things.

> The Highlanders *that* Bonnie Prince Charlie led were defeated at Culloden Moor in 1746.

The relative pronoun *whose* replaces possessive nouns, or nouns with apostrophes, such as:

> The impressionist did a takeoff of Humphrey Bogart.
> Bogart's lisp was easy to mimic.

> The impressionist did a takeoff of Humphrey Bogart, *whose* lisp was easy to mimic.

As stated in the introduction for this STEP, the punctuation of relative clauses is a problem for many students, in part because the writer must decide whether the relative clause is *nonrestrictive* (takes two commas) or *restrictive* (no commas). Here are some examples to help you make distinctions between the two types. Here, first, are the *nonrestrictive:*

Television commercials, which cost a good deal of money to make, are irritating.
(Two commas: no matter how much they cost, they are still irritating.)
There are many Italian restaurants, which stock lots of pasta, on the north side of town.
(Two commas: all Italian restaurants stock pasta, no matter where they are.)
Statues in the park, which serve as roosts for pigeons, honor forgotten generals and politicians.
(Two commas: even without the pigeons, few people would remember.)
The sauna, which originated in Finland, is now popular in many climates.
(Two commas: many people would still like saunas even if they came from Sweden.)

And now *restrictive:*

A car door that is damaged in an accident will never hang properly again.
(No commas: other car doors are all right; only those in accidents are askew.)
Money that is invested may pay a dividend.
(No commas: uninvested money just sits there and will never pay a dividend.)
Newspapers that come in tabloid form can be read easily on the bus.
(No commas: other newspapers are difficult to handle on a bus.)
Old Western movies that degrade Indians are an embarrassment to us now.
(No commas: not all of those movies are embarrassing, only some.)

The suggestion that *nonrestrictive* (two commas) relative clauses should begin with *which* and *restrictive* (no commas) should begin with *that* was once considered a rigid rule, but many accomplished writers today are rather casual about the distinction. Many teachers and editors would not consider the confusing of *that* and *which* to be a gross violation of standard English, but the student writer will always be in a stronger position by keeping the two straight. Distinguishing the punctuation of *nonrestrictive* and *restrictive* is certainly important. So would the restrained use of clauses beginning either *that* or *which*. Although selective use of sentences with relative clauses strengthens your writing, sentences with lengthy relative clauses tie knots in writing style.

Lastly, always put the relative information in the relative clause and the more important information in the main clause.

STEP 24   In the essay below, combine the following sentences using *who, which,* or *that:* 2 and 3, 4 and 5, 6 and 7, 12 and 13, 14 and 15, 17 and 18, 21 and 22. Copy everything else and proofread carefully.

Proofs of Love

---

¹Some famous lovers have indicated their feelings in memorable ways.

²For thirty years, Marion Davies was the "special friend" of William Randolph Hearst. ³He courted her intensely when he first fell in love with her. ⁴One night she was leaving a party. ⁵The party was one Hearst had also attended. ⁶Davies was with Angier Biddle Duke. ⁷He was her beau at the time. ⁸Hearst approached her and asked if he could shake her hand. ⁹She allowed it. ¹⁰He wished her good night and dropped something in her palm. ¹¹When she got home, she opened her palm and found a diamond wristwatch nestled there.

¹²Richard Wagner and the poet, Kenneth Patchen, were also prisoners of love. ¹³They showed their emotion through their art. ¹⁴Wagner hired an orchestra. ¹⁵It performed *Traume* beneath the bedroom window of his beloved, Mathilde Wesendonk. ¹⁶"Traume" was one of five poems by Mathilde that Wagner set to music. ¹⁷Patchen dedicated forty books of poetry to his wife. ¹⁸She had been his inspiration. ¹⁹He felt that because the poems had, in a sense, come from her, they should also go to her.

²⁰King Henry IV of France loved Antoinette de Pons greatly. ²¹He sent her a marriage proposal. ²²He wrote it in his own blood. ²³She turned him down.

As you proofread, underline the changes you have made.

STEP 24   In the essay below, combine the following sentences using *that, which,* or *who:* 6 and 7, 8 and 9, 10 and 11, 13 and 14, 15 and 16, 18 and 19. Copy everything else and proofread carefully.

When Money Hurts

---

[1]Money has been called "the root of all evil" and "filthy lucre." [2]Such statements warn people about the harmful effects of money on their character. [3]Dr. E. R. Plunkett, searching through medical journals, has found that money can also be detrimental to the physical well-being of people.

[4]Because bank employees used to handle a great deal of money, they became exposed to a variety of diseases. [5]Tellers in the 1870s handled many copper and silver coins. [6]They came down with Banking Clerks' Dyspepsia. [7]This was characterized by sneezing, a metallic taste in the mouth, and constipation. [8]In 1883 doctors diagnosed Money Counters' Disease. [9]It was caused by the arsenites used in paper money. [10]Modern bank tellers are sometimes rude. [11]They may be suffering from Money Counters' Cramp in their fingers.

[12]Gamblers have also been victims of illnesses that money has brought about. [13]Black Jack Disease is a dermatitis of the hands caused by chromium salts. [14]The salts are found in the green felt covering of gambling tables. [15]Poker Players' Palsy is a numbness and tingling of the fingers. [16]It is caused by the pressure of the elbow propped for a long while on a card table.

[17]Nowadays, as credit cards replace money, credit card-related diseases are substituting for ills money used to cause. [18]According to the *New England Journal of Medicine,* Credit Carditis is a sciatic nerve irritation. [19]It is caused by the pressure of a wallet filled with credit cards stuffed into a back pocket.

As you proofread, underline the changes you have made.

STEP 24   Some of the wordiness and choppiness of the following essay can be reduced by turning eleven sentences into relative clauses and joining them with nearby, more important sentences.

Join sentence 3 to 2: *whose* speaking voice . . .
Join sentence 4 to 5: *which* lasted more . . .
Join sentence 6 to 7: *who* was jazz's . . .
Join sentence 9 to 8: *which* was a red-light . . .
Join sentence 12 to 11:*which* fortunately had . . .
Join sentence 15 to 14: *which* skills he had . . .
Join sentence 17 to 16: *who* composed . . .
Join sentence 19 to 18: *who* recommended . . .
Join sentence 21 to 20: *which* was written . . .
Join sentence 23 to 24: *which* sounded like . . .
Join sentence 26 to 25: *which* was later . . .

Louis Armstrong

¹Born on the Fourth of July in the first year of this century, Louis Armstrong was one of the most influential and durable of all jazz artists. ²In his lifetime Louis Armstrong was one of the most famous people on the globe. ³His speaking voice was a distinctive as his music. ⁴His career lasted more than fifty years. ⁵His career had continuing success, despite many changes in popular taste.

⁶He was jazz's foremost ambassador. ⁷The man began life in unpromising circumstances. ⁸Born near New Orleans' Storeyville, the young Armstrong had a hard time staying out of trouble. ⁹Storeyville was a red-light district and the first home of jazz. ¹⁰On New Year's Eve, 1914, Armstrong was arrested for firing a pistol and sent to the Colored Waifs' Home, where he first learned to play the cornet. ¹¹His skill increased as he stayed in the home. ¹²It fortunately had a marching band. ¹³When he was released from the institution, he already was accomplished enough with his horn to play for money. ¹⁴Befriended by his idol, King Oliver, Armstrong quickly began to develop jazz skills. ¹⁵Those skills he had, until then, been able to admire only from a distance.

¹⁶When Storeyville closed down and King Oliver left for Chicago, a place opened for Armstrong in the band of Kid Ory. ¹⁷Ory composed the famous "Muskrat Ramble." ¹⁸A success, Armstrong was invited to play with other bands, including that of Fletcher Henderson. ¹⁹Henderson recommended that he switch from the cornet to the trumpet. ²⁰By the time Armstrong played New York, he had scored his first big hit with "Ain't Misbehavin'." ²¹The song was written by Fats Waller.

²²Some people thought Armstrong's singing voice was terrible, but many more loved it. ²³His voice sounded like a rusty cement mixer. ²⁴His voice earned him his first nickname back in New Orleans, "Dippermouth." ²⁵While he was in London in 1932, musicians began to call him "Satchelmouth." ²⁶The name was later shortened to "Satchmo."

Step 24

Writing Assignments:
Combining with Relative Pronouns

Relative clauses are also known as adjective clauses. They modify nouns (person, place, thing, concept) and sometimes give additional information about the nouns (or pronouns) they modify. When they supply additional information, punctuation is more complicated. Refer to the beginning of STEP 24 for explanations and examples on the punctuation of relative clauses.

1. Rewrite any sentences in your other essays that your instructor considers worthwhile combining with the use of relative pronouns.
2. Introduce someone, using a series of sentences that follow the pattern: This is the person who _____ .
3. Sell an item—a car, hamburger, television set—mentioning the virtues of the item. Use the pattern: This is an *item* that _____ .
4. Discuss the advantages or disadvantages of some of the schools that you might have considered attending. Use the pattern: (Name of School) was the school that _____ .
5. Discuss some jobs you have held, noting what you liked and disliked about each. Use relative clauses that begin with either *that* or *which*. Include at least one nonrestrictive clause.
6. Try to remember the people in one of your elementary school grades. Identify them one by one, noting some memorable attribute or action. Use the relative pronouns *who* and *that*.

Step 25

Combining with Participles

Here is a description of an air battle in World War I:

> It was battered.
> It was smoking.
> The Sopwith Camel biplane reeled into a tailspin.

These three short sentences are a poor way of describing such a lively event. The style is both babyish and redundant. All three sentences have the same subject and describe different aspects of the same episode, the distress of an old fighter plane. Consider how the writing can be made more concise and emphatic through the use of participles:

> *Battered* and *smoking,* the Sopwith Camel biplane reeled into a tailspin.

Participles are forms of the verb that serve as adjectives, in this case by modifying the subject of the main clause, the Sopwith Camel biplane. Although they are best closest to the word they modify, they may go elsewhere in the sentence:

> The Sopwith Camel biplane, *battered* and *smoking,* reeled into a tailspin.
> The Sopwith Camel biplane reeled into a tailspin, *battered* and *smoking.*

Putting the participles last, as far away from the modifier subject as the sentence will allow, is the poorest of the three choices, but it is still acceptable and correct.

Participles come in only two forms, the present, which always ends in *-ing,* and the past, which usually ends in *-ed.* Irregular English verbs take past participles that do not end in *-ed.* Indeed, when we learn the three principal parts of a verb, the third is the part participle. Think, for example, of: draw, drew, draw*n;* fly, flew, flow*n;* made, made, made; sit, sat, sa*t;* write, wrote, writte*n;* and so on.

Notice that the construction of the sentence allows the use of both present and past participles although the tense of the main clause is past.

Phrases with participles in them are called participial phrases. They are punctuated the same way participles are, but they carry more information:

> *Battered* by the Red Baron's guns and
> *smoking* from both sides of the engine,
> the Sopwith Camel biplane reeled into a tailspin.

Forming participial phrases is often much like forming relative clauses; usually, you can just drop the relative pronoun and change the form of the verb to a participle. We can start with two short sentences:

Tanzania is a nation in East Africa.
It comprises what used to be known as Tanganyika and Zanzibar.

With a relative clause, it becomes:

Tanzania is a nation in East Africa *that* comprises what used to be known as Tanganyika and Zanzibar.

And with a participial phrase, it becomes:

Tanzania is a nation in East Africa, *comprising* what used to be known as Tanganyika and Zanzibar.

STEP 25   Some of the wordiness and choppiness in the essay below can be reduced by turning some of the sentences into participles or participial phrases and joining them to nearby sentences.

Make sentence 7 a participial phrase modifying sentence 6.
Make sentences 9 and 10 participial phrases modifying 8.
Make sentences 12 and 13 participial phrases modifying 11.
Make sentences 15 and 16 participles modifying sentence 17.
Make sentence 20 a participial phrase modifying sentence 19.
Make sentences 21 and 22 participial phrases modifying 23.
Make sentences 27 and 28 participial phrases modifying 26.
Make sentences 31 and 32 participial phrases modifying 33.

The Labors of Hercules

---

[1]Before Hercules (Greek Heracles) could become an immortal, he had to perform twelve, seemingly impossible tasks for Eurystheus, king of Mycenae.

[2]First, he had to slay the Nemean lion, a beast that could not be harmed by iron, bronze, or stone. [3]Hercules strangled the animal. [4]He skinned and tanned its pelt. [5]For his next task he tried to kill the hundred-headed Hydra, which grew two heads for each one Hercules severed. [6]He had his nephew apply a flaming torch to the stumps. [7]He burned the potential heads away.

[8]Hercules captured a wild boar for his third task. [9]He chased it into a snowdrift. [10]He threw a net around it. [11]He followed this by capturing the golden deer sacred to Artemis. [12]He shot an arrow into its forefeet. [13]He captured it alive. [14]For his fifth task he had to deal with birds sacred to Mars (Greek Ares). [15]They were iron-feathered. [16]They ate men. [17]Many were killed by Hercules and the rest driven away.

[18]His sixth task was less violent. [19]He diverted two rivers from their beds. [20]He cleansed the Augean stables of thirty years' accumulation of dirt from 3,000 cattle. [21]He declined help from King Minos. [22]He rode on the white bull's back. [23]He brought the animal back from Crete to Greece for his seventh task. [24]For his eighth, he captured the wild, flesh-eating mares of Diomedes. [25]For his ninth task, he obtained from Hippolyte, queen of the Amazons, the girdle Ares had given her. [26]For his tenth, and as he thought, final task, he stole the red cattle of the fearful, winged monster, Geryon. [27]He slew a giant herdsman. [28]He clubbed to death a two-headed dog.

[29]Eurystheus insisted that Hercules owed him two more labors. [30]Hercules then performed his eleventh labor. [31]He tricked Atlas. [32]He freed Prometheus. [33]He brought Eurystheus the branch he had wanted from the tree of golden apples. [34]Finally, Hercules fetched up from the underworld its guardian, the three-headed dog Cerberus.

STEP 25   Reduce the wordiness of the following essay by turning nine of the sentences into participial phrases and joining them with nearby, more important sentences.

Make sentence 3 a participial phrase modifying sentence 2.
Make sentence 8 a participial phrase modifying sentence 9.
Make sentence 11 a participial phrase modifying sentence 10.
Make sentence 14 a participial phrase modifying sentence 13.
Make sentence 16 a participial phrase modifying sentence 15.
Make sentence 18 a participial phrase modifying sentence 17.
Make sentence 22 a participial phrase modifying sentence 21.

Cards Come in Four Suits

[1]As long as there have been playing cards, players have organized them into different suits, usually four. [2]The four designated suits that we know originate in Italy. [3]They begin shortly after the invention of the printing press. [4]Face cards of the different suits have changed little since the sixteenth century. [5]They retain an essentially Renaissance design. [6]Although almost all European countries have used four suits most of the time, the symbols of the suits and the values they represent vary greatly.

[7]Hearts are the easiest to understand. [8]They represent the clergy. [9]They may be a kind of wordplay on the word "heart," as the clergy were the heart of the community in earlier times. [10]In Italy, Spain, and Portugal, hearts have a counterpart in cups. [11]These symbolize faith instead of the clergy.

[12]Diamonds in cards have nothing to do with precious gems. [13]Instead they represent the old merchant class. [14]They allude to diamond-shaped tiles on the floors of commodity exchanges. [15]In early times those diamond-tiled floors were where merchants met with farmers and tradesmen. [16]They dealt in wheat, vegetables, cloth, or shoes. [17]The counterparts to diamonds on the playing cards of Italy, Spain, and Portugal are the emblems of the national currency. [18]These symbolize the merchant class more openly.

[19]The suit of spades is not always called spades. [20]In France and Italy the suit we now call spades represents the landed nobility and is called swords. [21]A sword with a flared blade is on the playing cards of Spain and Portugal. [22]It represents the professional military class. [23]The Spanish word for "sword" is *espada*. [24]It gives us the English "spade," which is not even a shovel.

[25]The suit of clubs does not, of course, look like clubs at all. [26]The visual symbol is obviously a clover. [27]Clover represents the Peasantry. Because its counterpart in Spain is the stick or baton, in England the Spanish word was translated as "club," even when cardmakers substituted the French clover for the older symbol.

Step 25

Combining with Participles

Helpful Hints and Special Situations

One of the great dangers in using participles is that it is so easy to have them dangle—to put them in an awkward position in the sentence so it is not clear just what they modify. Here is an example:

> Laying a trap for speeders, the truckers were angry with the troopers.

Although any reader knows that truckers do not set speed traps for troopers, the sentence construction makes it look as though they do. Further, the sentence does not leave them a reason to be angry. The modifier obviously needs to be closer to what it modifies:

> Laying a trap for speeders, the troopers gained the truckers' anger.
> *or*
> The truckers were angry with the troopers for laying a trap for speeders.

Most often participles will dangle when they modify a subject that disappears, especially in the first person. Some writers intend to say, "I saw . . ." or "We knew . . . ," but they leave the words out:

> Jogging before breakfast, the letter carrier started his rounds.
> Wearing my teeny, tiny bikini, the husky lifeguard was ogling me.

The letter carrier was not jogging and the lifeguard was not wearing the speaker's bikini. In both instances, the subject of the main clause should be the first person, *I:*

> Jogging before breakfast, I saw the letter carrier starting his rounds.
> Wearing my teeny, tiny bikini, I could see the husky lifeguard ogling me.

The danger of writing dangling participles should not discourage the writer from using participles, however, as they are especially suitable for expressing lively action, speed, or abruptness. The example describing an air battle in World War I should indicate the pattern. Here are some other examples:

> *Hurtling* down the field, Dorsett carried the ball to a first down.
> *Smashing* her returns, King won easily.

Look how the motion of these sentences is flattened in another construction
with coordinate clauses:

> Dorsett hurtled down the field, and he carried the ball to a first down.
> King smashed her returns, and she won easily.

As these two sentences show, present participles do not have to modify
main clauses in the present tense. Instead, they imply the same time as the
main clause, whether it is in the present or the past. When Tony Dorsett
is described as *hurtling*, we mean he was hurtling along at the same time
he made the first down, at some time in the past. If we wanted to imply
something happened before the action of the main clause, we would use
the helping verb "have" in participle form:

> *Having* hurtled down the field, Dorsett crossed the goal line.
> *Having* smashed returns all week, King won the tournament.

Past participles are used in the passive. They describe something done
to what is being modified:

> Hurt*led* into a back room, Dorsett found himself kidnapped by a gang
> of terrorists.

Although present participles always end in -*ing*, forms of the verb that
end in -*ing* are not always participles. Depending on how they are used in
a sentence, the -*ing* forms may be gerunds, a form of the verb that acts as
a noun:

> Run*ning* is his favorite pastime.

Though gerunds always act as nouns and participles always act as adjectives,
they may be confused:

> She was not interested in his running. (*Running* is a gerund. His
> running may have bored her, but she was still interested in him as a
> person.)
> She was not interested in him, running for office every year as he
> did. (*Running* is a participle. She is bored with him because he runs
> all the time.)

Please notice that a participial phrase cannot stand by itself. It must
be attached to the main, or independent, clause. By itself, a participial
phrase is a *fragment*. Always attach a participial clause to a main clause. It
is the main clause that provides the participial phrase with a subject and
verb.

participial phrase	main clause
Smashing her returns,	King won easily.
↑	↑ ↑
participle	subject verb

STEP 25 Reduce the choppiness below by turning the specified sentences into participles or participial phrases. You will have to use the -*ing* form more frequently, but you will have to utilize the -*ed* form of the part, too. Proofread carefully.

Make sentence 3 a participial phrase modifying sentence 2.
Make sentence 5 a participial phrase modifying sentence 4.
Make sentence 8 a participial phrase modifying sentence 7.
Make sentence 10 a participial phrase modifying sentence 9.
Make sentences 11 and 12 participial phrases modifying 13.
Make sentences 17 and 18 participial phrases modifying 16.
Make sentence 21 into participles modifying sentence 22.

In the Twinkling of the Eye

---

[1]Nature has perfected a windshield wiper for human beings that auto designers might well envy. [2]The lids of our eyes automatically lubricate and irrigate our eyes. [3]They move so rapidly that vision is never disturbed. [4]We blink once every six seconds. [5]We pull the folds of skin across our eyes a quarter of a billion times in the course of a lifetime.

[6]One function of the blinking maneuver is lubrication. [7]Along the edge of each eyelid there are twenty to thirty tiny glands. [8]They contain a secretion. [9]Each time the lids close, these glands between the lashes open. [10]They moisten the eyelids and eyelashes. [11]They catch dust. [12]They keep out foreign matter. [13]Eyelashes are both windshields and windshield wipers.

[14]The other function of the blinking procedure is irrigation. [15]In each eye there is a tear gland. [16]The eyelid, during blinking, applies a suction to the opening of the gland. [17]It draws out some fluid. [18]It prevents the eye from drying out. [19]In a sense, each time we blink, we are crying.

[20]Eyebrows are also part of the "wiper" mechanism. [21]They are plucked and they are painted. [22]They divert rain and perspiration from the eyes, keeping their vision from being impaired.

STEP 25   Reduce the wordiness of the following essay by turning thirteen of the sentences into participial phrases and joining them with nearby, more important sentences.

Make sentence 1 a participial phrase modifying sentence 2.
Make sentence 4 a participial phrase modifying sentence 5.
Make sentence 7 a participial phrase modifying sentence 6.
Make sentences 9 and 10 participial phrases modifying 8.
Make sentence 11 a participial phrase modifying sentence 12.
Make sentence 13 a participial phrase modifying sentence 14.
Make sentence 15 a participial phrase modifying sentence 14.
Make sentence 17 a participial phrase modifying sentence 16.
Make sentence 19 a participial phrase modifying sentence 20.
Make sentence 21 a participial phrase modifying sentence 22.
Make sentence 23 a participial phrase also modifying sentence 22.

Scott Joplin

---

[1]He was known once only for such favorites as "The Maple Leaf Rag." [2]Scott Joplin is recognized today as one of America's most distinctive composers. [3]His remains are still buried in an unmarked pauper's grave in New York's Borough of Queens, but his music is played throughout the land by small combos and symphony orchestras alike.

[4]He was born in the ghetto of Texarkana, Texas. [5]Joplin got his first music lessons, free, from a traveling German musician who recognized his talent. [6]He left home in his teens. [7]He was hoping to make a living by playing the piano in honky-tonks and bordellos. [8]When he was still in his twenties, he settled in Sedalia, Missouri. [9]He was performing in a local concert band. [10]He was studying composition in a local black college. [11]He rejected his own attempts to write waltzes and other European music. [12]He decided to adapt the popular music of the day, ragtime, and make it the classical music of America.

[13]He refined the rough vitality of ragtime. [14]He produced "The Maple Leaf Rag" when he was thirty-one. [15]It made him a rich young man, temporarily. [16]For the next six years he wrote some of his best-known music. [17]This included "The Entertainer." [18]But his success did not last; a child died in infancy, his marriage dissolved, and ragtime fell out of favor. [19]He summoned his best remaining efforts. [20]He worked for five years on an opera, *Treemonisha,* which flopped. [21]He was rejected by the public and by the critics. [22]Joplin went into a personal decline, from which he did not recover. [23]He died in a charity hospital in 1917.

[24]Although a few devotees kept ragtime alive over the years, few people knew the name of Scott Joplin until Nonesuch issued a collection of his piano rags for the classical market in 1970. [25]Within a year, an all-Joplin concert was held at New York's Lincoln Center. [26]By the time his "The Entertainer" was used as background music for the movie *The Sting* in 1974, Joplin had begun to appeal to all segments of the music market.

STEP 25   Reduce the wordiness and choppiness of the following essay by turning eleven of the sentences into participles and participial phrases and joining them to nearby, more important sentences. You will use both present and past participles.

Make sentences 1 and 2 participles modifying sentence 3.
Make sentence 5 a participial phase modifying sentence 6.
Make sentence 7 a participial phrase modifying sentence 8.
Make sentence 10 a participial phrase modifying sentence 11.
Make sentences 14, 15, and 16 participial phrases modifying 13.
Make sentence 18 a participial phrase modifying sentence 17.
Make sentence 20 a participial phrase modifying sentence 21.
Make sentence 25 a participial phrase modifying sentence 24.

Sentence 5 becomes a participial phrase modifying sentence 6 in this way: *Solving both the smoke and the building problems, Henry Greathead made the modern urban subway possible.*

The Better Subway

[1]They coughed. [2]They smoked. [3]The world's first subways in London looked like nuisances that no city would want. [4]Smoke and soot were bad enough, but, worse, subways could not be built without tearing down everything on the surface. [5]One man solved both the smoke and the building problems. [6]Henry Greathead made the modern urban subway possible.

[7]He saw that coal-burning steam engines did not work well underground. [8]Greathead recommended alternate forms of energy. [9]He first thought that cars might be pulled by cables, much as elevators are now. [10]He recognized the impracticality of cables. [11]He seized upon the developing technology in electric motors that allowed cars to be driven underground without producing smoke.

[12]More important was a way to build subways that did not completely disrupt life on the surface. [13]Work on previous subways had been by the "cut-and-cover" method, by making trenches along the street. [14]This method gave the trenches brick sides. [15]It provided girders or a brick arch for the roof. [16]And it restored the roadway on top.

[17]Greathead, instead, dug two tunnels. [18]He put them one on top of the other. [19]By digging in one while transporting dirt in the other, workman could burrow under downtown London like mechanical earthworms. [20]The men would have a place to retreat to in time of danger. [21]Not one workman was killed in the construction of Greathead's tunnels.

[22]Greathead's techniques also solved a legal problem. [23]Bankers and landlords had wanted to charge rent on the earth beneath their properties. [24]Now the subways ran many yards below the surface. [25]This made it impossible for landlords to claim ownership of the earth.

Step 25

Writing Assignments: Combining with Participles

Use participles to indicate different aspects of the same episode or different aspects of the same item. Participles liven up the sentence, relating parts to each other at the same time.

1. Rewrite the essay "Blitzkrieg" in STEP 14, combining sentences with participles whenever possible.
2. Rewrite the essay "The Two-Dollar Bill" in STEP 14. Use participles to combine sentences in the essay.
3. Consider the essay "The Flight." Combine the sentences in the second and third paragraphs with participles. (The essay is in STEP 3.)
4. Use participles in combining sentences in the essay "Heat from Beneath the Earth" in STEP 8.
5. Use participles to combine sentences in the essay "Soap" in STEP 14.
6. Write a paragraph in which you tell of a trip. Use simple sentences that simply inform the reader of what you did. Then add participles that modify each of those statements.
7. Describe a memorable scene in a movie. State the central events in simple sentences, adding participles as modifiers.
8. Rewrite one of your own essays, combining sentences with participles.

Step 26

Combining with Subordinators

Here are two sentences describing events that happened at almost the same time.

Juan and Maria ordered full-course meals in a Chinese restaurant. They got free eggrolls.

Many teachers would call such writing "choppy." More than that, ordering the meals and getting free eggrolls are related events; they should be discussed together. Most Chinese restaurants give eggrolls as a bonus with certain orders. We could ease the choppiness of the sentences and show the relationship between the two events by joining the sentences together with a subordinator (or subordinating conjunction) like *because, since, when,* or even *in that*.

$$\left.\begin{array}{l} \text{Because} \\ \text{Since} \\ \text{When} \\ \text{In that} \end{array}\right\} \begin{array}{l} \text{Juan and Maria ordered a full-course dinner,} \\ \text{they got free eggrolls.} \end{array}$$

Notice that we have included a comma at the end of what used to be an independent clause and is now a subordinate clause. We do this because the subordinate clause comes first in the sentence and is fairly long (five words or more). We can choose not to use the comma if the subordinate clause comes first and is fewer than five words:

When the eggrolls came Juan and Maria ate them right away.

We can choose not to add a comma when the subordinate clause comes after the main clause, no matter how long the subordinate clause is:

$$\text{Juan and Maria got free eggrolls} \left\{\begin{array}{l} \text{because} \\ \text{since} \\ \text{when} \\ \text{in that} \end{array}\right\} \text{they ordered full-course meals.}$$

When we put the subordinate clause after the main clause, we might also use the rather formal-sounding subordinator *for*, which would sound undiomatic when the subordinate clause comes first.

Thus far we have assumed that the main clause should deal with getting the free eggrolls. Although it may seem less likely, we could make "Juan and Maria ordered full-course meals . . ." the main clause.

Because they got free eggrolls, Juan and Maria ordered full-course meals in a Chinese restaurant.

Such a construction would imply that Juan and Maria ordered full-course meals only when they heard about the free eggrolls. If we take the two sentences out of context, it is difficult for us to know for certain which

269

is the more important. When the writer is certain, the more important idea should always go in the main clause.

Here is a list of words that may serve as subordinating conjunctions and the kinds of relationships they may describe:

Cause: because, for, in, that, since, in that.
Condition: if, although, unless, whereas
Manner: as though
Result: in order that, so that
Time: after, before, since, until, when, while

We say these words may *serve* as subordinate conjunctions because in other positions in the sentence and in other constructions they may also serve other functions, such as prepositions, adverbs, and so on.

STEP 26   In the essay below, connect the specified sentences with the subordinators that are listed alongside. Notice how combining reduces the choppiness of the sentences and establishes relationships between them.

Connect sentences 1 and 2 with *when.*
Connect sentences 4 and 5 with *although.*
Connect sentences 7 and 8 with *since.*
Connect sentences 10 and 11 with *when.*
Connect sentences 13 and 14 with *while.*
Connect sentences 16 and 17 with *although.*
Connect sentences 18 and 19 with *although.*
Connect sentences 20 and 21 with *when.*

Black Settlers and Patriots

¹Christopher Columbus sailed toward America thinking he was heading toward the riches of the Indies. ²According to some historians, he was accompanied by a black pilot, Pedro Alonso Nino. ³Other blacks helped settle North America, and many fought against the British in the Revolutionary War.

⁴History texts state that the first settlement in North America was established at St. Augustine, in 1565. ⁵Nearly forty years earlier, five hundred Spaniards, accompanied by one hundred slaves, settled near the coast of South Carolina. ⁶Soon after their arrival, the slaves turned on their Spanish captors and escaped into the surrounding forests. ⁷The remaining Spaniards abandoned the settlement; ⁸The black slaves were the first permanent settlers in North America. ⁹There were also eleven blacks in the Dutch company that set up a trading post on Manhattan Island in 1624. ¹⁰Ten years later, Cecilius Calvert, the second Lord Baltimore, sent an expedition to settle the lands north of the Potomac River. ¹¹Three blacks, Francisco Peres, Mathias DeSousa, and John Price, were with the party. ¹²Blacks were thus among the first settlers of what is now Maryland.

¹³The first casualty of the fight against the British is not known. ¹⁴One of the first was Crispus Attucks, a runaway slave from Massachusetts, who was one of five Americans shot in Boston in 1770. ¹⁵During the Revolutionary War blacks fought in every major encounter. ¹⁶Many fought at Bunker Hill. ¹⁷Peter Salem stands out as the one presented to Geroge Washington for his bravery. ¹⁸George Washington later crossed the Delaware River in the famous surprise attack on the Hessians. ¹⁹A black man, Prince Whipple, was in Washington's own boat.

²⁰In the winter of 1783 a black soldier calling himself Robert Shurtliff was "unmasked." ²¹Shurtliff turned out to be Deborah Gannett, a woman. ²²By the time her identity was discovered, she had served for a year and half in the Fourth Massachusetts Regiment.

STEP 26   Reduce the choppiness or wordiness in the following essay by subordinating seven of the sentences to nearby, more important sentences. In some instances the new subordinate clause will come before the main clause, and in some others it will come later; you must decide whether the new construction requires punctuation. The first two sentences may be joined this way: "**Although** *golf has traditionally been seen as a game for men who belong to country clubs,* **one** *of the top golfers today is a young lady of Mexican-American, or Chicano (feminine: Chicana), parentage."*

Join sentence 1 to sentence 2 with subordinator *although.*
Join sentence 3 to sentence 4 with the subordinator *where.*
Join sentence 8 to sentence 9 with the subordinator *when.*
Join sentence 10 to sentence 11 with the subordinator *when.*
Join sentence 12 to sentence 13 with the subordinator *although.*
Join sentence 14 to sentence 15 with the subordinator *because.*
Join sentence 17 to sentence 18 with the subordinator *when.*

Chicana Golfer

[1]Golf has traditionally been seen as a game for men who belong to country clubs. [2]One of the top golfers today is a young lady of Mexican-American or Chicano (feminine: Chicana) parentage. [3]Nancy Lopez grew up in the Chicano section of Roswell, New Mexico. [4]Her father, Domingo, still runs the East Second Street Body Shop. [5]At age seven she was following her parents around the Roswell public golf course. [6]When she was eight, her father gave her a sawed-off four wood club. [7]In less than a year she was playing rounds with her father, and in another year she was beating him. [8]Her parents realized her potential. [9]They released her from household chores such as doing the dishes so she could perfect her skills.

[10]She played on the otherwise all-boy golf team at Godard High School in Roswell. [11]She ranked first and led the team to a state championship. [12]She looks like a pretty, middle-American girl and speaks English without an accent. [13]She experienced some anti-Chicano discrimination, especially at Roswell's most exclusive country club. [14]She was offered one of the first athletic scholarships for women by the University of Tulsa. [15]The government had encouraged universities receiving federal aid to provide equal athletic opportunities for women under a ruling usually known as "Title IX."

[16]In her first year as a professional, at age 21, she finished first in nine tournaments, including a record five in a row. [17]Her mother died that year. [18]Nancy took renewed courage to fulfill her parents' expectations of her. [19]She won $189,813, the highest ever for a female professional golfer. [20]At the end of her first year as a professional, she was named Female Athlete of the Year by the Associated Press with an impressive 336 of 412 votes.

Step 26

Combining with Subordinators

Helpful Hints
and Special Situations

Subordinate clauses present students with only a few problems. One of them is that some students write fragments when they write subordinate clauses that somehow slip away from main clauses. Here is an example:

> Although the new coin dollar, bearing the likeness of suffragist Susan B. Anthony, had been circulating for some time. It was difficult to find them in many areas.

Some students do not see the first part of this as a fragment. They see a subject, "the new coin dollar," and a verb, "had been circulating," and perhaps fearful of writing overlong sentences, they just stop there. What such students overlook is that the subordinator "although" gives the reader a sense of expectancy. *Although* all this may be true about the Anthony dollar, something else—something apparently more important—is going to be said. The fragment can be corrected simply by putting a comma after "some time," and giving "It" a lowercase letter "i."

Subordinate clauses may tempt some careless students to write fragments, but they also serve to correct another plague in freshman writing, comma splices or fused sentences. These occur when the writer jams together what should be two short, simple sentences with only a comma to hold them:

> The concert ended early, the police arrested the band.

The writer may feel these two sentences belong together and like the rather understated phrasing. By looking closer, we see the two clauses are related to one another. The second is an explanation for the first. Look how much better they fit together when the second is made a subordinate clause:

The concert ended early $\begin{cases} \text{because} \\ \text{in that} \\ \text{since} \\ \text{when} \end{cases}$ the police arrested the band.

As stated in the introduction to the STEP, subordinate clauses usually take a comma if they come first in the sentence and are five words long or more. Further, subordinate clauses do not usually take punctuation when they come, without interruption, after the main clause. That "usually" means that some writers might choose to put in a comma because putting one there feels right to them. This is more likely to happen if the subordinate clause is fairly long:

> Mail service went from bad to worse because the creation of a private corporation to make the mails "run like a business' magnified more problems than it solved.

This is one instance where there is no hard-and-fast rule. Most informed contemporary writers would not put a comma before the subordinate clause beginning " . . . because the creation . . .," but others might just as easily put one in. Either choice works.

Some readers may have noticed that the list of subordinators or subordinating conjunctions does not include the word "like." That is because "like" is not classed as a subordinator in standard English. It is probably needless to say that "like" is used as a subordinator in informal English all the time. How many times in your life have you heard these two advertising jingles?

> Winston tastes good like a cigarette should.
> Nobody can do it like McDonald's can.

Both of these should use "as" in formal English, if anybody wanted to restate these formally. Does this mean that "like" is always substandard usage in a subordinate clause? Obviously, using it in everyday English does no harm to the cigarette or hamburger business, but the student writer would be wise to avoid using "like" as a subordinator in a letter of application to Harvard or in applying to be hired in any very responsible job—maybe even working for Winston or McDonald's.

Is "like" ever completely correct? Yes, it is used as a preposition or an adverb in comparisons that do not include full clauses:

> A Land Rover is like a Jeep.
> He did a report on the book *Black Like Me*.
> A trombone slides like this.
> They are like two peas in a pod.

In short, "like" is standard English when no form of the verb follows it, even in elliptical clauses where the verb is understood but left out:

> He took to campus politics like a fish to water.

STEP 26   The choppiness in the essay below can be reduced by using subordinators to join some of the sentences. Be careful about punctuation. Underline the title of the play.

Join sentences 1 and 2 with *although.*
Join sentences 3 and 4 with *when.*
Join sentences 6 and 7 with *although.*
Join sentences 8 and 9 with *because.*
Join sentences 11 and 12 with *when.*
Join sentences 16 and 17 with *if.*
Join sentences 19 and 20 with *while.*
Join sentences 21 and 22 with *because.*

Show Business Superstitions

[1]The world of show business is exciting and glamorous. [2]It is also quite superstitious.

[3]Friends come to wish performers well. [4]They have to be extremely careful with their choice of words. [5]Saying "Good luck!" is absolutely forbidden. [6]"Break a leg!" is not used frequently. [7]It is still preferable to "Good luck!" [8]Actors believe that Macbeth is bad luck. [9]They never quote lines from the play inside the theater. [10]Many show business people avoid mentioning Macbeth altogether, referring to it only as "that play."

[11]Performers visit each other backstage. [12]They avoid wearing green, a color of ill omen. [13]Whistling in the dressing room is another taboo. [14]An actor guilty of whistling must leave the dressing room immediately. [15]He can return only if he knocks on the door three times. [16]A play sometimes folds. [17]People in the cast immediately perform a number of rituals to ward off additional bad luck. [18]They burn all congratulatory telegrams they had received for opening night and clean their dressing rooms of the tiniest sliver of soap.

[19]Some performers are convinced that ghosts haunt many Broadway theaters. [20]They are still willing to work there. [21]One famous actor believes that actresses are accompanied by either good luck or bad. [22]He will not work with any he believes is a bearer of bad luck.

STEP 26   Reduce the choppiness of the sentences, and establish relationships between them by connecting them with subordinators. Be careful with the punctuation of the newly created sentences. Proofread carefully.

Join sentence 1 to sentence 2 with *when.*
Join sentence 4 to sentence 5 with *when.*
Join sentence 6 to sentence 7 with *while.*
Join sentence 10 to sentence 11 with *although.*
Join sentence 13 to sentence 14 with *although.*
Join sentence 15 to sentence 16 with *while.*
Join sentence 18 to sentence 19 with *because.*

Wealthy Ballplayers

[1]Johnny Vander Meer, who eventually pitched back-to-back no-hitters, began to get paid for pitching in semipro ball. [2]He received ten cents for each batter he managed to get out. [3]If he walked a batter or allowed him to get a hit, he received no pay at all. [4]Dave Parker comes to bat for the Pittsburgh Pirates. [5]He gets about $1,500 for each time at bat even if he strikes out. [6]Vander Meer and Parker represent the extremes in ballplayers' salaries. [7]The numbers for average salaries are equally startling.

[8]In 1967, the average salary for a player in the National Basketball Association was $20,000 per year. [9]By 1972 it was $60,000 per year. [10]The ratio of the increase has not continued. [11]In 1979 the average salary of a basketball player was $120,000 per year.

[12]Salaries in other sports have been affected by the rise in salaries paid to basketball players. [13]Football salaries merely doubled between 1967 and 1979. [14]Baseball and hockey salaries kept pace with the basketball salaries. [15]Baseball players in 1979 received $76,000 on the average. [16]Hockey players averaged $96,000. [17]This was five times the size of the average hockey salary in 1967.

[18]An arbitrator's decision in 1979 allowed Atlanta Braves' rookie Bob Hoerner to add the bonus he had received for signing in 1978 to his base salary for 1979. [19]Salaries rose even higher in baseball. [20]When the great Bob Feller signed his first contract, he received a dollar bill and an autographed baseball.

STEP 26   Some of the choppiness and wordiness of the following essay can be reduced by subordinating eight of the sentences to nearby, more important sentences. In some instances the new subordinate clause will come before the main clause, and in some instances it will come after; you must decide whether the new construction requires punctuation.

Join sentences 1 and 2 with *although*.
Join sentences 3 and 4 with *because*.
Join sentences 7 and 6 with *where*.
Join sentences 8 and 9 with *as*.
Join sentences 13 and 12 with *because*.
Join sentences 14 and 15 with *by the time that*.
Join sentences 18 and 19 with *in that*.
Join sentences 24 and 23 with *where*.

The first two sentences may be joined this way: **Although** *Ray Charles is a favorite of jazz professionals,* **he** *has a large following in the general public, even among people who otherwise would not listen to jazz.*

Ray Charles

[1]Ray Charles is a favorite of jazz professionals. [2]He has a large following in the general public, even among people who otherwise would not listen to jazz. [3]He has become a universal favorite. [4]It hardly seems worth mentioning now what people used to notice about him first, his blindness.

[5]Charles was born with normal vision, but he was blinded in an accident at age six. [6]Leaving his native Georgia, he attended a school for the blind in Saint Augustine, Florida. [7]He received his first musical training there. [8]His talent was recognized early. [9]He began performing professionally by the time he was fifteen. [10]Within a few years he formed a trio and met real success touring the Northwestern States.

[11]The jazz scene at that time was dominated by the cool sound of such white musicians as Dave Brubeck and Gerry Mulligan. [12]Charles admired their skill, but he did not like their music. [13]He felt it was overscored and underfelt. [14]His first LP was released in 1957. [15]It was clear that Charles wanted to restore Gospel and pop elements to the jazz idiom. [16]We now say that he was the man who put soul back into jazz.

[17]One of Ray Charles' best-known compositions is "Georgia on My Mind," about his home state. [18]It was so popular! [19]The Georgia Tourist Office began to use it in advertising. [20]Finally, the Georgia legislature made it the state song. [21]Charles was invited to play "Georgia on My Mind" in the state capitol building on the day of the vote. [22]What a scene it was! [23]There was Ray Charles, filled with funkiness. [24]A Confederate, slave-holding government once sat there.

Step 26

Writing Assignments: Combining with Subordinators

Subordinators begin adverbial clauses. Adverbial clauses answer questions of *how, when, where,* and *why* in sentence patterns. When writers use subordinators, they often create fragments. This was probably why high school teachers might have told you not to begin sentences with *because. Because* can, of course, begin a sentence. Do make sure, however, that you are not writing a fragment. If subordinators answer questions, make sure that the sentence contains both the question and the answer. I came on time (why?) because I remembered to set the alarm. By itself, *because I remembered to set the alarm* is a fragment.

1. Rewrite the essay "How Did They Begin?" in STEP 1, using the subordinator *although* to connect the jobs people held with what they did that made them famous.
2. Choose among the essays in STEP 23. Rewrite any of the sentences you have combined by using *but.* Combine them with *while.*
3. Describe the activity going on in the three rings of a circus. Use the subordinators *as, while,* and *when* to combine sentences.
4. Describe two people dancing, where one partner has to react to the steps of the other. Combine the sentences, using subordinators. (*Because he stepped on her feet, she tried to stand further away from him.*)
5. Observe two people having a conversation. Describe how they react to each other's words, gestures, body movements. Use subordinators to join sentences.
6. Rewrite sentences from your own essay that need to be combined by using subordinators.
7. Set up a series of *if, then* clauses as you list some expectations for the future.

Appendix 1

Working with Fragments:
Additional Exercises in Combining

Much of the essay below is written in outline form. As a result, the numbered items are fragments. They cannot stand by themselves if written into paragraph form. Rewrite the essay, making the fragments into complete sentences. Either connect them to other sentences or add words that would complete them. Consider using the methods for combining you have practiced in STEPs 23–26.

Garlic Power

According to legend, garlic has magical powers.

1. cures the common cold
2. wards off evil spirits, including vampires
3. induces strength and bravery

Recent experimental work suggests that there may be a scientific basis for these beliefs.

Studies in India and West Germany indicate that garlic helps break up cholesterol in blood vessels.

1. preventing the hardening of arteries
2. decreasing the incidence of heart disease

Additional experiments in Russia and Japan show that cloves of fresh garlic help eliminate toxic metals from the body.

1. collecting lead mercury and cadmium
2. enabling the body to remove them during bowel movements

Other research has found that garlic may contribute to treatment of diseases.

1. anemia, arthritis, diabetes
2. even cancer

Paava Airola, author of *The Miracle of Garlic* and a physician-nutritionist, recommends a minimum daily requirement.

1. two or three small cloves of garlic a day
2. from a fresh garlic only

While a clove a day may keep the doctor away, it may also keep close friends further away in the process.

Some of the essay below is written in outline form. As a result, the numbered items are fragments. Rewrite the essay, making complete sentences out of the fragments. Either connect the fragments to the complete sentences or add words that would make them into complete sentences. When you are done, proofread carefully. Consider using some of the methods for combining you have practiced in STEPs 23–26.

Jim Brown's Records

Jim Brown, who played his college ball at Syracuse, was perhaps the greatest running back in pro football history. During his nine seasons in the NFL with the Cleveland Browns, he set numerous records.

Among his accomplishments were:

1. rushing for 1,000 or more yards per season 7 times
2. rushing for 100 or more yards per game 58 times
3. leading the league in rushing 8 times (1957–1961 and 1963–1965)
4. leading the league in rushing for five consecutive years (1957–1961)

These various accomplishments, all of them records, add up to a number of career records for Jim Brown. He has amassed:

1. 126 career touchdowns
2. the most total yards gained (12,312)
3. the highest average gain of 5.22 yards per carry

Unitil 1973 Brown had also held the record for most yards gained rushing in one season, but O. J. Simpson rushed for 2,003 yards that year, topping Brown by 140 yards.

Parts of the essay below are written in outline form. The items that are numbered are fragments. They cannot stand by themselves. Rewrite the essay, making the fragments into complete sentences. Either connect them to other sentences or add words that would complete them. In your rewritten version of the essay you would have no numbers, of course.

Would You Walk a Mile for an Avon?

Some of the most successful trademarks and names were selected on the basis of personal whim, rather than scientific research.

Avon's history goes back to 1886.

1. a door-to-door salesman
2. a peddler of books

D. H. McConnell would hand out free samples of perfume to housewives before making his pitch. He did not sell many books but the perfume kept doors from being slammed in his face. McConnell took a chance.

1. renting an office in New York City
2. starting the California Perfume Company

His firm a success, McConnell renamed it Avon.

1. because of his admiration for Shakespeare
2. Stratford-on-Avon, the Bard's birthplace

Another easily recognizable symbol, the camel, was chosen by Richard Joshua Reynolds, founder of the R. J. Reynolds Tobacco Company. He thought that camels were exotic and so was his blend of Turkish tobaccos.

1. needing an actual picture of a camel
2. hearing that the Barnum and Bailey circus was in town

Reynolds sent an employee to photograph Old Joe, one of the camels. Old Joe was not very interested in the honor.

1. tossed his head and tail about
2. threatened to bite the cameraman

The unintentionally indignant pose of Old Joe became the symbol on billions of packages of Camel cigarettes.

Finally, trademarks that seem unusual to the public were once the ordinary names of individuals. The perfume "Charlie" is simply named after Charles Revson, owner of Revlon Cosmetics, while Birds Eye was the actual name of Clarence Birdseye, "Father of Frozen Foods."

In the essay below, all of the phrases in **boldface** type are *fragments.* They cannot stand by themselves. Eliminate the fragments by inserting them in the sentences that come before them. Then, set each phrase off by commas on either side.

July is blueberry and hitchhiking month. **Known for its dog days.**

The boldface words cannot stand as they are. They can be inserted:

July**, known for its dog days,** is blueberry and hitchhiking month.

July in History

¹July is named after Julius Caesar who was born on the twelfth day of the month. ²At the time of his birth, however, it was called the month of Quintilius. ³In 46 B.C. Marc Antony convinced the Roman Senate to name the month after Julius. ⁴**With Caesar safely dead.** ⁵The Latin spelling was "Iulius." ⁶English speakers used the "J" sound eventually, but as late as the time of the American Revolution, the word was pronounced to rhyme with "Julie," not with "lie." ⁷The month is filled with events of importance for Americans. ⁸**Called mild month and meadow month by the Anglo-Saxons.**

⁹Among the lesser-known events of July is that in 1835 the Liberty Bell cracked. ¹⁰**Whole at the time of the Revolution.** ¹¹In July 1848, bloomers were first worn. ¹²In July 1903, the Ford Motor Company sold the original Model A. ¹³**Its first car.** ¹⁴In July 1908, the letters S.O.S. became the international signal for distress. ¹⁵**Which do not stand for "Save Our Ships."** ¹⁶In 1935, the world's first coin-operated parking meter went into operation in Oklahoma City. ¹⁷**A major source of revenue for cities and of frustration for motorists.**

¹⁸Among the better-known events in July is July 1620, when the Pilgrims sailed for America. ¹⁹**Persecuted in England and unhappy in Holland.** ²⁰July 4, 1776, was, of course, Independence Day, although John Adams wrote to his wife on the third of July that it would be July 2 that would be "celebrated by succeeding generations." ²¹In July of 1863, the Battle of Gettysburg took place. ²²**Perhaps the most significant battle of the Civil War.** ²³The first A-bomb was exploded in July 1945, and the first moon walk took place in July 1969.

²⁴July birthdays include Ernest Hemingway, George M. Cohan, Gerald Ford, Louis Armstrong, Nelson Rockefeller, Henry David Thoreau and P. T. Barnum. ²⁵July deaths include Presidents John Adams, Thomas Jefferson, and James Monroe. ²⁶**July 4th, in fact.** ²⁷Nathaniel Hawthorne also died on Independence Day, in 1864. ²⁸**The author of *The Scarlet Letter.***

In the essay below, all of the phrases in **boldface** type are fragments. They cannot stand by themselves. Eliminate the fragments by inserting them in the sentences that come before them or by joining them to those sentences in some other way. Pay special attention to your punctuation.

Houdini

¹Harry Houdini was born Ehrich Weiss (Weisz Erik in Hungarian), reputedly in Budapest, on March 24, 1874. ²**"Master Mystifyer."** ³He was an infant when his parents emigrated, and his father became the first rabbi of Appleton, Wisconsin. ⁴**Mayer Samuel Weiss.** ⁵Erich ran away from the family's next home in Milwaukee. ⁶**Hoping to earn enough to contribute to his destitute family.** ⁷While working as an assistant cutter in a necktie factory in New York City, he developed his great physical strength and agility. ⁸At seventeen he set out to be a magician. ⁹**Inspired by the memoirs of Robert-Houdin.**

¹⁰His first successes were as an escape artist, however, not as a magician. ¹¹He freed himself from a Siberian prison van, from a handcuff with six locks and nine tumblers, from death row of the federal prison in Washington, and from Cell 77 of the "escape-proof" Boston Tombs. ¹²**Generally stripped of all his clothes.** ¹³Because he saw something magical in flying and filming, Houdini got involved in both. ¹⁴He made a successful flight over Australia and directed himself in a series of films where he shared top billing with a mechanical monster. ¹⁵**The Automaton.** ¹⁶He also wrote books that revealed the various methods mesmerists, illusionists, and mediums have used. ¹⁷**To dupe the unsuspecting public.** ¹⁸Still, he was known as the "master of manacles" and the "king of handcuffs," not as a magician.

¹⁹Finally, he was acknowledged to be a master magician. ²⁰**In 1914.** ²¹He made people disappear, conjured gold and silver out of thin air, and read minds, including that of Teddy Roosevelt. ²²**Aboard a ship bound for New York.** ²³In 1918 he made a 10,000-pound elephant vanish nightly. ²⁴**For nineteen weeks.** ²⁵As far as can be determined, it was Houdini's skill that enabled him to perform his magic. ²⁶**Not hidden devices.**

²⁷Before his death, Houdini said he would send a message from beyond the grave. ²⁸To this day seances are held on the anniversary of his death. ²⁹**October 31.** ³⁰But so far, the man who said he could escape from anything has not communicated from the beyond.

Appendix 2

Principal Parts of Irregular Verbs

Thousands of verbs in the English language are what we call "regular," which means that they take the same form in the past (used alone) and in the past participle (used with *have, has,* or *had*). This is the way the three principal parts of the verb look:

Base	Past Tense	Past Participle
ask	asked	asked
deliver	delivered	delivered
love	loved	loved

The *base* form is used in the present tense, such as: They *ask* for your passport at border crossings. The past tense is used without any helping verb, for example: Bonita *delivered* the paychecks. And the past participle always takes a helping verb, either *have, has,* or *had:* Frances *has loved* making Italian cookies.

Only a few more than one hundred verbs are irregular, but they are familiar verbs that are used all the time. Here is a list of the ones you are most likely to encounter:

Base	Past Tense	Past Participle
awake	awaked, awoke	awaked, awoke, awoken
be	was, were	been
beat	beat	beaten, beat
become	became	become
begin	began	begun
bend	bent	bent
bite	bit	bit, bitten
bleed	bled	bled
blow	blew	blown
bring	brought	brought
build	built	built
burst	burst	burst
buy	bought	bought
catch	caught	caught
choose	chose	chosen
cost	cost	cost
cut	cut	cut
deal	dealt	dealt
dig	dug	dug
dive	dived, dove	dived
draw	drew	drawn

Base	Past Tense	Past Participle
dream	dreamed, dreamt	dreamed, dreamt
drink	drank	drunk
drive	drove	driven
eat	ate	eaten
fall	fell	fallen
feed	fed	fed
feel	felt	felt
fight	fought	fought
find	found	found
fit	fitted, fit	fitted, fit
fly	flew	flown
forget	forgot	forgotten, forgot
get	got	gotten, got
give	gave	given
go	went	gone
grow	grew	grown
hang (an object)	hung	hung
hang (a person)	hanged	hanged
hear	heard	heard
hide	hid	hidden, hid
hit	hit	hit
hold	held	held
hurt	hurt	hurt
keep	kept	kept
kneel	knelt, kneeled	knelt, kneeled
knit	knit, knitted	knit, knitted
know	knew	known
lay (put)	laid	laid
lead	led	led
lean	leaned, leant	leaned, leant
leave	left	left
lend	lent	lent
let (allow)	let	let
lie (recline)	lay	lain
light	lighted, lit	lighted, lit
lose	lost	lost
make	made	made
mean	meant	meant
meet	met	met
pay	paid	paid
prove	proved	proved, proven
put	put	put
quit	quit, quitted	quit, quitted
read	read	read
rid	rid, ridded	rid, ridded
ride	rode	ridden
ring	rang	rung

Base	Past Tense	Past Participle
run	ran	run
say	said	said
see	saw	seen
send	sent	sent
set	set	set
shake	shook	shaken
shine	shone, shined	shone, shined (trans.)
shoot	shot	shot
show	showed	showed, shown
shrink	shrank, shrunk	shrunk
shut	shut	shut
sing	sang, sung	sung
sink	sank	sunk
sit	sat	sat
sleep	slept	slept
slide	slid	slid, slidden
speed	sped, speeded	sped, speeded
spend	spent	spent
spin	spun	spun
spring	sprang, sprung	sprung
stand	stood	stood
steal	stole	stolen
stick	stuck	stuck
sting	stung	stung
strike	struck	struck, stricken
swear	swore	sworn
swim	swam	swum
swing	swung	swung
take	took	taken
teach	taught	taught
tear	tore	torn
think	thought	thought
throw	threw	thrown
wake	waked, woke	waked, woke, woken
win	won	won
wring	wrung	wrung
write	wrote	written

Index